Lines on a Map

UNPARALLELED ADVENTURES
IN MODERN EXPLORATION

by Frank Wolf

FOREWORD BY JOHN VAILLANT

RMB

RMB | Rocky Mountain Books Ltd.
rmbooks.com
@rmbooks
facebook.com/rmbooks

CATALOGUING DATA AVAILABLE FROM LIBRARY AND ARCHIVES CANADA
ISBN 9781771602891 (paperback)
ISBN 9781771602907 (electronic)

All photographs are by Frank Wolf unless otherwise noted.

Interior design by Colin Parks
Cover design by Chyla Cardinal
Maps designed by Jerry Auld / Otago Computing

PRINTED AND BOUND IN CANADA BY FRIESENS

DISTRIBUTED IN CANADA BY HERITAGE GROUP DISTRIBUTION
AND IN THE U.S. BY PUBLISHERS GROUP WEST

For information on purchasing bulk quantities of this book, or to obtain media excerpts or invite the author to speak at an event, please visit rmbooks.com and select the "Contact Us" tab.

We acknowledge the financial support of the Government of Canada through the Canada Book Fund and the Canada Council for the Arts, and of the province of British Columbia through the British Columbia Arts Council and the Book Publishing Tax Credit.

Contents

For Shannon and Mom...

Foreword

by John Vaillant

The first time I saw a map of Frank Wolf's self-powered routes lacing their way across North America from coast to coast to coast, I wasn't sure what I was looking at. At first, I thought those meandering, colour-coded lines must be river systems, or maybe old trade routes. They were so long — hundreds, even thousands of kilometres — and they seemed unrelated to any modern boundary or road system; I could see no pattern, and I knew of no precedent. Looking more closely, I realized the problem lay with my own imagination: I simply could not conceive of one human being, especially one from this century, travelling so far, through such a variety of terrains, under his own steam. I was genuinely amazed to learn that such a person existed, and that he lived in my hometown of Vancouver. But when I did eventually sit down with Wolf and a gallon of beer, it still took some doing to pry the superhuman details out of him.

This invigorating book will save you the bar tab, even as I believe it will inspire the same amazement and admiration I felt across the table that evening when Wolf recounted highlights and backstories from this collection's nearly two dozen epic adventures. Any one of them would qualify as the trip of a lifetime for most of us, if we could manage it at all. After all, this is the guy who, in 1995, led the first successful expedition to cross Canada by canoe in a single season. Already he was in Mackenzie, Fraser and Franklin territory, and he was just getting started. Since then, Wolf has criss-crossed this continent and several others by canoe, kayak, bike and ski; when the going was too rough for any of those modes, he persisted by sheer force of will. This is not hyperbole; each stunning vista and thrilling rapid Wolf describes has been paid for dearly — in days of brutal portages and bushwhacking, days when progress is measured in blisters and metres per hour, and marked by lost canoes, fresh wounds, broken ribs and giardia — days, in short, that most of us work really hard to avoid. But these are merely details, call them the entry fee to Wolf's world, where, as he puts it, "working through the unknown, seeing with your own eyes what few if any have seen, is true adventure."

It is this philosophy, brought to life by his extraordinary fortitude and ambition, by his writing (and also by his films!), that places Wolf among that rarified tribe of adventurer-athletes that includes Alex Lowe, Alex Honnold, Henry Worsley, Kate Harris and Laval St. Germain. These people appear so different from the rest of us and yet, simply by virtue of existing and doing what comes naturally to them, they challenge us: what if we believed in the power of our minds and bodies, and loved the world, as they do?

As you make your way through these pages, and into Wolf's wild hinterland, you may feel justifiably glad it's not you in the boat, but I guarantee there will also be moments when you'll wish to hell you could have been there. Wolf is truly lucky to be alive, and we are lucky to have him share with us what he's seen, and survived. It's an honour to know Frank Wolf, and to introduce this remarkable collection.

Introduction

My aunt tells the story of visiting my mother at our house in the Toronto suburbs in 1973. I was 3 years old at the time, running around sticking random things in my mouth, knocking stuff over, ignoring my mother's pleas to stop — generally being a pain in the ass. It freaked my mother out whenever I got revved up like this, and for good reason. The year before, I'd landed myself in the hospital for three months after swallowing a handful of reachable peanuts and inhaling them down my windpipe, all the way into one of my lungs. The doctors thought they may have to amputate the lung, but I luckily pulled through intact.

Anyhow, on this day, my mom finally snapped. She grabbed me by the arm and led me downstairs, where she stuck me in the pitch-black root cellar, locked the door and said she'd let me out once I decided to behave.

My aunt and my mother worked quietly in the kitchen afterwards, keeping one ear out for my inevitable begging cry of forgiveness. But there was no sound, not a peep. After about ten minutes, as my aunt recalls, my mother became worried (and felt more than a bit guilty), so she and my aunt went down to retrieve the sure-to-be-traumatized child from the cellar. However, instead of finding a blubbering boy, they found me perfectly content, singing and playing in the inkiness of the dank cellar with an empty jar I'd found, rolling it around on the ground like a barrel. I grinned broadly when they opened the door, but made no move to leave the cellar. I was having a good time, apparently. My aunt thought to herself, *Hmm, this kid's a bit different.*

I have no memory of this, and I'd never heard the story until my aunt recounted it to me a few years ago. It made me realize why I do what I do — why I'm innately attracted to long, difficult trips in remote areas. A shin-deep portage through a mosquito-ridden swamp is not so dissimilar to a cold, dark root cellar. From the outside, both places seem to be hostile environments, and yet I enjoy them. The new, the mysterious and the strange are far more interesting than the predictable day-to-day existence we've been told to strive for since birth. There is something highly satisfying in making the best of difficult situations — it's what we're hard-wired to do and is the most engaging way I know how to live. While our society races toward absolute predictability and comfort, I run the opposite way.

My first big self-propelled journey was in 1995, when Roman Rockliffe and I became the first people to travel coast to coast across Canada by canoe in a single season. The 8000-kilometre, 171-day journey hooked me. I loved the simplicity of moving under my own power daily through an ever-changing landscape, of solving the inevitable challenges of the expedition.

A week after this epic traverse, I traced our route with a red pencil right across a detailed map of Canada. It was a thing of beauty. Looking outward at a map of the world, I saw that there were so many more lines to be had — to travel self-propelled where motorized vehicles could not. Year by year, I slowly laid down line after line — theoretical mysteries in the planning stages that became fully realized experiences once the journey had been successfully completed. I can look at a map of any one of my journeys and instantly form an image in my mind of the landscape and experiences I had along that route. These lines are old friends I'll never forget.

In 2007, after about a dozen years of adventuring, I realized I literally wasn't seeing the forest for the trees. I certainly enjoyed my journeys, but also began to notice the degradation of the wilderness

I travelled through — and also realized I was doing nothing to help out these wild areas that had given me so much.

I began to write and create films to increase awareness of issues threatening the ecology and Indigenous cultures of these remote areas. I've since tackled issues like climate change, oil pipelines and destruction of the boreal wilderness, trying to do what I can to preserve these fertile adventure grounds for the foreseeable future.

The stories in this book are collected from my journeys through the proverbial root cellars of the world — from the frozen landscape of Bylot Island to the steaming jungles of Indonesia. Some tales are pure adventure, some misadventure and some celebrations of threatened areas. The common thread is the pure joy to be found in stepping outside your comfort zone and breathing life into a line on a map.

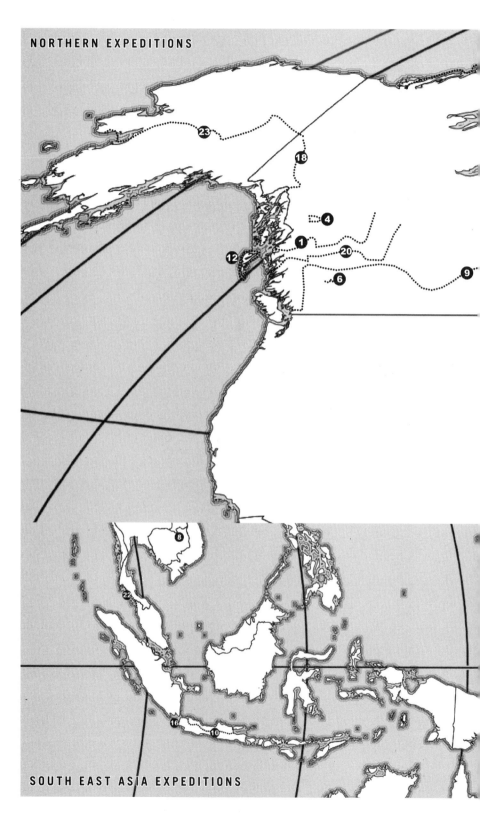

NORTHERN EXPEDITIONS

SOUTH EAST ASIA EXPEDITIONS

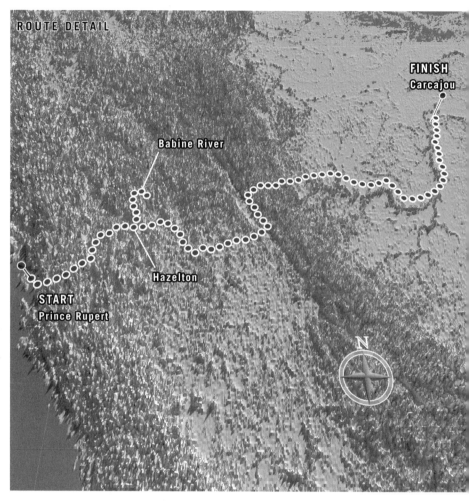

ROUTE DETAIL

FINISH
Carcajou

Babine River

Hazelton

START
Prince Rupert

N

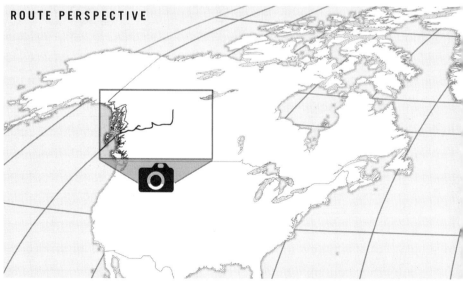

ROUTE PERSPECTIVE

A Quest Unfulfilled

A dance with death in an icy northern British Columbia river derails an attempt to cross Canada by canoe.

ORIGINALLY PUBLISHED IN MARCH 1999 ISSUE OF *RIVER MAGAZINE*

In earlier centuries, Alexander Mackenzie and Simon Fraser followed thousands of kilometres of northern Canadian waterways in the name of exploration. In the 1980s, modern-day explorer Don Starkell paddled 20,000 kilometres from Winnipeg to the Amazon River and captured the spirit and adventure of former famous explorers. In the spartan, unsupported manner of earlier explorers, I wanted to travel via the water "veins" that criss-cross Canada. The window of time to paddle Canada's northern waterways from coast to coast is limited. The journey must begin at spring thaw and finish before winter freeze-up.

On April 21, 1998, Ben O'Hara and I launched our 17-and-a-half-foot canoe into the calm water of the Pacific Ocean. It was the beginning of our attempt to follow, if not in the footsteps, at least in the spirit of earlier explorers. Our plan was to paddle 9000 kilometres of canoe routes from Canada's West Coast to East Coast — and to do it in a single season. We found sponsors, gathered gear, named our canoe *Groovy Gravy* and made a plan. Our expedition would go through the Coast Mountains of British Columbia, through the Rocky Mountains and over the Continental Divide into northern Alberta, Saskatchewan and Manitoba. From there we planned to paddle across James Bay, continue into northern Quebec and New Brunswick and finish at the Bay of Fundy.

The crux of the expedition came early. We had to paddle and portage our way upstream on the mighty Skeena and Babine rivers of BC during spring flood. The Babine provides the only continuous waterway over the Continental Divide. To keep our goals, we had to exclusively follow water upstream or down, without shortcuts. I'd done several thousand kilometres of upstream paddling on another expedition and felt confident we could make our way up the Skeena and Babine rivers as well.

Pushing off just south of the town of Prince Rupert, we left the misty Pacific coast behind and headed past a tidal-island-filled delta to reach the Skeena's 200-metre-wide rushing course. The Skeena is a robust river that cuts through the Coast Mountains in northern BC just below the southern tip of the Alaska panhandle, eventually wending its way to the Pacific Ocean, where we began our journey. For nine days and 262 kilometres, we worked our way up the Skeena, pushing toward Hazelton, BC.

Snow from the surrounding Coast Mountains melted and fed the river, rapidly causing the frigid water to rise higher as the hours and days progressed. Equipped with drysuits, we paddled the slower-moving water along the shore and got into the river to pull up over rapid sets, slowly progressing against the river's flow. Both Ben and I found excitement in our toil, and we took to our daily grind with enthusiasm. As we slogged upriver, we found ourselves grinning at each other, overjoyed to be on this grand adventure. In time, our grins would turn to grimaces, but at this point nothing hinted at the difficulties to come. Not that this section didn't have its unforeseen challenges.

On our very first evening, we arrived in camp after dark and made the lazy mistake of drinking water straight from the Skeena. Within a week, we both had giardia — a water-borne parasite that attaches itself to your bowels, forcing frequent purging stops and dimming your energy. We ground our way upriver in this state for the last couple of days before Hazelton. Once in town, we got Flagyl — an antibiotic cure for giardia — from the local clinic. A couple of days of waiting in a motel room for the Flagyl to kick in, and we were good to go again. I fear that motel bathroom has never been the same since.

On the Upper Skeena after Hazelton, the river sharpened its claws and a deep canyon forced us into a brutal, back-breaking, 36-kilometre portage over steep logging roads. I carried the 80-pound canoe, paddles, personal flotation devices (PFDs), a 40-pound pack and lunch, while Ben carried our 100-plus-pound pack. My shoulders and upper back ached badly at the end of each day, and Ben severely chafed his lower back, producing two large, oozing sores. Our first portage finished, we rejoined the Skeena and paddled up its last seven kilometres before getting to our next river vein: the wild Babine River.

The serpentine length of the Babine is predominated by narrow canyons and boulders. For centuries, it's been a valuable source of salmon for the Babine tribe. D.W. Harmon and James McDougall were the first white explorers to set eyes on the river, in 1812, but because of the Babine's fierceness, it escaped becoming a regular thoroughfare. More recently, wilderness rafting and kayak trips run from its source at Babine Lake down to the town of Hazelton. Several kayakers, canoeists and fishermen have died on it over the past few years, a reminder of the Babine's formidable power. To minimize risk, trips usually run in the late summer and fall, when water levels are low. After the last road ends, the expansive area is a wildlife-managed, no-roads wilderness with dense populations of grizzly bear and moose.

Few with a desire to live paddle downriver during flood, because of huge standing waves, powerful hydraulics, waterfalls and a current that can top 20 kilometres per hour. Fed by melting snowpack, the Babine in front of us had the classic brown, silty, frothy look of a river in flood. Seeing it for the first time made me realize the immensity of our task. A nervous gnawing in my gut began its rumblings in the raging torrents of this river. It wasn't giardia this time, more of a primeval foreshadowing of what was to come — the depths of my being knowing what my head did not. It wanted me to run away, but my stubborn will drove us forward.

We planned to paddle, drag and portage our canoe upriver, avoiding the 25-kilometre-long canyon at the Babine's mouth. This intimidating section of the expedition was our only way through, so we put our fears aside and focused on our task despite the labour required. The initial surges of joy in our adventure gradually dimmed, and we soon endured the most mentally and physically challenging moments of our lives. The river, flooded to the banks and deep, forced us inland, above the canyon, where we slowly and painstakingly hauled our gear through steep, dense terrain 100 metres or so inland from the cliff edge. At best, we could only move two kilometres each day, putting in gruelling 10- to 12-hour days.

The underbrush was so thick we could often see no more than five to ten metres ahead. We moved through a relentless tangle of alder thickets and devil's club. At the end of each day we picked hundreds of the minuscule devil's club thorns out of our hands and legs. We hardly spoke — our focus was on the canyon, plowing forward and getting around it so we could return to the river and make better progress. We couldn't carry our full loads over the fallen logs and dense brush, so we shuttled our gear back and forth, leapfrogging one load past the next, slowing the pace even more. Between shuttles, we marked our gear (obscured in the underbrush once we placed it down) with orange raincoats and navigated by compass and GPS. While sharing the rugged experience of wilderness adventure of earlier explorers, we avoided some of their struggles by relying on modern devices. They navigated by the sun, stars and other natural means, with no maps to guide them. Even though we toiled too, we had a few luxuries to help our progress.

On our third day in the dense bush, we ran into two straight 50-metre-deep canyons that forced us to lower the canoe down 40- to 50-degree slopes with ropes and carabiners. It took us over a day to cross two unnamed creeks that cut through the canyons flowing to the Babine. Because of our slow pace, we were running desperately low on food. Our meagre rations were insufficient to satisfy our bodies' needs, and we ached from hunger and exhaustion. After five days of bushwhacking, we passed the main canyon and reached a spot on the Babine where we could finally paddle and slog through the water close to shore. After about a kilometre of dragging the canoe, another canyon forced us to climb with rope and carabiners, at first 200 metres straight up, then 500 metres across and down again. The river was close to breaking us — we had only seven days of food left and many more days than that to travel before we could resupply.

After our portage around the side canyon, we ate quickly and decided to put in a couple of hours' water travel before bedtime. We got into the deep, thin eddies that abutted two-metre-tall standing waves, and managed to make it up one and a half kilometres before disaster struck. I was lining the canoe around a log that jutted three metres into the river when the current caught the boat, turned it, filled it with water and swept it under the log. A loud *crack* came from the hull, and our canoe headed downstream. Ben and I dove after the canoe and wrestled it into an eddy, untied the gear inside and began throwing it onto shore. A wave surge from the rapids hit and tore the canoe loose again. Ben grabbed the boat. One bag and a camera broke free and floated downstream. I swam after them, plucked them from a tangle of branches along the river's edge and heaved everything onto shore. When I inspected the canoe, I found a metre-long hairline crack in the centre of the hull. In addition, the river had claimed our map.

Damn, damn, damn. While Ben sat quietly, I swore at the river, myself and our predicament. We had 75 kilometres of hard upstream travel to go and only six days of food and a damaged canoe. As we were moving only a few kilometres per day, our best option was to return to Hazelton, pick up some mid-wheels for the canoe, repair it and reroute by overland portage to Babine Lake, where we would access the Continental Divide. I had wanted to go solely along waterways on this journey, but the river had other plans. Checkmate Babine River.

Next morning, I woke feeling edgy. The Babine raged. Yesterday's escapade had ruined my fondness for the river, but it was our only way down. Notwithstanding the intolerable mental and physical challenges, it would take too long to bushwhack back to Hazelton the same way we'd come. We would paddle downriver as far as we could, to the edge of the main canyon, and then begin portaging from there, which would save us several days of toil. After a paltry oatmeal breakfast, we packed *Groovy Gravy*, placed her in the current and set off.

Immediately the river bucked us onto massive two- to three-metre standing waves, bigger by far than anything I'd seen. We stabbed at the waves with our paddles, our control marginal in the Babine's flooding current. A wave suddenly caught us sideways and overturned us. Wide-eyed and shocked, we swam downriver with the canoe. As we rounded the bend, a moose onshore spooked and dove into the rapids, barrelling down alongside us. Its dark, glistening eyes were wide with fear as it thrashed wildly in the current. It was a truly surreal moment: two men, a canoe and a moose, plummeting down the Babine River. If it hadn't been so terrifying, it would have been funny. Luck plucked us from the river, but the moose was less fortunate. We were able to pull the boat into a corner eddy, but the moose swept downstream, sucked through the short canyon below us where it disappeared from view.

We emptied the canoe on the river's edge. Ben was wet, deathly pale and gripped by fear. My heart pounded in rapid staccato beats. I thought, *We're both okay, we have all our gear and there's not much farther to go. Just have to stay cool and make our portage.*

We ran the next short canyon with its surging eddy lines and boils and took a break below to empty water from the canoe. After a calm, forgiving stretch prior to our portage point, we encountered more colossal standing waves. The canoe tipped, and we swept helplessly past our planned exit and dropped through the 50 to 75-metre sheer walls of the main canyon. Deeper and deeper we tumbled through towering waves standing three metres from trough to crest, with absolutely no calm spots. Desperately, we tried to get to the canyon walls, to hang on and pull in the canoe. Our hands clutched at the rocks, but the water ripped us away and repeatedly sucked us back to the central flow. I heard Ben yell, "I can't make it much longer." He held intrepidly to the canoe with me, trying not to lose it, but he was now coming dangerously close to drowning. We were like a pair of ants being sucked down a kitchen drain.

I shouted, "Leave the canoe, Ben! Get out! Get out!" He finally lunged for a pile of crumbled rock and pulled himself out, slumping down in shock and exhaustion. Our eyes locked for an instant before I was swept away down around the corner with our boat. "I'll get it out somewhere downstream!" I shouted.

Alone now in the canyon, I wrestled the canoe, holding its line in my teeth, trying at all costs not to lose our expedition gear. The water was cold and began to seep under the latex cuffs of my drysuit. The river flushed me and *Groovy Gravy* into a series of big hydraulic drops, at one point pinning me under the canoe for 15 seconds. I pulled myself to the side of the canoe and realized the camera that National Geographic had lent me to film this expedition was still running, mounted on the deck in a waterproof housing. The red *on* light was blinking, and for a second I morbidly thought that I was perhaps filming my last moments on this earth.

I wrapped my arms over the canoe and hauled myself up, managing to straddle its upside-down belly. Around me, the river surged, violent, fast and loud. Everything seemed distorted and in slow motion. In the maelstrom, I felt strangely detached and calm, looking down the walls of the narrowing canyon, which seemed to go on forever. In that brief, delusional daydream, I thought I could actually ride the canoe like a bucking bronco down the rest of the Babine.

The illusion was instantly ripped apart as I went over another drop recirculating the full muscle of the Babine, with a deep, two-metre whirl-pool flushing through it. I was separated from the canoe and pulled down, set free to pop to the surface for a half breath, pulled backwards into it again, and then submerged for another half minute. Finally, I came up for another half breath before being taken back a third time and tugged deep under the brown, frothy whitewater. The river held me there until my lungs felt close to bursting. My next breath would be the icy water of the river — and I wanted desperately to breathe. I was sure I was about to die. In the darkness at the bottom of the river, I used the last vestiges of my energy from that last breath to swim hard to the side of the river, where I was finally released from its grip. I dragged myself onto a small pile of rubble at the base of the canyon wall.

Staggering to my feet, I turned and watched *Groovy Gravy* speed down the canyon, and let out a huge, bellowing scream at the river — a combination of adrenaline and elation. In that moment nothing else mattered: I had oxygen and flesh. I was alive. Then I thought of Ben. He was quite a ways farther up the gorge, probably weak and hypothermic. I scaled the steep, crumbly, 50-metre canyon wall, my body chilled and feeble. For over an hour, I bushwhacked along the river until I came to the end of the logging road where we had originally portaged. For two hours I stumbled along the road, hoping to bump into someone. If I didn't, I had an 80-kilometre hike back to Hazelton.

Around a bend, Gary Arnold appeared like a mirage. He was a forestry manager checking how the spring flood was affecting the new road. I jogged toward him and blurted out my story about Ben's predicament. He gave me some peanut butter cookies and Coke, and called the RCMP to have the provincial emergency patrol dispatch a helicopter and rescue team. Three hundred years ago, I would have hunkered down, built a fire and made a shelter. I would have had no one to turn to for help and likely would have been the first white man on the Babine. I probably would have survived the summer and fall, and perhaps died the next winter. The luxuries of my modern exploration didn't escape my awareness. For my sake and Ben's, I was grateful.

I flew up the canyon with the helicopter search crew, looking for Ben. We made several passes but saw no sign of him. I was getting worried. If we couldn't find him by nightfall, the search would be called off until morning. A ground rescue was impossible in this dense forest at night. I hadn't seen him since approximately ten a.m., and it was now seven p.m. Finally, we saw him waving his brightly coloured PFD on the shore below. Tears welled in my eyes as we came down to pick him up. Ben and I had persevered through much in the last three weeks and had become tight friends. Although all of our gear had disappeared downriver, the two of us were alive. The RCMP told us that of four searches on the Babine in the past two years, we were the only people found alive. Six others before us had not been so fortunate. The fact that Ben had survived for five kilometres in the canyon and that I had ridden out ten kilometres through the canyon on a flooding current was, to them, unfathomable.

The night of Ben's rescue, we stayed in the Hazelton hospital for overnight observation. I was convinced the expedition was over. All of our gear was gone, including our video, photographic and written documentation of our experiences to this point. I contacted every newspaper, radio station, fishing lodge, river patrol and RCMP detachment along the river, but none of our old gear had shown up — and never would. The only thing ever found was the canoe, discovered a couple of weeks later, split into halves found ten kilometres apart down on the Skeena. The footage probably ended up somewhere in Japan — perhaps I'm a big hit there.

And yet, whatever urging had compelled me to begin the expedition initially still voiced itself. After some discussion, Ben and I decided to commence our trip again, and we managed to re-outfit ourselves and set out six days after the Babine incident. We began overland from Hazelton and managed to cover another 1200 kilometres over the next three weeks through the lakes and rivers of BC and Alberta. Things certainly didn't get much easier. I cracked two of my ribs on a portage; Ben had severe Achilles tendonitis. Eventually, we surrendered. By the time we were on the Peace River, a relatively easy portion of the trip, we were both mentally exhausted. Physical pain can be overcome to some extent, but without mental fortitude, we were in trouble. Up until the Babine incident, we had been inspired, driven and motivated. Once we were resupplied and on our way again, the desire, drive and spirit of the expedition evaporated.

On June 6, 1998, Ben and I made the very difficult decision to end the expedition. We pulled out near Carcajou, about halfway down the Peace River, and packed up our gear. The joy was gone. Every day seemed forced; a chore, contrived. We weren't taking the trip paddle-stroke by paddle-stroke anymore, and we thought of nothing but the trip's end. With 1500 kilometres behind us and 7500 ahead, we were in a tough situation. We had become apathetic.

Early explorers like Alexander Mackenzie lived off the land and moved slowly. Every bend in the river was a new discovery, and ending an exploration because of apathy was not an option. There was no net to catch them if they fell — but fame, fortune and a place in history were their rewards for a successful exploration. Discovering the Northwest Passage was equivalent to landing a man on the moon. The world was limitless, its resources infinite. Europe was Earth, North America was Mars.

Modern exploration is more about human discovery and less about geographical exploits. Much of the world's surface has been mapped; there is nowhere to truly explore except within ourselves. Today's expeditions seek to be the fastest, longest or most unique. By succeeding in these endeavours, the modern explorer pushes the limits of what was once deemed humanly possible.

Despite failing to be the first to go from West Coast to East Coast by canoe, I succeeded in other ways. I found the courage to attempt a dream. I've grown as a person, have no regrets and am moving on. It is better to have dreamt, tried and failed than never to have dreamt and tried at all. Some dreams will flush out successfully, and others will be quests unfulfilled — but they will always be successful explorations of inner discovery.

ROUTE DETAIL

Angilaaq Mt.

START

N

FINISH
Pond Inlet

ROUTE PERSPECTIVE

The Ice Kingdom

Skiing the glaciated hinterland of Sirmilik National Park's Bylot Island.

ORIGINALLY PUBLISHED IN FALL 2017 ISSUE OF *EXPLORE MAGAZINE*

It's 11 at night, but the sun is shining like it's the middle of the afternoon here in Pond Inlet. I'm walking the frozen dirt streets of this Inuit hamlet, trying to shake off jet lag after the milk run of flight connections I took to get from Vancouver to here. "Pond" is situated on the northern tip of Baffin Island at a latitude of 73 degrees north; in the month of May, the only time is daytime.

No matter where my stroll takes me, the jagged, snow-capped peaks of Bylot Island, 25 kilometres away across Eclipse Strait, jump from the horizon. Everything on this side is rolling terrain, but Bylot resembles a huge chunk of the Rocky Mountains torn out by a giant and dropped into the Arctic Ocean. Named after the mutinous first mate of Henry Hudson, it lies shrouded in mystery, like Scaramanga's island in the Bond movie *The Man with the Golden Gun*.

I'm here to spend 12 days ski-touring and climbing peaks on the island with my partner Dave Garrow. Bylot is fully within Nunavut's Sirmilik National Park, a 22,000-square-kilometre wilderness area rarely visited at any time of year. Dave and I are the only skiers to journey into Bylot's Byam Martin Mountains this year, and park manager Carey Elverum told us only about a dozen groups of skiers have ventured in during the 17 years he's spent at the helm of Sirmilik since it was established. "We get skiers in there about every other year or so."

I stop and chat with a group of tween boys hanging out on their bikes. A nice kid named Joey, the de facto leader of the crew, puffs on a cigarette, straddling a BMX and wearing only a hoodie and jeans to ward off the minus-12-degree-Celsius air. As with most Inuit I've met, his answers are short and to the point — the pretence and elaboration of city slickers like myself a seeming waste of time.

"What's your favourite time of year here Joey?"

"March — it's best time to get Polar Bear."

"Why is it best to get them in March?"

"Their fur is the best"

"You mean the coat is the thickest?"

"Yup."

"What time does it get dark this time of year?"

"It doesn't."

I ask if any of them have been to Bylot island. They all shake their heads and smile.

I then ask if they have a pump track or any jumps for their bikes in town. A kid named Gordon shyly peeks up from under his toque

"Nope."

"You guys should build some — you'd have a blast."

They look at me blankly, then laugh to each other and ride off.

"Bye, Frank!" a couple of them yell. The seed I plant seems to take root as I spot the crew throwing themselves off a series of freshly built jumps by the school the next day.

I walk farther down the street and chat with James Simonee, who's building a qamutik for his brother-in-law. The 25-foot-long wooden sled is based off a dogsled design, but today's qamutiks usually haul gear and people behind snowmobiles instead of teams of canines.

I ask him if he's ever spent time on Bylot.

He looks across at the island, then me.

"Nope."

"Why not?" I ask.

"Never had a need to."

"When do the kids go to bed this time of year?"

He laughs. "Whenever they want… my nephew Jassie" — he points to his teenage nephew whittling slats for the qamutik a few feet away — "he'll work on this until eight a.m. or so, then sleep until four in the afternoon."

Jassie nods and smiles. "Time doesn't matter here."

"Ever get polar bears in town, James?"

"Only happened a couple times I know of, and only in the fall. Once had a mother and two cubs hanging around a shed with rotten seal meat in it at the end of town. The wildlife officer told me to go shoot them, but I didn't. I just kept an eye on them, and after a couple days they went away. This is their home too."

Sirmilik means "Place of Glaciers" in Inuktitut, and there is no better symbol for the place than the polar bear — or "ice bear" — which makes its living in this frigid zone, hunting the abundant ringed seal. Although there's a large denning area for the bears on the north side of the island, we're unlikely to see any, as they'll still be out on the sea ice, getting their fill before the lean months of summer. That said, just a couple of weeks ago the tracks of a mama bear and her cubs were spotted leaving a den on Bylot near where we'll be travelling.

*   *   *

Our first few days on the island will see us climb 5,400 feet along a 40-kilometre stretch from sea level to a central hub of ice from which the glaciers emanate outward through valleys like spokes on a wheel. Once there, our primary objective is to summit Angilaaq Mountain — at 6,401 feet, the highest peak in the Byam Martin Mountains.

To expedite our adventure in the mountains, Brian Koonoo has agreed to transport us by snowmobile the 25 kilometres across Eclipse Strait to the toe of Sirmilik Glacier. At the end of our journey, we'll ski back across the sea ice to the hamlet. Brian is a local, born and raised in Pond, and the longest-tenured National Parks staff here. A wiry man with an easy smile, he's spent a fair bit of time on Bylot — more than anyone else in town, probably. But he has never seen Angilaaq.

"Hope to one day."

Another Inuk and fellow Parks employee, Terry Kalluk, earlier told us "It's my dream to climb Angilaaq." It seems few people in town have ever set foot on Bylot, and even Parks staff haven't ventured very far in. It's fascinating to me that they look over at the Byam Martin Mountains every day but have never actually *seen* them.

Groups of dogs chained to the ice and covered in their own feces dot the shoreline. These are not pets — they are descendants of the dogs that pulled Inuit ancestors across the ice bridge over the Bering Sea a few millennia ago. Tough as nails, they live outside all year round, even through the bitter days of December and January, when highs average minus 30 degrees Celsius and lows can dip to minus 60.

I spoke to a woman named Jen yesterday as she fed her four dogs out on the ice. A non-Inuit who's lived here for ten years, she'll occasionally go for a sled run with her dogs, which are clean and treated well.

"My guys are sweet... but those Inuit dogs" — she points to a couple of packs of the ragged beasts farther down the ice — "they're vicious. I fed one of those teams last year as a favour to the owner, and a couple of them got a hold of my arm and tried to drag me into their circle. If I hadn't yanked my way free they would've mauled me badly."

"You ever been to Bylot Jen?"

"No, I've never gotten that far. I stick closer to home."

I walk by the Inuit packs and pet a couple of the more timid ones but avoid the big mangy fellas who strain at their chains and snap at me.

I'd be ornery too, if I was in their place. These dogs have been rendered obsolete by mechanization. Born to run, they're instead doomed to an existence of chained servitude, watching the snowmobiles that have replaced them go back and forth on the far-flung adventures that they once led.

As we finish loading, a burly, middle-aged Inuk man with the deeply tanned face of someone who spends a lot of time on the land asks us where we're headed.

"Over to ski Bylot." Dave replies.

With the man are four other Inuit guys and one portly Caucasian fellow who's obviously not from around here. He's dressed head to toe in moss-coloured camouflage hunting fatigues, ironically standing out more conspicuously than anyone else against the stark white background of the landscape.

I get the picture pretty quick and ask the guy, "You after polar bear?"

"Yup."

"Where you from?"

"Wisconsin."

"How long do you have to get the bear?"

"Ten days."

The conversation ends there, awkwardly, as the guides and their client say nothing more and turn away. There's a stigma attached to what they do, and they're wary of criticism. Guided polar bear hunts are a lucrative source of income for the Inuit, and the few tags made available to trophy hunters are a boon to the community — although so is ecotourism, driven by wildlife watchers who come up here to shoot animals with cameras, not guns.

This time of year is "floe-edge season," when tourists come to hang out 60 kilometres east of town, where the ice meets open sea. It's the best time to spot narwhale, polar bear, beluga and other exotic arctic species. We see a few of these tourists walking around town, conspicuously overdressed in identical outfitter-issued parkas and snow pants.

Dave hops on the snow machine with Brian, while I ride with the cargo. Just over an hour later, we are at the toe of Sirmilik Glacier, ready to set the first tracks of the season.

*　　*　　*

We part ways with Brian and head onto the island. The sleds are heavy with our assorted gear, but it's much better than having the weight on our backs. We joke that we are "man-hauling" our way to Angilaaq — a term used by 19th-century British explorers like Sir John Franklin who would harness several men like dogs to half-tonne sleds and steadfastly drag them over the ice into inevitable misery and death. Meanwhile, Inuit of the time would visit them out of curiosity, gliding quickly and easily in their pooch-powered sleds while the "man-haulers" stubbornly stuck to their methods, thinking themselves better than the Inuit and their dogs. Though mechanized travel is forbidden in Sirmilik, I suppose Dave and I are no different than the man-haulers of yore. We stubbornly drag our sleds while guys like Brian coast along easily on the sea ice in their snowmobiles. The more things change, the more they stay the same.

As we don't know the terrain at all, we stay roped up during our entire time on the glaciers to avoid plummeting into hidden crevasses. To the naked eye, the way seems fairly benign; the obvious crevasses are along the edges. However, this is an arctic desert with very little snowfall, so any chasms that may be lurking will be hidden under a very thin layer of snow that will not likely hold the weight of a 180-pound human and his gear sled.

At camp, Dave probes the radius of our site to ensure we don't set up on a crevasse and wake up plunging into its inky depths. We melt snow for water, have our freeze-dried meal, sip some whiskey and adjourn to our tent. Inside, Dave attends to his freshly blistered feet while I dig into a forbidding book — *In the Land of White Death*, about the crew of an early 20th-century Siberian hunting ship trapped in pack ice for two years who attempt to escape their fate through a perilous journey across the arctic waters. It puts any difficulties we experience on our journey into stark perspective.

I wear an eye mask to convince my body it's nighttime, but I still wake up every couple of hours from twitchy, dream-filled sleeps. Over 11 nights of mystical ice-and-light-injected visions, I have vivid adventures with just about everyone I've ever known. I awake from a sailing trip in the South Pacific with my now-dead father, and it takes me a minute to realize where I am. The dream seemed so real. I feel suddenly sad realizing he's still gone, and quickly fall back asleep, hoping to find him on the other side again.

*   *   *

Thunk, thunk. The points of my crampons bite into the thin ice slope of the south ridge of Angilaaq Mountain. Breathing steadily, I work my way up a winding, narrow strip of white through broken rock. Dave follows behind me as we kick our way to the top of the ridge. We pause for a break at a distinctive menhir and look back at where we came from. Our tent is not even discernible from up here, lost seven kilometres away in the vast white plain of a seemingly endless glacier. It's warm today: the thermometer says minus three degrees Celsius, but it feels like it's plus ten. There's not a puff of wind as we toil under the beating, ever-circling sun.

We rope up for the final section along a snowy ridge that leads to the summit. Both sides fall away steeply for 1,000 feet. If one of us stumbles and begins to fall down either slope, the other has to dive down the opposite side to arrest a nasty, careening tumble to the bottom.

Angilaaq means "the highest" in Inuktitut, and the mountain lies in the geographical heart of Bylot. With no motorized vehicles allowed in the park, there's no easy way to get here. It took four days of dragging sleds up the length of Sirmilik Glacier and then three passes to get to our camp at the base of Malik Mountain — the second-highest peak in the park.

We rose at five this morning with a plan to nab both Malik and Angilaaq in a day, then head back down one of the passes to set up a lower camp before forecasted bad weather sets in. Malik was a straightforward snow slope with a bit of rock. From the summit, we could clearly see Angilaaq, its classic diamond shape and prominent snow ridge seducing us like a snow-cloaked siren.

We crest the summit of Angilaaq and look north over an army of peaks to Lancaster Sound, the northern entrance to the Northwest Passage, where Franklin and other noble failures sailed to their doom again and again like proverbial lemmings over a cliff.

From here, it looks peaceful and calm — an albescent blanket stretched over a sleeping sea, with Devon Island visible beyond. I spin slowly on the spot to take it all in, on top of a frozen world. Thousands of peaks and ridges jut up from glaciers that extend like petrified serpents through every valley until their terminus at the ocean. It's hard to believe that only a handful of people have ever stood here before us, but that's what remoteness, and a one- or two-month ski season between the dark and bitter cold of winter and the quick melt of summer, will do.

Standing here is far more interesting than being, say, on Everest or Denali — two peaks of great height that have been bludgeoned into mere bucket-list items, having long lost their adventurous aspect. Objectives have to be obscure, remote and off the radar to truly be considered adventure. There's nothing adventurous about the well known — there is difficulty, but not adventure. I take a height measurement with my GPS and find that the summit is actually 6,480 feet high — 79 feet more than stated on official maps or in other research materials we've seen.

*   *   *

Over the course of the following few days, we return the same way we came, with excursions up a few side valleys to the peaks at their terminuses. So few people have been here that these places have no names. For all we know, no one has ever travelled up these summits — and why would they? They don't connect to any efficient traverse routes, and there's little good hunting here for the Inuit.

About halfway down Sirmilik Glacier, we set up our camp, and then we ski east up one of these side basins, climbing steadily to the back of a crescent bowl. The scale here is so vast, we're rendered into two insignificant specks of dust in the porcelain of the landscape.

We choose an appealing peak in the northeast corner of the bowl with a steep, rocky ridgeline. Though the peak is 1,400 feet lower than Angilaaq's, we climb twice as far (2,000 feet) because our starting point is much lower on the glacier. Back at camp, it was minus 20 degrees Celsius in the chill of the north wind, but now we're sheltered, and the climb is quite pleasant. Snow begins to ball on our crampons as we work our way up the south-facing slope, forcing us to pause and clear them from time to time by tapping them with the shafts of our ice axes. It's the most challenging summit of the trip, and we're treated at the top to a spectacular view of Sirmilik Glacier on one side and an expanse of peaks that extend to the floe edge on the other.

This unnamed mountain may have just had its first ascent — none have been recorded before, and there are so many unclimbed peaks in this park that more likely than not it's ours. There aren't many places on Earth where humans haven't set foot, where a beautiful view hasn't been gazed upon by someone else. This makes it more special to me even than Angilaaq: a wonderful combination of adventure and obscurity. We name it Mount Koonoo, after Brian Koonoo, our lift to the island.

On our last day on the island, we ski up to a small knoll and notice Arctic fox tracks leading to bare patches on the slope. Scat from fox, pika and jackrabbit lies among the grasses, heather and broken rock. A couple of ravens circle overhead. A lone snow bunting sings its shrill song as it swoops across the sky. The first signs of spring have come to Bylot. Ski season is over, with a grand total of two members of the 2017 club.

*   *   *

The next morning, we cross 25 kilometres back over the sea ice, the occasional seal disappearing into its breathing hole before we ever get close enough for a good view. They're a regular part of the Inuit diet and also used almost exclusively to feed the Inuits' dogs. Back in Pond, we pass by their frozen carcasses scattered about the chained dogs, who yap greetings to us as we return.

A freshly skinned polar bear is stretched out in front of the house of one of the Inuit guides, its humanoid skeleton still piled in an awkward heap nearby. Apparently the camouflaged man from Wisconsin got what he paid for. One of the rulers of this ice kingdom has been reduced to a rug in front of someone's fireplace. This unpleasant realization is tempered by the knowledge that his Inuit guides got paid and probably tipped well too, money that will go a long way in this community.

Glancing back at the wall of peaks we've been immersed in for the past 12 days, I feel content that a place barely grazed by humanity still exists — a place of true adventure where future rulers will be born in north-side dens and hundreds of peaks remain unclimbed. Long live the Ice Kingdom — long live Sirmilik.

ROUTE DETAIL

START (Saint John)

(Montreal)

FINISH (Vancouver)

Lunch with Mr. Trudeau

A private lunch with former Prime Minister Pierre Trudeau during an 8000-kilometre canoe journey across Canada.

What sets a canoeing expedition apart is that it purifies you more rapidly and inescapably than any other travel. Travel a thousand miles by train and you are a brute; pedal five hundred miles on a bicycle and you remain basically a bourgeois; paddle a hundred in a canoe and you are already a child of nature.

—PIERRE ELLIOTT TRUDEAU

"*Allo?! Vous ne pouvez pas camper ici.*"

The unfamiliar voice wakes me from my slumber.

Lance unzips the tent door. A police officer is crouched down in the vestibule, peering in at us. Montreal's rush hour traffic rumbles by on Avenue de Lorimier behind him.

"Excuse me?" Lance asks.

The officer switches seamlessly to English "Ah, you cannot camp here — this is a public park — no camping in downtown Montreal."

Lance explains that we're canoeing across Canada and had no place to camp but here late last night. The officer seems amused — the canoe beside the tent will give him a good story to tell later on. Regardless, we still can't camp there.

"I'll give you an hour to clear out of here... Good luck on your trip."

The previous evening, we were paddling upstream, hugging the shore of the St. Lawrence River, looking for a spot to get our canoe and gear onto shore. The whole south shore of the city consists of ten-metre-high shipping docks — made for freighters, not canoes, so it was impossible for us to get out there. The big ships are from places all around the globe — Singapore, China, Portugal, Spain — a collection as diverse as the population of our country.

We paddled on and on into darkness, working our way to the centre of the city underneath hulking freighters docked along the way. Every time we encountered a freighter, we were forced around it into the main current of the St. Lawrence, having to paddle with all our might just to inch around the metal beast before ferrying back close to the wharf, where the current eased.

As we approached the lights of the Jacques Cartier Bridge, low-lying Île Sainte-Hélène came into view at the other side of the bridge, so we ferried over the fast-moving water to the island. We landed in the shadows along shore, just below the large terrace of a bar on the edge of La Ronde, a large amusement park on the island. It was packed with patrons, completely unaware of us as we set up our portaging mid-wheels on the canoe. We loaded our gear into the canoe and rolled toward the bridge, the pulse of music and din of conversation slowly fading into the white noise of the city. The amusement park itself was closed, and we passed underneath a large Ferris wheel patiently waiting for the next day's influx of riders. It's one of the strangest places I've ever portaged a canoe through.

We pulled the canoe onto the bridge and walked over it, moving in the shadows of the sidewalk, oblivious cars passing only feet away, all in a hurry to get somewhere. We were in no hurry, moving slowly, the lights of the city twinkling around us in all directions as far as we could see.

At the far end of the bridge, we entered the park and found a clump of trees to set up the tent and stash our canoe. We bedded down at one a.m., after a 16-hour day on the water.

*   *   *

When you're attempting to be the first people to cross Canada by canoe in a single paddling season, long days are the norm. We're 26 days into what will end up being a 171-day, 8000-kilometre journey from Saint John to Vancouver. This day, though, is unique. The reason we pushed to get to downtown Montreal for May 12th is that we're having a rendezvous with former Prime Minister Pierre Elliot Trudeau. He heard about our trip and wants to meet us.

When I was growing up, in the 1970s and into the early '80s, I was always aware of Trudeau and proud he was our prime minister. There are two photos that captured his essence for me — one of him paddling a canoe in a tasselled buckskin jacket, the other of him doing a solo pirouette behind the Queen's back. Could any other prime minister pull that off? The answer is no.

Mr. Trudeau is an iconoclast — a playful, intelligent, adventurous man with a great sense of humour — as comfortable in the wilds of the boreal forest as he was in the stateroom. Before or since, there has never been a person who better exemplified the ideal of "Canadian-ness." He is someone I aspired to be like — plus he's my mother's favourite prime minister, so I have to meet him for her sake at the very least.

After the police officer leaves, Lance goes to find a phone to figure out in exactly what context we'll be meeting Mr. Trudeau. I stay with the gear. Lance is keen on drumming up some media attention about our trip and is hoping the former PM will help out in that regard. I don't care about media, I just want to meet the man.

*　　*　　*

It's morning now, and I feel like a bit of a homeless person. In fact, I am a homeless person. This tent is my only home — I ditched my rental in Vancouver to spend a half year on this trip. The problem now is that I *really* have to do my morning business — number two, so to speak.

The gear around me in this park is essential to our journey, so I don't dare abandon it to run around the city looking for a bathroom. Besides this porous little clump of trees, there's no privacy from the bustle of cars and people walking by. I don't need to be arrested for public indecency on the day I'm about to meet one of my heroes. Things are so much simpler in the wild.

The crucial moment is upon me, so necessity being the mother of invention, I slip into the vestibule of the tent. Pulling out my Leatherman tool, I unfold the saw and cut a perfect one-by-one-foot square in the manicured grass. After quickly digging out a functional amount of dirt from underneath the square, I relieve myself in the hole, fill dirt around my business and then replace the square of grass over top. It's as if nothing had happened there whatsoever. The coverage is seamless, and I'm proud of my bit of craftsmanship. Figuring out how to solve crises on the fly during the course of an expedition is one of the joys of the process. This twisted delight is something I decide to keep to myself — no need for Lance or Pierre Trudeau to know about it.

Lance comes back and tells me he got in touch with Mr. Trudeau's secretary and we've been invited to have lunch with the former prime minister — he won't talk to any media, he just wants to talk to us about our trip.

We pack up our gear into the canoe and roll it into downtown Montreal. Lance never notices anything amiss in the vestibule area. A perfect crime.

In the bustle of downtown Montreal, we draw sideways looks from passersby as they make way for the big yellow boat rolling down the sidewalk.

Tonight we're laying over in the city while we resupply, so we stop at the Ramada and get a room. The concierge helps us stash our canoe and gear in a safe spot in the underground parking area, and we're free for our lunch date.

*　　*　　*

The IBM building is a 47-story skyscraper in downtown Montreal. We're in the elevator of this glass and steel structure, hurtling up to the 25th floor. Our clothes are dirty and worn after a month on trip, and their pungent smell is a mix of dirt and sweat — not exactly the attire you want to wear when meeting a dignitary, but it's all we have. You don't bring natty city clothes on trip. A couple of business people cling to the side of the elevator opposite us, trying, it seems, to get as far away from our aroma as possible. In the city we're homeless vagrants, and treated accordingly.

On the 25th floor, we step onto the polished office floors of the Heenan Blaikie law firm, where the former prime minister is counsel. We step up to a desk blocking the entrance to a posh room with a spiral staircase and a broad view of the city. A pretty woman glances up at us and smiles.

"Frank and Lance?"

"Yes, ma'am," Lance replies.

"Mr. Trudeau will be right down. Have a seat."

We do as she asks, and she picks up her phone.

"Mr. Trudeau? The canoeists are here... okay."

About a minute later, a man blurs down the stairs from an upper room — at a full run — and hits the carpet striding straight toward us, a big grin on his face. We both stand quickly at attention. He throws out his hand to me first.

"Welcome to Montreal! Lance?"

"No, sir, I'm Frank."

"Excellent, Frank, excellent, pleased to meet you!"

After shaking hands with Lance, he pauses for a beat to look at us. He's shorter than I expect, about five-foot-eight, but wiry and fast in his movements. It's him — but older of course than the man I remember from the newspapers when I was growing up. The creases in his face are deep, showing the wear of a life well lived. Beneath the weathered features are the bright blue eyes of a child — full of energy and wonder. I like him instantly. I wonder where we'll be eating — an upscale patio of a Montreal cafe, perhaps?

"How about chicken gyros for lunch?" he asks. "The cafeteria downstairs has pretty good food."

We nod agreeably and follow him into the elevator, joined by Jean and Claude, two of his friends from the firm. All three of them are canoeists and eager for a little shop talk to break up the day.

The cafeteria is, well, a cafeteria. Workers from all walks of life are lined up with their plastic trays, putting through their orders at a cash register before moving down the line to pick up their food. We fall in behind Mr. Trudeau with our trays. He orders us chicken gyros with fries, and we chit-chat about our trip. He peppers us with questions as we stand in line: "How many days have you been out?" "What's your route across the country?" "What kind of food are you eating?"

With gyros on our trays, we find a small, round table and stuff five plastic stools around it. No one seems to recognize our most famous PM, or, if they do, they pay him no mind. Perhaps seeing him ordering lunch on a plastic tray in a cafeteria convinces them he couldn't be a dignitary. He blends right in. It is 1995, of course — had this been 20 years later, a circle of smartphone vultures would be uploading his image to Instagram, making a casual public get-together like this an impossibility. But it's 1995, and respect for an individual's privacy is something that still exists.

The conversation flows easily within the group. I talk about doing two 32-kilometre portages with the canoe on my back along an abandoned railway in order to get around ice-choked sections of the St.

John River at the beginning of our trip. Mr. Trudeau counters with a solo trip he did as a young man, paddling his canoe from Montreal to James Bay. He also completed trips with Canadian canoeing icons like Bill Mason and Eric Morse. When dialled in on the subject of canoeing, he speaks with joy and energy.

Lance tries to steer the conversation in a different direction, to see if the PM will help us drum up some publicity for the trip.

"Would you consider joining us for a meeting we have with the press later this afternoon?" he asks.

Mr. Trudeau visibly deflates. He speaks suddenly very slowly, as if the life had been drained from his body.

"The media and I... we've had our time together."

An awkward silence follows, with Mr. Trudeau glancing down at his half-eaten gyro. Jean slides in to fill the void and steer the conversation back to tripping, "We're going on a ten-day trip down a river on Baffin Island this summer — it's never been paddled before."

The PM suddenly comes back to life and fills us in on the details of this next venture. In that moment I realize that even though he is a revered politician who led our country for almost two decades, his journeys in the wilderness are far closer to his heart. His eyes turn to dead lumps of coal when politics and the media are brought up, but he's an illuminated soul when we chat about canoe tripping. In the golden years of his life, his experiences in nature mean far more to him than political success and accolades.

Talk turns to his children — in particular to his youngest son, Michel. Mr. Trudeau beams with pride as he describes his lifestyle: "Michel is a ski bum in Whistler in the winter, and in the summer he's a canoe trip guide. It's a good life."

Lance and I bring up a conundrum we have — our route through Montreal is blocked by the Lachine Rapids, and we'd ideally like to avoid a long portage through the city.

Mr. Trudeau's eyes light up, "Let's go back up to my office and look at some maps. I'm sure there's a better way around."

Up in his spacious perch, Jean, Lance, myself and Mr. Trudeau spread out a map of the city on his desk. The PM points to a canal that runs alongside the rapids.

"There — that's how the freighters get around the rapids — you can go there too. Let me make a call to confirm it."

The next thing we know, he's making a call to the lock master of the canals. After a couple of minutes of conversation, he hangs up and smiles at me.

"No problem — he says your canoe can use the canal — it will be an easy paddle from there." I chuckle — it's nice to have Pierre Trudeau running logistics for you.

We've spent over two hours talking canoeing with Mr. Trudeau, and our time is up. After presenting us with a six-pack of Canadian maple syrup as a parting gift, he walks us down to the elevator doors of his office, both of us trying to keep up with his quick cadence. He shakes our hands and bids us a warm farewell and good luck. As the elevator door closes, he smiles and gives a little wave.

Three years later, Mr. Trudeau's son Michel — whose vagabond wilderness lifestyle he so admired — is killed in an avalanche in British Columbia. It devastates the PM, and he passes away less than two years later. Michel was a child of nature, and so was his father. May they both rest in peace.

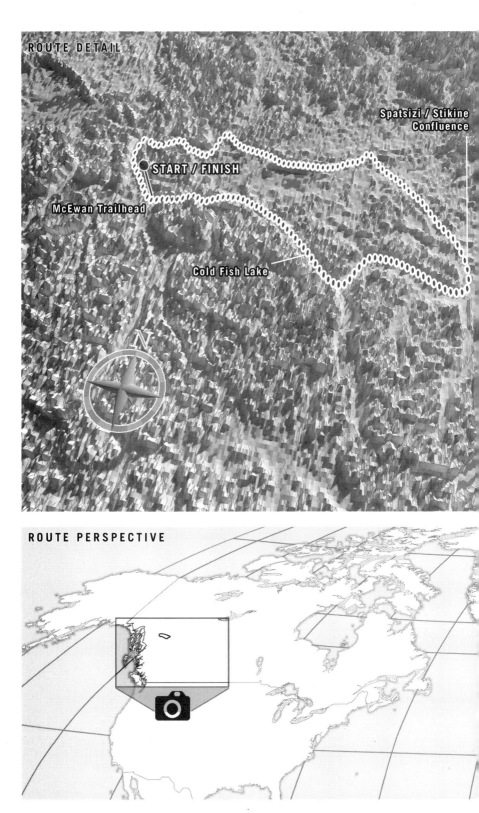

ROUTE DETAIL

Spatsizi / Stikine Confluence

START / FINISH

McEwan Trailhead

Cold Fish Lake

N

ROUTE PERSPECTIVE

Place for a Mission

A 280-kilometre pack rafting and hiking journey through one of British Columbia's most threatened places.

ORIGINALLY PUBLISHED IN SUMMER 2016 ISSUE OF *EXPLORE MAGAZINE*

"Why is he here?" I wonder to myself. I'm thinking about Shawn, who is sitting beside me, driving his Matrix 130 kilometres an hour northward on the Cassiar Highway, hell-bent on getting to the start of our journey. It's late in the afternoon, middle of August, and only a couple of weeks earlier Shawn said yes to this excursion.

By evening (and after two days of driving from Vancouver), we'll be at the McEwan trailhead beside the Klappan River, our entrance to the Spatsizi Plateau Wilderness. The mission: a 280-kilometre hiking and pack-rafting loop that will bring us through the protected heart of one of the world's ecological gems — the Sacred Headwaters.

We are taunted all the way up the Cassiar by the gleaming towers of the 344-kilometre-long Northwest Transmission Line (NTL) — a $716 million white elephant constructed by the provincial government to encourage a rush of resource extraction in the North that threatens to forever alter the landscape.

Industrialization is what we came here to escape, not see more of... but back to Shawn, and the "why." Why does a guy drop everything to take on a challenging wilderness mission with someone he barely knows. Why do I for that matter... why does anyone? Is it an escape? Is it a sense of accomplishment? Or is it simply the experience itself? Perhaps the answer lies somewhere up on that splendorous plateau...

* * *

Quagmire

Shawn is crotch-deep in the swamp, about halfway through the first 60-kilometre hiking section to Cold Fish Lake from the Klappan River. The map to the area describes the zone we're passing through simply as "Muskeg-Bog." Churning his way out of the black, foot-sucking quagmire, he emerges with a wide smile — more mud than man. Our 70-pound packs, loaded with 12 days of food, pack rafts and camping gear, make moving through the sludge that much tougher — turning a pair of 170-pound guys into 240-pound monsters.

I falsely assumed that record drought conditions throughout the province this summer would have dried everything out — that the footing would be firm and the rivers low. Up here, though, it's exactly the opposite — it seems to have its own weather system — drought be damned. Two weeks of steady, torrential rain preceded us, absolutely saturating the grounds and turning trails into creeks.

This is completely unpredictable terrain, where I have to watch every step in the muck so I don't break one of my overloaded legs in the matrix of roots and rocks that lie hidden beneath. Though it's a seemingly miserable experience, I find great joy in this.

I've discovered that Shawn, like me, also revels in the punishment. As I said earlier, we don't know each other that well, our main acquaintance having been made when we were part of a larger group at a backcountry ski cabin a few years earlier. He let me know that if I ever needed a trip mate, he'd be keen — so when my original partner fell through a short time ago, Shawn stepped into the void.

After 20 years of undertaking extended wilderness missions with various partners, I've discovered that most humans seem to revel in the difficulty of moving under their own power. Like bears, wolves or elk, people are made to move all day, every day — and ideally we move in unspoiled nature. It's hard-wired into our million-year DNA. Only in the past century have we bought into the marketed idea that retiring to a rocking chair on a porch is the holy grail we should aspire to.

In the sprawling terrain of the Spatsizi, the routine of "nine to five" and Netflix is replaced by a world where all our senses are wholly alive. In the wild, especially areas unfamiliar to us, every stride or paddle-stroke reveals something we've never seen before, thrusting us into the moment.

Conversely, civilization leans toward the predictable. Every surprise is accounted for. I'm as duped as anyone, for as I write this at my home in North Vancouver, my lizard brain feels the urge to check my Instagram account... which is reason enough to go rambling in the Spatsizi, where the closest thing to Instagram is thousand-year-old stone petroglyphs.

The local Tahltan First Nation name for this area is Klabona (Sacred Headwaters), which refers to the source of the four salmon-bearing river systems here: the Klappan and Spatsizi (which run north into the Stikine), and the Nass and Skeena.

Just west of the park boundary, Todagin Mountain looks across the Klappan Valley to the plateau. The flank of that peak is currently being eviscerated by the Red Chris Mine, which was recently approved and is currently the sole beneficiary of the aforementioned NTL.

If not for the foresight of an earlier generation, the vast protected area Shawn and I are travelling would also have been staked by industrial interests. Even with parks status, though, people interested in the preservation of this unique ecosystem have to be ever vigilant: that protection is now under threat, with the current provincial government's passing of Bill 4. The bill allows feasibility studies that could lead to the construction of pipelines, power lines and roads through BC's sacred parks.

*   *   *

High Water

On our second evening, a pair of mountain goats scurry away as we descend a scree slope down to Cullivan Creek. Usually a wade, the creek is high and humming, with grey flood waters that will surely sweep us away if we try to ford it. This is where our pack rafts come into play for the first time. Within minutes we have the five-pound rafts inflated and four-piece kayak paddles assembled. We ferry across the torrent without incident, but a thought creeps into my mind that this water level could make things interesting in a few days when we reach the big rivers.

Breaking from the clutches of the muskeg a day later, we amble in meadows surrounded by rust-coloured peaks that break in a line from the emerald forest below. The clanking of cowbells alert us to... a pair of horses. The collared duo are wandering freely and we stop to say hello. A little farther on, we find a dozen more horses in a corral but no sign of their keepers. They are beasts of burden at rest. We're beasts of burden too, but our rest lies a couple of kilometres ahead, at Cold Fish Lake.

The deep blue lake is nestled in a broad cirque. Alongside its western shore we come upon a cluster of cabins maintained by BC Parks that are typically accessed by float plane. No one is there except Patricia and Eric — a middle-aged couple who volunteer as park hosts.

Confirming my suspicions about the water level, Eric tells us, "The bush pilot that brings in hikers and supplies was in a few days ago and he says he's never seen the Stikine River as high as it is right now, *ever* — and he's flown this area for 30 years."

We stay the night in one of the cabins, taking advantage of the luxury of the wood stove to dry out our wet gear. The next morning, Pat sends us off with a care package of chocolate chip cookies and a side of bacon. We inflate the rafts, wave goodbye to her and Eric and paddle the eight kilometres across Cold Fish Lake, where we pick up the trail again.

The path becomes overgrown, strewn with logs and then washed out when it reaches Mink Creek. We bushwhack for a couple of kilometres through forest, meadows and beaver ponds until the Spatsizi River reveals itself.

The river looks fast but inviting — apparently our days of hiking with only an occasional rain burst here and there have given the waters time to settle down from peak flood. We camp in a thicket of Jack pine along the banks of the river, and the bright smells of the forest, water and mountain air combine into a freshness I wish I could bottle and reapply every day for the rest of my life. In the shadow of Mount Skady, Shawn and I talk in the waning light beside our fire, savouring this moment in the geographical heart of the Spatsizi Wilderness.

For 40 kilometres the next day, we paddle the twists and turns of the Spatsizi Valley through light wave trains before being spit out into the mighty Stikine River. We camp at the confluence. A rain shower moves through, followed by a rainbow and gorgeous sunset. Shawn and I play a best-of-three round of bocce with the portable set we have carried with us to this point. The game becomes our post-dinner ritual for the rest of the trip.

*　　*　　*

Nemetchek

Nemetchek. NEM-ET-CHEK. The name rolls abrasively off the tongue, sounding rough and hard as sandpaper. And Ron Nemetcheck personifies that sound. We're sitting in the living room of his two-story log house alongside the Stikine River. His wife, Maria, waved us in for coffee as we drifted by. I'm five cups deep and getting to know all about Ron's world.

He and Maria own North River Outfitting, and their clientele is the richest of the world's rich, who come to hunt big game in the region, with Ron's guidance. He's as gregarious and outrageous a man as you'll ever meet, with one-liners flowing out of him like water from a spring: "Don't piss on my back and tell me it's raining" (said to a haughty client who spoke down to him), or "You may have met better men, but not one as sincere" (his favourite pickup line).

Like the Sacred Headwaters region — a bastion of wilderness bordered by transmission lines and mines — Ron is full of contrasts. On one hand he wants the surrounding area to maintain its pristine quality so it can support trophy animals like the grizzly bears that his clients come to hunt. On the other, when I mention the ugliness of the NTL, he simply shrugs and says, "People got to work."

Though Ron is a sort of conservationist, he pokes fun at Wade Davis, the famed ethnobotanist who has been highly critical of the Red Chris Mine. Noting that Davis's residence faces the mountain, Ron quips, "Ha! He's just a rich guy who's pissed that his view is ruined."

Ron has his opinions, but what shines through about the man is his generosity — he and Maria would have fed and housed us for as long as we wished. No matter your politics in the North, people here are friendly and will go the extra mile to help out a stranger.

We part the outpost with our bellies full of moose stew, coffee and our heads full of enough Ron Nemetchek stories to last us the rest of the trip.

* * *

End of the Mission

Our run through Jewel Rapids the next day is invigorating as we manoeuvre around the large holes and collapsing waves driven by the higher-than-usual water levels. I lead the way and Shawn follows behind, hooting with joy.

As we exit the rapid, I spot a grizzly on the shore for a few moments before it bolts back into the forest. It reminds me that we are just part of the food chain here, utterly irrelevant except in our own hubris. My anonymous insignificance in this landscape is comforting. We camp in a sandy site beside an old burn, have an excellent best-of-three bocce session and then drop away to sleep beside the hissing Stikine under a star-blanketed night sky.

A couple of mornings later, we arrive at our final transition point at the mouth of the Klappan River, where we pack up our rafts and hike out the remaining 20 kilometres to the vehicle via an abandoned rail grade. After nine days in this paradise, our mission is nearing completion as we return full circle to our starting point. Shawn and I are good friends now — bonded through the experience of working together to accomplish our route. We've already planned another big one for next summer.

As we walk side by side during our final few hours along the overgrown grade, I mention how much I appreciate him joining me on this venture.

"How could I say no?" he replies "This is what life is all about. Cool journeys in the wilderness are what I live for."

It's true. It's why he's here. It's why I'm here. Shawn is searching in life, I'm searching in life — and I think to a great degree most people are. When we're in the midst of an immersive mission, though, the search is over — we've found "it." In areas like the Spatsizi Plateau Wilderness, the noise of society disappears into a landscape unchanged for millennia. We are at peace here. We are home.

Towns and cities produce few of these life-affirming missions — it's mostly dinner dates, meetings and smartphone-tapping. Intrusive projects like the NTL and Red Chris Mine bring these comfortably numbing elements of modernity to the wilderness — an intrinsically strong argument for these schemes having no place up here.

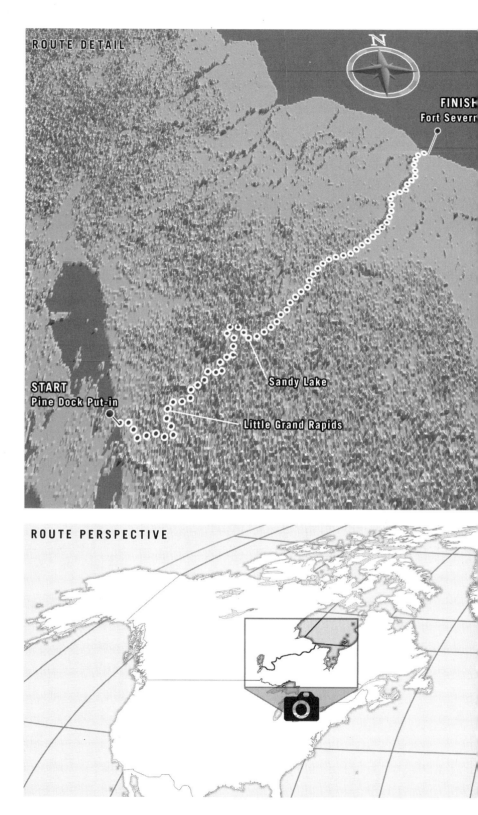

ROUTE DETAIL

N

FINISH
Fort Severn

START
Pine Dock Put-in

Sandy Lake

Little Grand Rapids

ROUTE PERSPECTIVE

Spirit of the Sasquatch

Seeking the truth about the existence of Sasquatch in northern Ontario during a 1350-kilometre canoe expedition through the remote Little North.

ORIGINALLY PUBLISHED IN SPRING 2015 ISSUE OF *EXPLORE MAGAZINE*

I believe that imagination is stronger than knowledge.
That myth is more important than history.

—ROBERT FULGHUM

On day eight of our 1350-kilometre canoe journey from Pine Dock, Manitoba, to Fort Severn, Ontario, my partner Rob and I are in the Ojibway community of Little Grand Rapids, sorting our oats into bags on the dock in front of the Northern Store. We've just come through the "character-building" section of our trip, having travelled 275 kilometres upstream on the Bloodvein River and then through a series of lakes connected by densely bushed portages. Ahead of us lies a waterway matrix that will take us to the source of the mighty Severn River, which we plan to follow to its conclusion at the southwest corner of Hudson Bay.

An imposing 300-pound man ambles by and strikes up a conversation. After pleasantries about our trip and the weather, he asks if we've seen any animals along the way. We mention the usual bear/moose/beaver combo of boreal mammals — but this doesn't seem to satisfy Enil Keeper, a member of the band council. He has a very specific creature in mind.

"How about Sasquatch — you guys see any Sasquatch?" I hold back a smirk and check his face to see if he's putting us on. He isn't. He's serious.

"The Big Wild," "The Little North" — or whatever else people call the vast swath of taiga north of Lake Superior and east of Lake Winnipeg — is one of the few areas on Earth where man is peripheral to nature. Since the region's First Nations there shifted from nomadic to settled life, it's wilder and more free of human contact than ever before.

This expansive "dark zone" is one of the few areas not tainted by artificial light or able to be penetrated in detail by anyone with a computer, tablet or smartphone. Here, the possibility remains that millennia-old mythical creatures may actually exist.

Twenty years of annual wilderness expeditions have yet to yield a trip in which I don't learn a lesson of varying degrees of significance. Last year I got pummelled in the Northwest Passage and learned that travelling while looking in the wrong direction the entire time (i.e., rowing) is not a pleasurable way to go about things. This year, Enil put the hairy head of the Sasquatch on my radar.

*   *   *

A Scourge

Before we turn the focus to Bigfoot, another, smaller beast demands our rapt attention. Three years ago, I did a trip from Thunder Bay north through the Winisk system in the worst fire season in Ontario history. Fifty-five thousand hectares of forest burned to a crisp and so, it seems, did all the mosquitoes. There were none to be found.

It was pure pleasure. This year, however, a colder than usual winter combined with a cool, moist spring provided flourishing conditions for the wee beasts.

The Bloodvein became Manitoba's first Canadian Heritage River in 1987 and has been used for centuries as a travel route by the Oji-Cree and Ojibway to go back and forth from the interior to Lake Winnipeg. These days it's a popular two- to three-week downstream canoe trip.

Few if any people still travel upstream on the river, but it's necessary in order to earn our payoff at the beginning of the Severn. I've always preferred traditional travel methods over the convenience, cost and carbon dioxide of a bush plane. After all, nothing worthwhile is easy.

Paddling upstream can be as satisfying as going down. The key is to find the path of least resistance and exploit it. Like the spatial challenges inherent in a game of chess, working your way up eddies and dragging through rapids is an engaging and immersive activity — and the best way to learn the intricacies of a river.

It's our first evening on the Bloodvein. We've just enjoyed a leisurely swim in the rapid in front of the campsite and are having a sip of whiskey as we watch the sun set below the fringe of spruce on the far bank. As the last sliver of orange disappears, the sky suddenly darkens as clouds of mosquitoes descend upon us like one of the seven plagues of Egypt. We've made the horrible mistake of not being in our tent at the onset of the "witching hour."

We scramble to put on bug jackets and DEET, hurriedly brush our teeth and then dive into the tent. About a hundred of the vermin enter with us and we slap, crush and smear them all over the inside walls before stripping down to underwear in the muggy evening so we can ease into sleep.

An inch-thick layer of the *kitturiaq* black out the mesh above our heads. Their chorus, ominous yet soothing, is so loud it sounds like someone has hung a high-voltage power line over us. We slip into slumber to this bedtime lullaby.

At about two a.m., Rob is busting to pee. He decides that the bug danger has dissipated and elects to step outside to relieve himself. In the course of this action, he is assaulted by a thousand thirsty suitors, many of whom he proceeds to bring back inside the tent with him. I abruptly wake as he steamrolls over me, and find myself in a half-dazed nightmare, clawing at my face before realizing the situation and resuming the slaughter from earlier that evening.

I'm not stoked about Rob's action but quickly forgive him — he's from the West Coast, and this is his first canoe trip with the Eastern mosquito. From that point on in the journey, each of us converts our spare water bottle into a urine receptacle so that if the urge arises at night, we can take care of business inside the protected confines of the tent.

*   *   *

Bushwhack Portage

"There's lots of them up where you're going."

"Really? You've seen them before?"

"Oh, yeah — a couple of times."

"What happened?"

"I was fishing with my friend just north of here. We were walking along a portage trail from one lake back to where we had our boat. Then from the forest I heard this growling and grinding of teeth and the whole bush where it came from shook. Fear shot up my spine and I almost shit my pants on the spot... and it was no bear — I know what bears sound like. We both ran to the boat and jumped in. I looked back and saw more bushes on the shore shaking wildly — he'd followed us to the end of the portage. I've never been so scared in my life."

The thing about creating a modern route via the ancient waterway paths of the North is that portages that were once there have largely been absorbed back into the flora. Where, decades ago, people would take a month or so to travel by canoe to hunt or reach a trading post, the advent of the airplane has left these routes abandoned — returned to nature and her creatures, be they real or imagined.

We're in the middle of a one-kilometre bushwhack portage from Giraffe Lake to a smaller, unnamed lake on the other side. This route was once part of a standard connection from Sasaginnigak Lake to the Dogskin River but is now barely discernible. A faint mossy trail is covered by a dense stand of spruce with only a few inches of space between the trees — a literal wall that blocks our progress. The forest is so impenetrable that Enil's Sasquatch could be looking at us from ten feet away and we'd never even know it.

We painstakingly work our way forward with the canoe, sliding it through, over and around the seemingly endless barrier. The mosquitoes, blackflies and moose flies have definitely not abandoned the area and draw liberally from our blood bank.

The trail disappears completely at a rock outcrop, after which we progress more easily through open old-growth forest, eventually breaking out onto the lakeshore. After a refreshing dip, I reverse my compass course and back it up with GPS. I zip the device into my pants pocket, then double back for our remaining pack.

Moving quickly, I follow the general direction of the bearing and at about halfway decide to confirm my position with the GPS. I reach for it and discover it is gone. Somewhere along the way a branch must have yanked the tether of the unit and pulled it free.

I briefly try to retrace my steps in order to recover it, but quickly realize the hopelessness of the task. Strangely, I smile and feel liberated. As this portage has returned to the forest, I've been reverted to good ol' map and compass. The loss means I have to be absolutely "present" in my navigation from now on, perpetually aware of my location at all times in relation to a paper map — no more lazy dependence on technology to get me out of a jam.

* * *

Another Furry Critter

"What do you think would happen if it caught you — would it eat you?"

"Oh, no — Sasquatch are herbivores — but I'm not going to fight something that's twice the size of me."

"How come no one actually sees them — you only saw bushes shaking."

"They're too smart — they know how to stay away from people and stay out of sight. And there's lots of room up here to stay away from people."

Enil's story of his Sasquatch encounter was something Rob and I discussed in the canoe throughout the journey. Farther along, the possibility of seeing a Sasquatch was reinforced when, unprompted, a woman in the community of Muskrat Dam Lake also asked us if we'd encountered one along the way. She claimed people in town had seen tracks over by their airport only a week earlier.

This second mention really propped up our Sasquatch antennae — to the point where we were actively looking for them all the way down the length of the 981-kilometre Severn River. Inevitably, though, any "Sasquatch" we spotted on shore seemed to be leaning up against the stump of a tree — and then ended up merely being the tree's root ball.

On our final day of the trip, we're having lunch among the bleached limestone boulders of the Wapakopowistik Rapids. The previous evening, we intentionally camped 90 kilometres from our destination town of Fort Severn — the northernmost community in Ontario. Pregnant female polar bears often wander 50 kilometres or more upstream from Hudson Bay at this time of year in search of a den, so we tried to sleep out of their range. Having one poke its head into our tent to say hello would not be ideal, to say the least.

As we eat, I stand up from time to time to periscope the surroundings. We are much closer to the bay now, and an encounter is a possibility. These rocks would provide perfect camouflage for a sneaky critter. I feel a bit exposed, as I usually travel with a gun in polar bear country. Since we were only going to be in their habitat on our last day, I decided the weight and maintenance of carrying a firearm 1300 kilometres to this point was not worth it.

About an hour farther on, Rob and I ferry our canoe over from the mainland to cruise the edge of one of the many islands that mark the Severn delta. My eye suddenly catches movement directly in front of us and, as if appearing from nowhere, a fat, healthy polar bear ambles along the shore of the island toward us. I couldn't be more surprised or delighted if I'd seen an actual Sasquatch. We are 20 metres from land and the bear doesn't seem agitated, so we drift slowly by, watching it in awe. It yawns, stretching open its jaws to reveal an impressive set of teeth, then half-interestedly stares at us before continuing on its way.

* * *

Sasquatch Revealed

Our journey concludes, and we never see an actual Sasquatch — but my interest is piqued. My post-expedition research offers little evidence to support the belief that the Sasquatch is part of local First Nations legend. The cultural origin of this particular anthropoid actually comes from First Nations of the Pacific Northwest.

On day 17 of our 26-day journey — not far from the Oji-Cree community of Sandy Lake — brothers Jesse and Adam Fiddler pull up to our campsite in their boat and generously cut us a fresh steak from a moose they've just shot. We've already eaten, but it's no problem for two hungry trippers to put back a second dinner — particularly such delicious local fare.

As luck would have it, we bump into Jesse on our paddle into town the next day, and he invites us up to his family's property to share in a traditional feast they're having that afternoon.

In between bites of fried moose liver, pickerel, fried bannock, moose soup and boiled moose meat, we have a fascinating conversation with the patriarch of the clan — Ennis Fiddler — whose encyclopedic knowledge of the area is startling. However, I must have slipped into a food coma, because I completely forget to ask him about the history of Sasquatch in the region.

I track him down later, after our trip is completed, reaching him by phone just as ice was beginning to form on Sandy Lake. I ask him about the Sasquatch in Oji-Cree folklore. He thinks for a moment, then states flatly that he's never heard of Sasquatch in their oral history — not from his parents, his grandparents, anyone.

In Ennis's words, "The idea of a Sasquatch is relatively new, there's nothing in our oral history about it. It's a legend from somewhere else that's been imported and adopted into the culture of some of the communities up here. I think this is because our world today is shrinking, and cultures are colliding. Everyone is connected to everyone else. People are borrowing ideas from every corner of the earth and adapting it to their environment."

It all suddenly made sense. The Sasquatch is a creature who embodies the wilderness, who requires wilderness to exist. So even though it did not originally arise in northwestern Ontario, the Sasquatch made its way there — if not literally, then emblematically — because that's one of the last areas in which it fits.

Like the Sasquatch legend, the ideal of wilderness is mysterious, endless and impenetrable. The region through which we did our trip is the largest pristine forest left on Earth. At twice the size of England, it's an area that has remained largely unchanged since the last ice age. Protected by a phalanx of mosquitoes, disappearing portages and polar bears, in many ways this zone is more primeval than ever. It's the perfect place to transplant and grow the Sasquatch story.

If, through the relentless clawing of industry, sweeping wildlands like this cease to exist, so too will the Sasquatch. For now — through people like Enil Keeper who truly believe in it — the legend of the Sasquatch in the Little North has taken root and is growing. We can only hope it will continue to do so into the foreseeable future — for the myth is more important than human history furthering itself through our last reaches of wilderness.

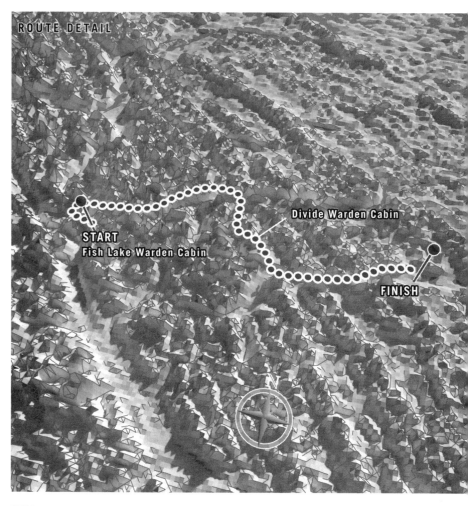

ROUTE DETAIL

Divide Warden Cabin

START
Fish Lake Warden Cabin

FINISH

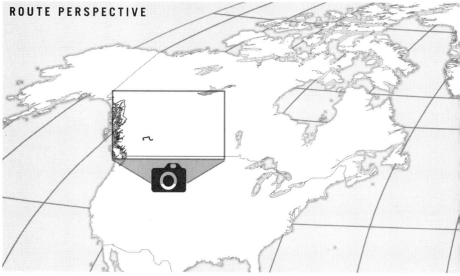

ROUTE PERSPECTIVE

In the Land of Hairy Beasts

Uncovering the heart of Banff National Park with wardens both past and present during a mammal-tracking survey on skis.

ORIGINALLY PUBLISHED IN WINTER 2015/16 ISSUE OF *EXPLORE MAGAZINE*

The massive metal door creaks open and I follow Dave Garrow into a cavernous freight container that's been converted into a freezer for the most unique of purposes. A variety of frozen mammal carcasses — mostly elk, deer and beaver — are piled in the back half of the unit in a tangle of body parts.

"We use these to bait grizzlies for study and relocation purposes," he says casually. "The elk and deer are roadkill from the highway; we get the beaver carcasses from a local trapper."

Next door to the freezer is a high-ceilinged abattoir where carcasses scraped off the highway are processed into usable pieces. As in a scene from a serial killer's lair in *Criminal Minds*, long heavy chains with menacing hooks hang over a bloodstained floor. The air is thick with the ripe stench of death. Welcome to the glamorous world of a Banff National Park "resource conservation officer" (not "park ranger," as I mistakenly first referred to him).

Dave is a strapping, dark-haired hulk of a man with piercing eyes, a stoic nature and an extremely dry sense of humour. He has a passion for journeying through wild places under his own power — and gets paid to do it.

Outside the abattoir, we walk past bear traps lined up neatly in a row. Pointing to one of the minivan-sized cylinders, Dave explains how they are used: "We put a beaver carcass in the back of the trap and wait for the bear to come. Some big males love it when we put these out. They know they're going to be trapped but don't care because they know we'll release them a short while later, and there's an easy meal there. Some younger bears and females get a bit more stressed in the cage. It's all part of the deal when trying to safely manage a large population of bears so close to a busy summer tourist town."

Human-caused mortality of grizzlies is a big problem in the park, particularly because of trains hitting the animals. One of the key problems for Parks staff like Dave is to figure out how to minimize these bear-train collisions.

A hundred metres away, a helicopter waits to take us on our mission for the week — a 120-kilometre ski traverse through the remote northwest corner of the park in order to undertake a mammal occupancy survey and to service dozens of remote camera traps designed to log the wild inhabitants of Canada's oldest national park. A third person — Ross Glenfied, a former Banff warden now on sabbatical — fills out our team for the journey.

Our pilot, Megan, flies us over endless jagged peaks on a bluebird day — a privilege in itself, as only Parks-sanctioned helicopters are allowed to fly within Banff boundaries. No commercial heli-tours or heli-skiing operations are allowed. Herds of mountain sheep stream over the ridges as we pass above. Although it's early March, the snowpack is exceptionally low, making me wonder how much actual skiing we'll be able to do.

We do a quick stop en route at the Indianhead Lodge Warden Cabin to drop off our midway food supply. The snow coverage looks okay but patchy. We fly on to our starting point at Fish Lakes Warden Cabin, where I'm happy to see the snow is easily more than a metre deep, a promising sign for the first few days of our traverse. With the chopper running, we quickly dump our skis and gear in the snow, and Megan flies off, leaving us to shuttle our stuff to the hut.

The cabin is in great shape, and one of five we'll use along the way. Not accessible to the general public, each warden cabin is set up with a horse corral and all the basics necessary for Parks staff to do their work while in the backcountry. Most work is done in the summer, when staff can travel by horseback — a tradition in the park since its inception in 1885.

That afternoon, we head down the Pipestone Valley to service the first of many remote cameras along our route. These devices collect data on the distribution and abundance of grizzly bears, wolverine, lynx and other mammal species. Banff staff use this information to identify changes in distribution of species and competition effects on them throughout the vast landscape of the park.

The afternoon sun is warm and the snow heavy, making for survival skiing in the "shmoo" with our lightweight touring equipment. The locations of the cameras are plugged into Dave's GPS, and we find the first one strapped to a spruce by an opening. Dave swaps in a fresh memory card and batteries, then locks the weather-tight camera back to the tree. Heading back, we slog on to the next camera, about a kilometre farther uphill, past the cabin. The day turns for the worse as Dave discovers his ski binding is broken just before the return descent. Ever the cool cat, he quips, "Guess I'm skiing back on one leg."

Pulling off his best waterski slalom technique, he manages to work his way on one plank back to the cabin, where we jury rig a fix using some old screws and pine sap to coax the binding back to life.

Day two is 22 kilometres long, with two 8,000-foot-high mountain passes to cross. We approach Pipestone Pass in the teeth of a howling wind, where the blowing snow feels like thousands of tiny needles bouncing off my face. Well above treeline, it's like we're moving inside a Ping-Pong ball of whiteness.

We pause to wait for Ross, who is slightly behind, grinding valiantly along on ski equipment from the 1980s. Dave and I muse about whether he still uses pine tar to wax them. The oldest of our group at 49 years of age, Ross is admirably tough — you can take the warden out of the mountains but not the mountains out of the warden.

As we drop over the other side of the pass, the wind eases, the sun returns and we ski by a porcupine drinking water from a small creek that has opened in the snow. Dave is surprised the porcupines are up this high, where only a few clumps of subalpine fir krummholz stick up from the snow.

After reaching Clearwater Pass, we ski down the frozen Clearwater River and arrive at the Clearwater Lakes Warden Cabin. A classic log cabin chinked with clay, it is one of the original warden cabins in the park and is officially recognized as a federal heritage building.

The structure sits at the base of Mount Harris, in a clearing in the Clearwater Valley. Built in 1930, it looks very much the same as it did over 85 years ago. A simple one-room design, it's just big enough to sleep three. Two in the bunk, one on the floor. I get the floor.

Ross explains to me that the wardens' role has changed significantly since they first started patrolling the park in in the early 20th century. Back then the wardens would literally stay year-round in the backcountry, hauling in their loads and patrolling by horseback in the summer and by snowshoe in the winter.

"By the time I was a warden in the 1990s, we only stayed out on patrol for ten days at a time. Nowadays, wardens don't patrol the backcountry at all. This trip here is one of the few extended backcountry projects that Parks still conducts." In fact, a majority of warden positions were reclassified in 2009 to more specialized titles, like Dave's "resource conservation officer" moniker.

A link to the history of these cabins is the logbooks that still reside there. The journals go back to the 1970s and give insight to the trials and tribulations of backcountry Parks staff of years gone by, who slept in these very same beds.

A telling excerpt from June 30, 1981, by P. Applejohn gives us a peek at the challenges they faced: "Miserable day, miserable time, miserable lost horse. Couldn't find him."

A couple of weeks later, on July 15th, P. Applejohn writes, "Caught miserable horse, Snow, rain, cloud, sun. Not necessarily in that order."

I imagine those wardens got quite lonely at times too, judging by the old copies of *Playboy* buried deep in the pile of old magazines in the corner. Apparently a sweep of such periodicals was conducted a few years ago, but in this little-used cabin a couple of well-worn issues still survive.

Besides servicing the cameras, the main objective of our journey is completing the "mammal occupancy survey" done annually by Parks at this time of year. By logging animal tracks along the same transect over a number of years and then plugging that data into an algorithm, occupancy rates of mammals within Banff can be accurately determined and then managed accordingly.

Dave keeps a booklet handy, and on every kilometre along our route he logs the mammal tracks he sees in the snow; Ross and I help out. In this way we get a good overall picture of which animals are out and about, and how many of them there are. In the course of the survey, I spot tracks of lynx, wolf, wolverine, hare, moose, porcupine and fox. As far as actual physical sightings, I spot a lone wolf on the river, and the aforementioned porcupine. The high number of tracks we see en route show the animals are there — but also that they are wary of us. This reaffirms the transect and remote-camera methods as the best way to determine numbers non-invasively.

Our most out-there mission to service a camera trap was up Indianhead Creek, a tributary of the Clearwater River that is rarely visited by people. Some horrible bushwhacking for nine kilometres in deep, soul-sucking, mashed-potato snow eventually gets us to the camera — and also produces great results when we review the memory card from the camera that evening at the hut.

Grizzly, wolves, cougar, lynx, bighorn sheep, wolverine... you name the critter, that camera took a photo of it. It shows how remote valleys, far from human influence, do indeed attract the wildest of animals. Wolverines in particular are sensitive to human encroachment on their habitat. As a result, Dave explains, "Sometimes we close off these remote valleys completely from human access if it's determined that populations of wolverines are dropping off." Shutting off the valleys allows this ghost-like but key member of the food chain to recover and repopulate.

Speaking of ghosts, as we shoot the breeze that night in the Indianhead Warden Cabin, Ross recounts the tale of Frank Burstrom, a former Banff warden. Frank was at the cabin alone and claims to have seen a ghost in the tomb-like basement there. After that, he apparently cowered upstairs for the three-day duration of his stay, sleeping little and refusing to go back into the basement.

More like a house than an actual cabin, the old residence at Indianhead is unique in that it has a concrete foundation and a massive wood furnace in the basement that forces heated air into the upstairs rooms via a duct system.

Curious, I descend into the black pit of the basement to check out the monstrous iron furnace that could easily be confused for a crematorium. Perhaps he did indeed see a ghost — although Mr. Burstrom was a bit of a character himself, preferring his own company to that of others, or ghosts. Here's an excerpt of his from one of the cabin diaries, dated February 6th, 2007: "My partner for the shift... has deserted me. Was it something I said? Was it something I did? Nope...she had a family emergency. The peace and quiet is great. I miss my own company."

My favourite cabin of the trip is the Divide Warden Cabin. The approach to get there is epic, as we initially ford back and forth across the flowing water of mostly open Peter Creek... until we hit the snow line. We inch forward in the deep heavy stuff once more, the three of us trading off exhausting trail-breaking duties every five minutes.

We arrive just before dusk after a 12-hour day, and the cabin appears like a vision in a picturesque opening along Divide Creek across from majestic Mount Tyrrell.

The original warden cabin here was built in 1922. Like Clearwater Cabin, it is also a federal heritage building and now serves as a feed shed, while the newer one, built in 1982, is a quaint, compact little number with anything you'd ever need inside. The entrance is protected from grizzly bear penetration by a pair of nail boards that are put in place when the cabin is not being used.

Despite the unseasonably warm temperatures and low snowpack we experience throughout our journey, the cabin journal entry from September 1977 reminds us of the bitter cold that can set in here — and that political correctness had not yet seen its time. The simple one-liner reads: "Colder than a whore's heart."

The snow almost completely disappears at the end of our second-last day as we drop down into the Red Deer River Valley. Dave points out a grizzly "rub tree" and the residual hair left behind. He collects a fur sample for DNA analysis to add to a study Parks is doing on grizzly population trends and density.

We spend the night at Scotch Cabin, a roomy structure set in front of a sprawling horse meadow along the river. The next day we hike with our skis strapped to our packs, finishing off the last 16 kilometres of our trek to the park border, where a vehicle has been parked in advance so we can drive the three hours back to town.

On our way out, Dave leads us to an old den where we discover the carcass of a dead wolf nearby. Seemingly expired of natural causes, the mummy-like remains of the creature lie perfectly displayed in the snow like a mosquito in a million-year-old piece of amber.

The cycle of life and death is present as ever in the Banff National Park, and the work done by people like Dave ensures it will remain so for years to come. It's a reminder that despite the park's reputation as a picturesque front-country destination, its backbone is the wilderness and wild animals that exist beyond the fringe.

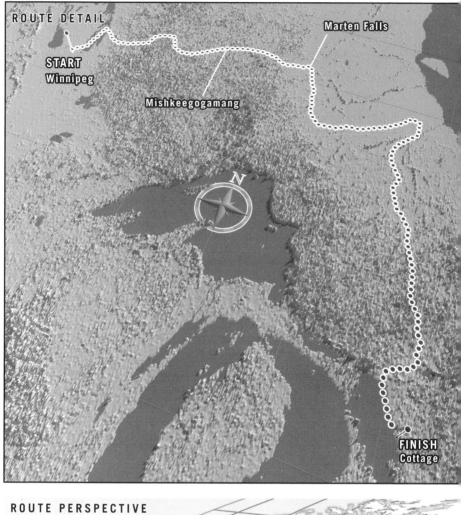

ROUTE DETAIL

START
Winnipeg

Mishkeegogamang

Marten Falls

FINISH
Cottage

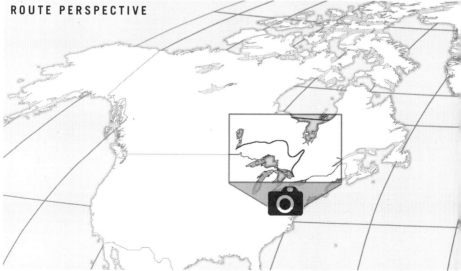

ROUTE PERSPECTIVE

Boreal Summer

Examining the industrialization of wilderness during a 75-day journey through the pristine heart of the boreal forest.

ORIGINALLY PUBLISHED IN OCTOBER 2008 ISSUE OF *WEND MAGAZINE*

I watch him, a curious-looking fellow crouched on the edge of the dock in Trout Lake Park. Located in the urban heart of East Vancouver, the park is a small oasis of green with a centrepiece pond not more than 200 feet across. Frequented by dog walkers, old men on benches and tai chi devotees, it's not the typical training ground for an extended wilderness excursion.

The guy in question is yanking away at the water with his paddle, with an effort that looks like he's trying to tear the dock from its mooring. I stroll toward him. He sees me and flicks his hand in acknowledgement between strokes, barely missing a beat as he continues to labour away on a makeshift canoeing treadmill. His name is Taku Hokoyama, and he will be my partner for a 3100-kilometre canoe journey through the heart of Canada's boreal forest. Every day for a month, he has run three miles from his home to paddle the dock for four hours — two hours on each side — in an attempt to get ready for the rigours of his first canoe trip. Taku is concerned about how he will perform. I am not. He is a good friend with whom I've spent a lot of time backcountry skiing in the Coast Mountains. I chose him for the mission because of his "personal intangibles." Anyone can learn to canoe, but compatibility, spirit and the toughness to see through a 75-day journey are rare and valuable commodities. He also writes one hell of a haiku.

*   *   *

City liquidates
Paddles and current
Push us to new horizons

Crossing a busy intersection, I almost get nailed by a minivan. I glance over at the driver. The woman looks perplexed for a moment and then laughs at me. I carry our red Royalex craft across the road to the safety of the sidewalk. Winnipeg's lunchtime crowd chokes the way ahead but parts like the Red Sea in the face of the oncoming canoe. Taku chugs along beside me with two packs. Apparently, the canoe is out of context enough in Canada's seventh-largest city to bring dozens of people to a complete, hysterical stop. One-line zingers like "Where's the water, buddy?" and "You're going the wrong way, dude!" fly at us from all directions. We've carried our load from Mountain Equipment Co-op, an outdoor retailer kind enough to store our gear until we arrived from Vancouver. We negotiate our way three kilometres through the downtown core along the aptly named Portage Avenue until we arrive at the Red River.

The turbid river is high with spring rain, snaking north through the muddy lowlands of Manitoba into Lake Winnipeg. A quick pack and we shove off for the summer — the canoe as our office, the tent our home and pushing on our job. Canada's unbroken boreal wilderness is staggering in scale and global importance.

Representing 25 per cent of the world's remaining ancient forest, the boreal is like a giant carbon bank account, with its forests and peatlands storing an estimated 67 billion tonnes of carbon in Canada alone — roughly ten times the amount of carbon produced worldwide each year.

Our route will take us through the largest area of intact boreal forest remaining. While southern parts of this forest have been heavily developed and logged, the area north of roughly 51 degrees latitude remains unallocated to industry and mostly undisturbed. Recent moves by forestry, hydro and mining interests now threaten the ecological integrity north of 51. Dropping above and below the 51st parallel along the route, we will see, intimately, the footprint of humans juxtaposed with undisturbed nature.

*   *   *

Canoe trip bottle
Lost in time for 40 years
Holding a message

Crashing through dense brush with a canoe on my head and a cloud of blackflies chewing at my face, I realize this is not the portage trail used by most to get from Embryo Lake to Upper Hatchet Lake. In fact, there's no trail at all. Taku is not far behind. Poplar and spruce saplings competing for space lash my shins, and fallen logs make me stumble as I work toward an opening in the canopy where the lake has to be. Mere steps before the water releases me from my burden, something in the forest catches my eye — a reflected light that stands out from the browns and greens of the forest. I drop the canoe abruptly and rush to the shiny bauble like a northern pike to a minnow. The empty bottle is half-buried in earth, reclining casually on its side. I pull it up and inspect it. It's a 26-ouncer of Schenley — standard-fare Canadian whiskey — but, alas, completely empty. A faded du Maurier king size cigarette wrapper is stuck to the inside. I see a faint scrawl — some sort of message written on the paper.

"Bill E. and Harry Harvey, Celebrating 50 days on trip. July 24, 1967."

"Yeah, boys!" I shout. Almost exactly 40 years earlier, these two fellow canoe trippers passed the same way as we — long before the area had been turned into a park. They were most likely carrying out one of the many canoe expeditions launched that year in celebration of Canada's centennial. The note from Bill and Harry reminds me that these wilderness waterways have been travelled not only by trippers for decades but by voyageurs (original French fur traders) and First Nations people for centuries before that. Here, I'm transfixed by time, realizing how crucial it is to preserve these places that haven't been bludgeoned by modernity, not only for environmental reasons but for our communal human psyche. These ecosystems exist in much the same state as they did millennia ago, and their increasing rarity gives me pause.

The evening sun slowly sinks over the sharp-pointed spruce fringe that lines Upper Hatchet Lake, its balloon of light ready to burst into darkness. Sitting on the broad slab of Canadian Shield in front of our tent, we pass a flask back and forth. We lounge under the light of a pink horizon, serenaded by four loons echoing across the calm water. It's a moment to savour, cut short by the night shift of swarming mosquitoes. Retreating to the tent, we drift off to the lullaby of millions of tiny, beating wings. We are content. As they did for the Schenley men of a summer long past, weeks and weeks of these evenings lie ahead.

*　　*　　*

Chance and circumstance
Stay open to the flow
And it will happen

The Mishkeegogamang First Nation is an Ojibwa community of 600 people located at the eastern terminus of Lake St. Joseph. We stash our canoe in the bushes and head up a gravel road to grab the two weeks of supplies I mailed before our departure. "Mish" is just 35 kilometres from the end of remote Highway 599; beyond it, the boreal wilderness stretches undisturbed for 1500 kilometres as the crow flies before petering out into arctic tundra. Once you get beyond the major Canadian cities that hug the US border, the dominant populations in Canadian towns and villages like Mish are the ancestors of the first immigrant wave — the hardy folks who crossed the Bering ice bridge more than 10,000 years ago.

A couple of plain, boxy, white houses appear on our left, surrounded by dozens of snow machines, ATVs and trucks in various states of repair. A red-and-blue Canada Post sign hangs on the second building, with the name "Osnaburgh House" stamped on it. The reserve only recently shucked off this moniker, coined by white traders 200 years earlier, in favour of its traditional namesake — which the federal postal agency has yet to update.

The reserve is just north of the 51st parallel, that line in the sand that extraction industries are pressing hard to cross. The area is traditional land for First Nations people who wish to maintain a long-standing moratorium on development, emphatically stating the region should be left alone to preserve its ecological integrity as well as their hunting and fishing rights. With metal prices booming, there has been a rush to stake the far North despite the moratorium, and the Ontario government is doing little to stop it. The first bowling ball to crash through the china shop was international mining giant De Beers, which managed to push through a proposal for the Victor diamond mine on the Attawapiskat River, in the northeast corner of the province. The mine will decimate 5000 hectares of ancient forest, generate 2.5 million tonnes of chemical leaching waste rock per year and pump 100,000 cubic metres of salty water per day from the pit into the Attawapiskat. All this for a mine forecasted to produce for only 12 years.

At the store, we bump into an activist named Neecha Dupuis. She has an easy smile, cherubic face and shiny jet-black hair tied in a ponytail. Neecha's T-shirt is adorned with renderings of great leaders of the past — Chief Joseph, Sitting Bull, Geronimo and Red Cloud stand side by side in front of Mount Rushmore, below the motto "The Original Founding Fathers." Part of the activist face of the First Nations, she recently returned from a boreal forest action tour through US campuses like Yale, NYU and the University of Illinois, raising awareness among the students about the onslaught of North American deforestation and where their paper comes from. Her main purpose was to promote the exclusive use of recycled paper because, as she says, "Every time you use non-recycled paper, it's the death of a tree."

Neecha is a force, speaking with passion about her home. She tells of how Mish was once ravaged by crime and drugs but is recovering rapidly through a growing movement to reconnect the people with their culture and its relationship to the landscape that defines them.

She gestures theatrically at the forest. "And this is for what's-his-name there... Al Gore? Is that his name? That guy?" We confirm that is the guy's name. "Well, he's talkin' about climate change and global warming. The answer is easy — quit clear-cuttin' the trees. The ancient trees are here; this is the last of the intact forest of Ontario. We're in the middle of it all, and it's not just for us; it's for the whole world. The rivers you're travelling down, they may be dried up ten years from now, seven years from now, three years from now, you never know. The time to fight is now, before it's too late."

Before we depart, she hands Taku a pack of cigarettes to use in tobacco offerings along our journey. She assures us that whatever gods we pray to will throw some luck our way if we squeeze some tobacco in our hands, make a wish and then place it on the land.

We're at the headwaters of the 980-kilometre-long Albany River, the longest in Ontario, laced with thundering waterfalls and rumbling rapids. Taku has never paddled whitewater save for the three times we practised on local rivers in Vancouver. A little luck will be welcome.

The Albany begins at its source on Osnaburgh Lake by Mishkeegogamang and runs crystal clear and unhindered through the heart of Ontario's pristine boreal forest. It crashes over the metamorphic Canadian Shield for 600 kilometres before flattening out on the Hudson Bay Lowlands for a broad 380-kilometre amble to James Bay. It is the crown jewel of the boreal — a ribbon of life that supports a healthy environment teeming with moose, black bear, bald eagle and pickerel. On average, only four or five groups canoe down this river every year.

Running rapids in such a remote setting takes some care. One mistake could be costly. A worst-case scenario would be our canoe pinned and one or both of us injured, leaving us stranded far from help. The key to successful negotiation of boulder-strewn current is a cohesive team in the canoe. In order to achieve this cohesion with a novice like Taku, I will have to call out each and every one of his paddling strokes.

*   *   *

Draw and pry
Side-slip the red canoe
Past gleaming wet rock

Day three on the Albany and we hear that now-familiar hiss — it gets my gut churning with excitement. The river is moving but flat, and we can't see anything past the bend in front of us — all we get is the siren song of the rapid bouncing off our eardrums. I'm eager to glimpse it, read it and chart a course down it. The river makes us wait, only providing the steady drone of water running over rock. But every moment, that drone grows more intense.

The bank straightens out, and the rapid begins to show itself. The tops of a couple of big boulders appear below a horizon line. I begin to wonder if we'll have to hunt around for a portage. We draw nearer, Taku silent and attentive in the bow. I stand up in the canoe 50 feet before the start to get a better look, and the rapid finally reveals itself fully. There is an obvious line on the right, some big standing waves to go through, a couple of holes, then an eddy below a boulder. After that, it looks like it mellows out around the next curve. It's a Class 3 set — very runnable.

We descend into it, and our canoe drives easily through the opening set of waves. Though not as nimble as an empty boat, a loaded canoe is stable and heavy, carrying enough momentum to plow through any hole or wave. I put on my best galley-master impression, shouting out Taku's strokes: "Forward hard! Hard! Hard! Draw! Draw! Draw! Back-paddle! Back-paddle! Back-paddle!" I call for a crossbow draw, and we swing into the eddy behind the boulder, pause to recheck the line and then peel out on the other side. We side-slip a few more boulders, then drive through a hole that buries the bow of the canoe. Most of the water spills off of our spray skirt, but a few gallons thunk Taku in the head, slicking his black curly hair straight back so he looks like he's going to a 1950s prom. We make it cleanly through and pull into the eddy below, euphoric.

The river has been a blur for Taku. He tells me at our campsite below Kagiami Falls, "Each time we approach a rapid, my heart rate goes up... rapid after rapid after rapid. It's relentless. Sometimes I hope you'll come back after a scout and say it's a portage. But no — no rest for Taku — it's inevitably a go. It can get exhausting sometimes." It's as close as he ever comes to a complaint.

*　　*　　*

Personal feelings
Dissipate like morning mist
Next to the mission

Taku sometimes snores at night in the tent; Taku is annoyingly, overwhelmingly positive in the worst situations; Taku is sometimes indecisive picking a line when it's his turn to pull the canoe upstream... and that's about all I have on the guy. These are the only things I can think of that ever bug me about him on this trip. We haven't had a single argument and, in the end, never will. Not a single one.

Ten weeks spent with another person, 24 hours a day, often under difficult circumstances, has the ability to amplify any and all perceived shortcomings you may discover about that individual along the way. Taku, though, is a different cat. He is the ultimate soldier — trusting my experience and learning from it, which allows me to run the trip and make final decisions. A natural tripper with loads of endurance, he seems to ease through our 10- to 12-hour days on the water.

As long as the expedition keeps moving forward, I'm happy. I don't let the small stuff get in the way. Successful long-tripping is best taken one paddle-stroke at a time, staying in the moment, never looking ahead. It's a philosophy that Taku seems to have taken to heart — and if he hasn't, he's a damn fine actor. We have a functional, weird ease with each other. It's a like-mindedness usually found only in married couples and life partners — but without the personal baggage or expectation of that sort of relationship. Ultimately, we are prostrate to the gods of this trip as the journey itself rises above any whiff of discontent.

*　　*　　*

Coffee and pork chops
Spread out on the tabletop
Feast fit for a dude

We pick up our next package at tiny Marten Falls First Nation. Only accessible by plane, the community of 285 people consists of a string of houses lining the banks of the Albany. A local named Norman "Dude" Baxter spots Taku wandering around the village and invites us into his house for a meal of pork chops, mashed potatoes and coffee. A barrel of a man with wire-rimmed glasses and a tight crewcut, he was given his nickname by a friend who thought Norm's lazy drawl was eerily similar to that of the main character in *The Big Lebowski*.

While we're chowing, down, a sudden storm blows through, bringing thunder, lightning and sideways rain. We hang out for a couple more hours, waiting out the squall, drinking coffee with the Dude. In his mid-50s now, the Dude is a part-time fishing and hunting guide. Unlike the Ojibwa we met up in Mishkeegogamang, he doesn't want to talk about environmental issues — he lives with the land, but conflict is not his style. He speaks proudly of his father, who 60 years ago would spend two weeks paddling his canoe from Marten Falls to the nearest town of Calstock to trade furs for supplies. His father is in his 80s now and still hunts and traps the surrounding land. There are no roads in the area even today, just waterways. The Dude gets around like his father once did — only his cedar freighter canoe is powered by motor, not muscle. He explains, "The Albany River is our highway — it's how we survive — our fishing and hunting, everything. It's how we get around, eh?" I ask him how long his people have depended on the river. The Dude pauses, then says, "Dunno. Way before our time, anyways."

After 650 kilometres and eight days being pushed by its power, we turn away from the Albany, heading upstream on the broad Kenogami River. It's the same route the Dude uses to bring clients to fishing spots and that his dad paddled over half a century ago to get supplies for his family before the age of bush planes. Despite the Albany River's provincial park status, the Ontario Power Authority has proposed that two major dams be built on it. The projects would carve up the surrounding boreal wilderness with roads and transmission lines as well as flood existing habitat and hunting grounds.

*　　*　　*

Gravel road creeps by
The body is racked with pain
Purgatory wheels

A sharp blast tears through the silence of the scrubby birch forest on either side of the gravel path. A gunshot? I wish. I look down and see that one of the two wheels on our canoe cart is flat. It has blown apart only half an hour into our 21-kilometre portage around four consecutive dams that choke this once-great river. The cart is rated for 150 pounds, and we more than doubled the capacity. It's our fourth day on the Mattagami River, 131 kilometres into a 580-kilometre upstream slog to get to the next divide. The dams sit by themselves, with no town around for over 100 kilometres. We've been horribly worked getting to this point, and the flat is, well, mentally deflating.

I crouch down, stare at the shredded tire and then look up at Taku. "Shit," I remark. He nods, agreeing that yes, indeed, this is a crappy moment. Paddling upstream, though brutal at times, gives one an intimate perspective on the character of a river. You have to find the path of least resistance, interpreting your course in reverse of downstream. The Bird, Kenogami and Kabina rivers earlier in the trip were straightforward. We hugged the edge, utilizing shore drag and back eddies to work our way up. If the current became too strong to paddle, we'd hop out and pull. Though hard work, it was a pleasure to slosh through clear water, mesmerized by the net of sunlight glinting off the kaleidoscope of smooth pebbles beneath our feet. Like the Albany, these are free rivers with an unharnessed power and spirit that personify the boreal above the 51st parallel. The Mattagami, located in the industrial zone below the 51st, is their kidnapped sibling — chained up and thrown into the cellar, where no one can see it, whimpering away for all eternity.

As we began up the Mattagami, it quickly became apparent that this river was far different than anything else we'd come across. The water was the colour of coffee and covered with brown foam along the river's edges. Our canoe skimmed through cappuccino eddies, leaving an imprint of filth on the hull. Due to high levels of mercury and other toxins, it is recommended that you not eat the fish in the river or drink the water. Every day we'd search out side streams for our drinking supply. The pollutants enter the river 400 kilometres upstream from the mouth, in and around the mining town of Timmins. Heavy metals leach into the water from millions of tonnes of waste rock strewn across the land from old and new mines alike, drawn into the great watershed of the Mattagami through the water cycle.

By our second day, we began to recognize a pattern. In the early morning, the water level would be dead low — sometimes only a few inches deep, so that we had to walk our canoe through a labyrinth of rock for a couple of hours until around nine a.m., when the water would suddenly rise and we'd have to hop back in the boat to fight a fast-flowing torrent. The water would drop again at noon and then rise again until around five p.m., when it would start to steadily drop through the night. We were experiencing first-hand what the river had to go through to satisfy the human demand for electricity.

Water is held back behind the four great dams until the collective moms and dads go to work and their collective kids go to school. In response, all lights and computers are running full blast by nine a.m., and so are the Mattagami dams. At lunchtime, people turn off their computers and head out for a bite, and the Mattagami dams close up a little. They open up again after lunch, then shut down for bedtime. It's an alien tide that rises or falls three feet in a matter of minutes: computer-controlled release based on the power demands of our hungry world. There is a famous rapid on the Mattagami called the Grand Rapids. Fur traders used to sing songs about running their birchbark canoes down it. When we went up this feature, it was essentially a gravel bed with perhaps six inches of water running through it. Unable to move any farther upstream, we were forced to camp and wait for the morning release. On the day of our portage around the dams, every drop of water in the channel we had paddled up the evening before was gone — it was dry land.

This dead, dirty river is what the Albany will become if the Ontario Power Authority has its way. Putting roads into the pristine Albany — one of only four large, free rivers remaining in Ontario's north — to dam it will bring in the inevitable charge of forestry and mining. It's a slippery slope. The world's biggest carbon bank — that which keeps us from launching off the tipping point toward desertification — is in jeopardy.

We stuff our flat tire with my fleece pants and a camp towel, keeping it together with a crafty matrix of knotted static cord that Taku created. It's a passable fix. Dragging our 300-pound anchor through the sand, we walk slowly and silently up the soft gravel road that passes around the dams for seven more hours. With dusk approaching, we crest the final dam and collapse, unable to move another inch — as broken as the Mattagami itself.

*　　*　　*

Seventy-five days
Living in the North land
A good, simple life

Taku and I transitioned out of the boreal forest 12 days ago, linking the popular canoe tripping areas of Temagami, the French River and Georgian Bay to arrive at Killbear Point. My family's cottage is six kilometres away, and that is where the journey will conclude. We are each 20 pounds lighter and tanned deep brown from a summer outside. My trip beard is bushy and bleached by the sun. Taku's facial hair seems relatively unchanged, thanks to his Japanese genes.

We are having a *Master and Commander* moment — borrowed from a scene in the film of the same name, where Captain Jack Aubrey breaks out the cigars and whiskey to celebrate sailing around Cape Horn. Taku stashed away a Cuban on day one for this very occasion. We alternate the Cohiba and a flask of Forty Creek rye. The hot afternoon sun beats down on us as we linger on the point, not quite ready to let go of the trip. Our experience has filled us with conviction to help protect the vast swath of green and blue we have come to know so profoundly. For now, though, we hang on to the last hour, bathing in the afterglow of the boreal.

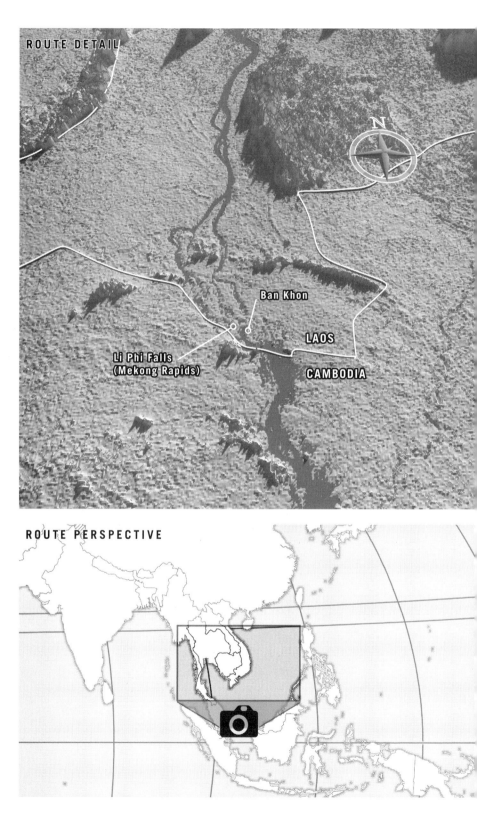

ROUTE DETAIL

Ban Khon

LAOS

CAMBODIA

Li Phi Falls
(Mekong Rapids)

ROUTE PERSPECTIVE

Spiritual Channels

Negotiating the cultural divide during a whitewater paddling expedition in Laos and Cambodia with Russian extreme kayakers.

ORIGINALLY PUBLISHED IN AUGUST 2003 ISSUE OF *ACTION ASIA*

Vissily from St. Petersburg sits hunched over the table, digging into his breakfast of spicy fish lap, sweating profusely, his pale skin flushing as red as his curly locks. At six-foot-six, with piercing blue eyes and a narrow, pointed nose, he strikes an imposing figure. Back home he makes his living as an abdominal surgeon, cutting and sewing the intestines and stomach muscles of Russia's finest. His profession, however, is only a means to an end. Vissily's passion is paddling his kayak over waterfalls in remote spots around the globe.

I turn and ask his compatriot Mikhail where their group will be kayaking today. Mikhail shakes his head and furrows his brow to indicate he doesn't understand the question. The day before, he spent the better portion of a minute at the bottom of the Mekong River after swimming out of his kayak during an attempted descent of a furious waterfall. His compatriots got a rescue line to him and it quivered, taught as piano wire, with Mikhail at the other end somewhere down and deep, holding on for dear life. He finally surfaced after we thought him drowned, clinging to a lone rock in the middle of the channel, violently puking brown water from his lungs. Needless to say, the experience shook him to his very core.

Vissily straightens up, swallows the minced fish in his mouth and wipes his brow. Raising his eyebrows, he looks at me and states matter-of-factly, "Mikhail no paddle today... yesterday, he see God." I scratch my head and say something about finding religion on the river bottom not being conducive to whitewater paddling success. They both stare at me blankly.

The Si Phan Don (4,000 Islands) area is located at the southernmost tip of Laos, a stone's throw across the water from Cambodia. The idyllic palm-and-sand-rimmed islands lie scattered over this widest stretch (14 kilometres) of the Mekong River, where the whole girth of Southeast Asia's main vein flows over a jagged fault line.

Vissily, Mikhail and the three other Russians (Alex, Mikhail #2 and Arseni) have come to this part of southern Laos to attempt first descents of the dozens of waterfalls created by the fault. They signed a deal in Moscow to film a four-part television series about whitewater paddling in Laos. At high water the Mekong splits into as few as 5 channels over the drop created by the fault, while at low water there can be as many as 20. We're here in December, when the flows are considered medium. No matter what the Mekong flows are at, though, there is no easy way down.

I spend a day watching and photographing the Russians, holding my breath every time they run a set of the thundering drops. I'm an experienced whitewater kayaker but would not even attempt what they're doing; for me it would be tantamount to putting a loaded gun to my head and pulling the trigger. These Russians, though, are a ballsy lot. Having grown up together in Soviet-era sports schools, they were hand-picked and trained as future kayak slalom champions for the USSR. With the breakup of the Soviet Union in 1989, they banded together as a group and have undertaken various whitewater expeditions all over the world ever since. Between trips, all except Vissily work as river guides to make ends meet. Vissily acts as their cut-man and is perhaps the craziest of the lot. Today he points to one Niagara Falls-esque drop, says to me, "Apocalypse Rapid," beams maniacally and then promptly kayaks the cascade, pumping the paddle in his arms all the way down like Stalin with an ice pick.

Thankfully, there's a lot more to see and do in the area than paddle down harrowing waterfalls. Most people come to simply bask in the splendour of the powerful display of hydrology and chill out reading in hammocks under coconut palms by the riverside. The best island to view the rapids from is Don Khon, where I take up residence in one of the thatch bungalows at Miss Phan's in the village of Ban Khon, located on the banks of the broad, idly flowing Mekong, a kilometre above the thundering falls. Accommodation is basic, and there is no electricity on the island. Power for the sparse lighting at the simple guest house restaurants is provided by car battery, while oil lamps are given to guests to illuminate their rooms.

The village itself is made up of a scattering of thatch and wood huts on stilts. A few old, crumbling, colonial French villas, their whitewashed walls streaked with black, remain as a reminder of the country's former rulers. A couple of the villas have been converted into guest houses by local people trying to capitalize on the growing popularity of the region, particularly among Thai tourists who hop across the border to enjoy the tropical, beach-like atmosphere.

A friend of mine, Mick, who lives in Vientiane, swears to me he saw a ghost when he spent a night in one of the Ban Khon buildings last year. Not one to believe in such things, he was awoken from beneath his mosquito screen by the distinct figure of a man hanging above the bed in mid-air, smiling at him. Mick screamed at him to get the fuck out of his room. His girlfriend woke up from beside him but could see no one. The apparition had disappeared. He looked up at the ceiling again and saw that it would have been humanly impossible for someone to be suspended there. The next day, Mick approached the owner of the guest house and told him about what had happened. The owner didn't act surprised, but merely shrugged and said many people had died in the house over the past century and some of their spirits still wandered around inside.

Other ghosts of the past can be seen just 50 metres off the main path in the centre of the village, where a rusting locomotive and boiler sit in a small opening beside an old track. They're remnants of a railway system built by the French in the 1920s that was an important link for supply lines between Saigon and Laos. Goods were transported above the waterfalls from boats that unloaded at a pier located on the southern tip of Don Khon. A still-intact rail bridge connects Don Khon from the village to another island, Don Det, where the goods were loaded back onto boats to continue their trip upstream on the Mekong. The 14-kilometre-long track, abandoned after Japanese attacks in 1945, is still the only railway ever built in Laos.

Moving southwest along the dirt trail, you pass through open rice fields for half a kilometre before turning off toward the Taat Somphamit rapids, where the Russians spend most of their time. Channel after channel of raging water plummets through the jagged volcanic rock, making for a breathtaking display of nature's power. Built into the bases of some of the smaller falls are crude bamboo fish traps installed by brave locals to catch the huge fish that navigate the Mekong waters. Anything caught in the traps is fair game to be served fresh in the village that day — stir-fried Russian, anyone?

Ambling another three kilometres along the trail, you pass the Buddhist Wat Khon Tai temple and descend through jungle to a sandspit at the other end of the island, where a dozen or so narrow wooden fishing boats sit pulled up on the powdery white sand. It's a great spot to go for a dip in the cool river water or negotiate a ride down the lower Mekong to view the Irrawaddy dolphins. These endangered animals — there are estimated to be only 20 to 50 left in the Don Khon area, 100 to 300 in the entire Mekong — grow to 2.5 metres and are believed by the Lao and Khmer to be reincarnated humans. Legend has it many a fisherman and villager has been saved by the dolphins from drowning in the Mekong or being eaten by crocodiles. Despite their benevolent reputation, the dolphins are still accidentally caught and drowned in gillnets used by the locals. Unfortunately, even if the fishermen realize their mistake, the cost of the nylon nets is too prohibitive for them to cut out the entangled dolphins.

A practice banned in Laos but still common in Cambodia is bomb fishing. The abundance of hand grenades and other explosives left from Cambodia's war-torn past make this an inexpensive way for fishermen from across the way to gain their catch. Although they aren't directly targeted, dolphins fall victim to this practice as well. Efforts at conservation so far have proven futile. The best chance for the dolphins seems to lie in ecotourism — which at this point is unorganized, limited only to fishermen sporadically taking curious travellers into the area for a chance to see them.

Mr. Sun, a wiry fisherman with a shock of black hair and a perpetual grin on his face, has been building a new long-tail — one of the 25-foot-long wooden boats that are the main source of transport and commerce for Straits of Malacca fishermen. He casually asks if I want to see the dolphins. I negotiate a price of 30,000 kip (four Canadian dollars) and agree to meet him at six a.m. the next morning, the best time to view the dolphins. In the past, Khmer Rouge activity in Cambodia stopped people from going to the dolphin area. As recently as 1998, access to the lower Mekong was halted due to a Khmer Rouge mutiny in nearby Anlong Veng.

We set out into the swift-moving water below the rapids with Mr. Sun's long-tail prop *chop-chopping* through the quiet of dawn. He skilfully negotiates the churning water through a forest of trees bent at perpetual 45-degree angles by the torrential floods that strain against their trunks every wet season. We eventually come out into a huge open bay of calm water, where he shuts off his engine and lets the boat drift. Using a paddle he's hewed from a chunk of wood, he strokes silently to the middle of the bay. After a few minutes, a pod of four dolphins appears, their gleaming backs and dorsal fins arcing out of and then back into the water as they hunt for their breakfast.

We watch them quietly for 20 minutes as they circle the bay, never getting closer than 40 metres to the boat.

They differ from my traditional image of dolphins. This freshwater variety has a smooth, rounded head with no protruding snout; they closely resemble miniature grey versions of the beluga. Their movement is graceful and mesmerizing as they dance about the Mekong millpond; it's a shame that their days seemed hopelessly numbered.

Before we leave, Mr. Sun asks me, "You want go to Cambodia?"

"Um, sure... but I don't have my passport with me."

"No need passport, just one dollar for guard."

He turns the boat toward the thick tangle of green that covers the hilly mainland on the far side of the Mekong. We soon come upon a yellow slash in the riverbank incut with dirt steps leading up to a Cambodian flag flying high atop a wooden pole. I walk up with Mr. Sun to a flattened-out area occupied by a crude bamboo hut and stand with "Police Border Post" painted in bold letters on the front. A plump man in military garb is leaning back on a chair with his feet up on the stand and an AK-47 hanging on a hook behind him. Another, leaner man in fatigues walks up, smiles and speaks to Mr. Sun, who then turns to me and says, "You give him one dollar now."

After accepting payment, the guard motions for us to join him. Wen sit down at the top of the dirt steps beside the flagpole. He lights a cigarette, puts it to his lips and inhales slowly. He grins wordlessly through a haze of smoke as he exhales and passes it over to share with Mr. Sun and me. The Irrawaddy dolphins, visible from here only as small black specks, bound along obliviously below as the three of us watch a fiery orange sun rise over the Mekong.

Under a midnight sun, sled dogs prowl seal meat left for them by their Inuit owners.

Camping on Sirmilik Glacier, Bylot Island.

Pond Inlet kids riding late into the never-ending light.

Dave Garrow ascends newly named 'Mount Koonoo' on Bylot Island.

A youthful version of the author in 1995 taking a breather at the end of the 13.7 kilometre Grand Portage during his cross-Canada canoe expedition.

Our camping spot in downtown Montreal a few hours before we had lunch with Pierre Trudeau.

Shawn Campbell pack rafting the Stikine River.

Shawn Campbell taking in the mountain splendour during our backpacking leg through the Spatsizi Wilderness.

Shawn Campbell working his way through the muddy quagmire that made up much of the route to Cold Fish Lake.

Rob Hart (front) and the author paddle through a hole on the Severn River.

A 'Sasquatch' (left) resembling the iconic Patterson-Gimlin version of the creature (right) is also eerily similar in appearance to the author.

Pushing the canoe through the trees during a bushwhack portage in Sasquatch country.

Water sloshes over the deck in the midst of a wave train on the Severn River.

Striking out into Sasquatch country with moose antlers as audience.

The author (left) and Rob Hart (right) hanging out with Ennis Fidler (middle) at a Sandy Lake cookout.

Wolverine captured on camera trap footage collected during a mammal survey in Banff National Park.

Dave Garrow with road kill and donated carcasses used to trap bears for relocation and study.

CHOPPED SOME WOOD FOR YOU GUYS.

PASSING THROUGH — ...

CLEAR, WINDY, AND ...

... SNOW. ...

... !

P. APPLEJOHN   JUNE 30/81   MISERABLE DAY, MISERABLE TIME MISERABLE LOST HORSE, COULDN'T CATCH HIM.

P. APPLEJOHN
P. CAMPBELL
D. WATERS
J. ISRAELSON
JULY 15/81
HAPPY CANADA DAY
CAUGHT MISERABLE HORSE, SNOW, RAIN, CLOUD, SUN. NOT NECESSARILY IN THAT ORDER. BACK TO SCOT

A 1981 cabin journal entry by Banff warden 'P. Applejohn' noting a 'miserable lost horse' which the wardens apparently caught the next day.

Ross Glenfield heading out for another day of tracking mammals at Banff.

Taku Hokoyama counting the days during a 75-day journey through the boreal forest.

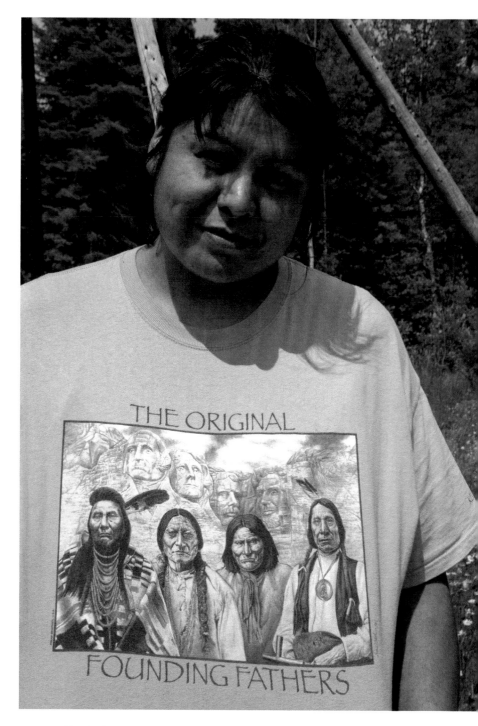

THE ORIGINAL

FOUNDING FATHERS

Neecha Dupuis showing off her 'Original Founding Fathers' shirt.

The author looking out over the Mattagami River left suddenly dry overnight by an upstream dam.

The author (left) and Taku Hokoyama show off a combined 50 pounds lost on day 50 of their canoe trip across the boreal.

Starting off a 75-day journey through the boreal forest with a portage through downtown Winnipeg.

The author cooks breakfast while Lance Weathers looks down from camp along the North Saskatchewan River during a cross-Canada canoe trip.

Kevin Vallely looks down from the summit of Gunung Slamet.

The author riding in a cloud of diesel smoke on the Jalan Raya, Java.

The author passes by a local field worker on the way down from Gunung Slamet.

School kids in Bambangen chase the author as he rides by.

Kevin Vallely (left) and the author tired and dirty after a day of riding the
Jalan Raya.

Sketch of a man aiming a gun at Kevin Vallely and the author as they ride through East Java.

A fisheye view of the canoe in the crystal clear waters of Lac Bienville.

The author portages around a cascading rapid on the Upper Great Whale River.

Peirson Ross (front) and the author looking fierce while running a rapid on the Upper Great Whale River.

The storm abates one fine morning on Lac D'Iberville.

Keith Klapstein exploring a cave on the outer coast of Haida Gwaii.

The Careys' cabin in Puffin Cove.

Todd Macfie shows off the bounty of Puffin Cove — a lunker ling cod hauled from the depths.

Camping on the vast Labrador Plateau.

Running rapids on the Natikamaukau River.

The author with his head sheath soaked in his own blood after being ravaged by blackflies during the Poungasse portage up to the Labrador Plateau.

The author 'being mosquito' during filming of a canoe trip across the Labrador Plateau.

Fred Wolki in Tuktoyaktuk, NWT.

Paul Gleeson (standing) and Kevin Vallely moor the rowboat with ice screws after being forced to cut its anchor.

Beluga tail at Brown's Camp.

Pushing the rowboat along the shore during a windstorm.

Interviewing Paul Atutuvaa and family in Baker Lake, NU.

The author covers up as apocalyptic-looking clouds gather over the Thelon River.

Remains of a wolf on the barren grounds.

Villagers in Sumur gather around our kayak before we paddle out to Ujung Kulon.

The author carrying the broken folding kayak along Cibandowah Beach.

The author (centre) posing with park rangers Arnasan (left) and Hutbi (right) in Ujung Kulon.

The author on Cibandowah beach with soaked gear shortly after wrecking the kayak.

Dene brothers Dallas (front) and Silas getting comfortable in our canoe in Lac Brochet.

Shawn Campbell staring down a long drag during a six-day 'mystery move' to the source of the Kazan River.

The author holding a tern chick that had fallen out of its nest, shortly before returning it and fleeing its angry parents.

Pounding through a drop on the Churchill River.

Caribou crossing a narrows on the Kazan River.

Voracious mosquitoes near the Saskatchewan/NWT boundary.

Portaging a set of falls on the Kazan River.

An inukshuk on the Kazan system.

Working upstream during the 'mystery move' section of the journey.

Navigating the transparent waters of Saskatchewan's Reindeer Lake.

The author jotting down journal notes in Coffee John's cabin.

Unpacking the kayak along the shores of Lake Laberge.

Coffee Grandma (left) with her granddaughter in foreground, in Porjus, Sweden.

Our journey across Scandinavia hot off the press as the cover feature in the local *Kuriren* newspaper.

Portaging over the Scandinavian Mountains along the Norway/Sweden border.

Crossing the Murray River on the way to the Rocky Mountains, following a proposed pipeline route.

Checking our route on the GPS during our trek through the Rockies.

Following the Northern Gateway route in Alberta.

More beautiful than any painting, the sun sets over Whiteclay Lake.

The author wild and free jumping off a cliff in Wabakimi.

Dave Stibbe crawling up rickety bamboo ladders into the bird nest caves.

Hong Island, Thailand.

The author cycling through overflow on the Yukon River.

Paddling the Amable du Fond River on the way to the next concert in Mattawa.

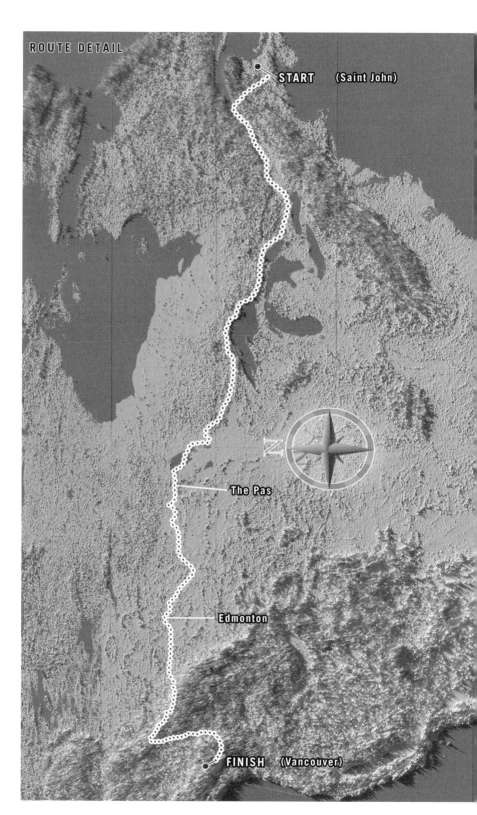

ROUTE DETAIL

START (Saint John)

The Pas

Edmonton

FINISH (Vancouver)

The Bear

A story of adventure and deception woven into the fabric of the first-ever single-season crossing of Canada by canoe.

He told me the story about "The Bear" the first time I met him. I'd driven to Oakville from Toronto to meet up with Lance Weathers. Lance had been planning a journey across Canada, had fallen out with his original partners for the trip and was searching for someone to fill the void. The expedition was an 8000-kilometre paddle that was to be the first coast-to-coast crossing of Canada by canoe in a single season.

I was known as a "hard tripper" from my time as a guide at Camp Onondaga. I would do things like run the canoe over portages — once transporting all four canoes from a trip in Temagami over a three-kilometre portage by sprinting back and forth over the rough ground, eventually finishing at the same time as the last camper struggling through the trail. I would squeeze in 160 kilometres of distance over a lake-and-river circuit during the course of a six-night trip, campers in tow. In the esoteric world of summer camp canoe tripping, word about this sort of thing gets around. When Lance began searching for someone to join him on the trip, a couple of people mentioned my name to him as a good candidate, and the connection was made.

But back to "The Bear."

I pulled into the driveway of the mansion where Lance lived. His family owned and rented out several apartment buildings and had apparently done quite well for themselves. I knew nothing of Lance; I only knew that he wanted to canoe across Canada, and so did I. It's every canoe tripper's dream.

I rang the doorbell, and Lance appeared. He looked every bit his name. He was six-foot-four, broad-shouldered, with a square jaw, hawk nose and narrow blue eyes. A blond Fabio mane spread gloriously down his back.

After a brief hello, he closed the door behind him and stepped outside. "Let's go for a walk."

We ambled down the tree-lined street of estates to the Lake Ontario shoreline. After a few minutes of chatting about canoe tripping and tree planting, he mentioned a face-to-face encounter with "The Bear." Before getting into it, he paused and lit a fresh cigarette.

"I was tree planting in Swan Hills, Alberta, with a crew a couple of years ago. The area has the densest population of grizzlies in Canada, so they kept a shotgun at every tree cache in case there was ever a problem with bears on the planting block."

He paused and took a drag of the cigarette, exhaled the smoke slowly while looking out over the lake, then continued.

"I had two dogs at the time — a Rottweiler and a half-wolf mix that I would plant with. I would also plant regularly with this chick called Everest — a pretty, blue-eyed blonde.

"One day Everest and I were working a new piece of land. I started at the top of the piece, and she began at the other end. We'd work toward each other through the course of the day. She planted with a Sony Walkman on, listening to tunes as she worked. As we began planting, there seemed to be something in the air. My dogs were acting squirrelly, and they were usually pretty calm. At about noon, I glanced down the piece to see where Everest was, and I suddenly realized why."

Again a pause as he drew in the smoke and exhaled with a thousand-yard stare.

"She was hunched over, planting her trees, and because she had her Walkman on, she didn't see or hear two grizzly bear cubs pop out of the trees on one side of her. Moments later, a mama grizzly appeared from the brush on the opposite side — so now she was between the mother and its cubs. Everest had no idea anything was going on, but it all happened right before my eyes. As soon as my dogs saw this, they made a beeline for the bears — but before they got there, the mother charged Everest and knocked her tumbling 15 feet along the dirt. My dogs reached the mother before she could do any more damage and ran interference, snapping and jumping at her. I immediately dropped my planting bags and ran to the tree cache to grab the shotgun. I returned a minute later with the gun and saw that my dogs were still preventing the mother from getting to Everest. It was a double-barrel break-action gun, and I quickly loaded two shells into it. I fired the gun in the air, and I immediately had that bear's..."

This time Lance's pause was the most dramatic of all. He stared out over Lake Ontario like he was right back there in Swan Hills, facing down that grizzly. He drew in his deepest drag so far and exhaled slowly before finally turning to me and finishing his sentence. I was admittedly gripped.

" ...undivided attention."

Pause, inhale smoke, stare, exhale.

"The mother immediately charged toward me, 50 metres away and closing distance fast. I calmly popped in a couple more shells and fired at her. I hit her but she kept coming, a little slower now. I popped a couple more fresh slugs into the chamber and aimed it at her again. She came within ten metres of me and suddenly reared up on her hind legs in front of me, and I put both rounds right into her chest. She dropped to the ground."

Pause, inhale smoke, stare, exhale.

"I walked toward the big bear and chambered one final round, walked up to it, pointed the shotgun at its head and finished her off."

Pause, inhale smoke, stare, exhale.

"The Ministry of Natural Resources sent in a couple guys to inspect and remove the bear. They weighed it and said it was 1,200 pounds — a record for a female grizzly. The two cubs were given to a nature sanctuary, so they were okay in the end. Everest was not too badly off, all things considered — she had a broken wrist and three broken ribs. Her planting season was over, but she recovered fully."

Wow. I was blown away by Lance's encounter with the bear. It was a great story and immediately elevated his stature in my eyes.

A couple of weeks later, we began to canoe across Canada, beginning in the Bay of Fundy and eventually finishing in Vancouver. I spent 171 days with Lance in a canoe that year, and we did indeed become the first people to canoe across Canada coast to coast in a single paddling season.

When you spend that much time with a person, portaging, lining, paddling and dragging a canoe across Canada, you get to know them intimately. I didn't know Lance at all when we started — I just knew he wanted to canoe across Canada, and that's all that mattered. I wanted to immerse myself in the experience and achieve the goal so badly that Adolf Hitler could have been in a canoe with me and I would have made it work.

Lance wasn't Hitler, but I wouldn't do a trip with him again. It took us getting lost three times for me to convince him that the compass was better than his sense of direction when navigating in fog on Lake Superior. For no discernible reason, he threatened several times to replace me on the trip, but backed down when I said I'd just continue on alone and beat him to the finish in Vancouver.

Lance would often brag about his "black book" — a list of over 100 women he'd bedded and could call up for an intimate rendezvous. He had two girlfriends on the go at the same time during our journey. I met one of them in Montreal and then the other in Toronto. He corresponded with both separately but at the same time, in secrecy. Easy to do in the pre-smartphone-and-internet era, apparently. A real piece of work. Even so, almost until the very end, I figured everything we went through to achieve our goal would positively bond us for life.

The final straw was when he threatened me with legal action on the very day we concluded the trip, paranoid that I would write a book about the journey and gain all the perceived glory that he sorely desired. I kept a very detailed journal of the expedition and snapped all the trip photos, while he wrote and photographed nothing.

We spent the last few months of the trip mostly in silence. I paddled steadily and fell into the rhythm and meditation of the water and land, while Lance chain-smoked and listened to his Walkman in the stern. I'm not sure how he paddled and chain-smoked at the same time; I didn't look back to check. It didn't matter — we were moving forward, and that meant we would get there eventually. The only time I was in the stern was during a five-week stint paddling upstream on the Saskatchewan River from The Pas to Edmonton. At the very start of that stretch, Lance claimed that he had somehow separated his shoulder while canoeing. That left me to do the brunt of the work — paddling hard and dragging up the rapids while he gingerly paddled in the bow or walked alongshore. His shoulder had miraculously healed by the time we finished the upstream section.

Despite all this, Lance's "Bear Story" remained the glue that kept the trip together throughout. Whenever we were invited to spend a night under a roof by friendly people we met en route, I would encourage him to tell his story. He would pull out his cigarette and recount it with conviction, using the same dramatic pauses and smoke exhalations as when I'd heard it the first time. It always worked like magic.

His tale enthralled small-town folks, park rangers, even Pierre Trudeau when we had lunch with him in Montreal. "The Bear" had people on the edge of their seats, eyes wide as the story unfolded; Lance was immediately established in their eyes as a god of the wild. The story maintained my respect for him, despite the way he seemed to want to sabotage our relationship along the way.

Needless to say, we didn't maintain any sort of friendship past the journey. Lance did call me a year later to tell me he would allow me to write a book on the trip. I politely declined. At the time I didn't have the desire to talk in depth about an event long past — I was embroiled in new adventures. It's the last I ever heard from him.

Not too long after that call, I was having a beer at the Raven Pub in North Vancouver, close to where I now live. I met up with my buddy Kevin Rehill, who was a ski patroller at Cypress Mountain, a local resort. He brought along a co-worker of his: a beautiful, blue-eyed blonde named Everest. Well, what are the chances? It was her — in the flesh.

I immediately made sure that this wasn't just coincidence — how many blonde, blue-eyed Everests could there be in Canada?

We huddled around a small round table, beers in hand, and got into it immediately.

"Do you know a fella named Lance Weathers?" I asked her.

Everest had to pause for a moment, thoughtfully looking at the ceiling before recollection set in.

"Yeah... yeah, I know Lance — he was at our planting camp up in Swan Hills a few years ago."

My eyes widened.

"So, how are you — how was your recovery after the bear attack?"

She looked confused.

"Bear attack?"

I told her Lance's story of "The Bear." Kevin laughed. Everest was absolutely perplexed.

"I didn't really know Lance, he was just some guy in camp. I never planted with him either. I regularly planted with a different guy. The only bear story I have from that season is when a grizzly walked onto our land one day, and we both went to grab the shotgun from the cache. By the time we returned, the bear was long gone. It had just been passing through. We told people about it when we got back to camp, but that's the only thing I can think of."

Wow, her revelation blew me away. Lance had basically taken a simple bear-sighting story and turned it into a fantasy rescue scenario where he saved a beautiful woman from being killed by a wild animal. He was apparently infatuated with Everest but had never approached her, instead concocting a hero story that he hoped would elevate him in the eyes of anyone he met. It worked on me, it worked on everyone. The truth comes out in strange ways sometimes, and this truth from the proverbial horse's mouth made me suddenly reflect on everything Lance had told me during our six months together. Was any of it true? Or was his whole world built on a house of lies? Working in an AIDS hospice for kids in Nigeria? His black book? His expeditions on the Thelon and Nahanni? Those stories could be real, but I could no longer be sure, as his seminal establishing story had been exposed as absolutely fake.

In the end it didn't matter. We succeeded in our mission to be the first people to canoe across Canada in a single paddling season, and there were new tales to tell. Perhaps that was what this journey was all about, in the end. Forever languishing in a fantasy world of his own creation, Lance broke free and replaced "The Bear" with something that was actually real.

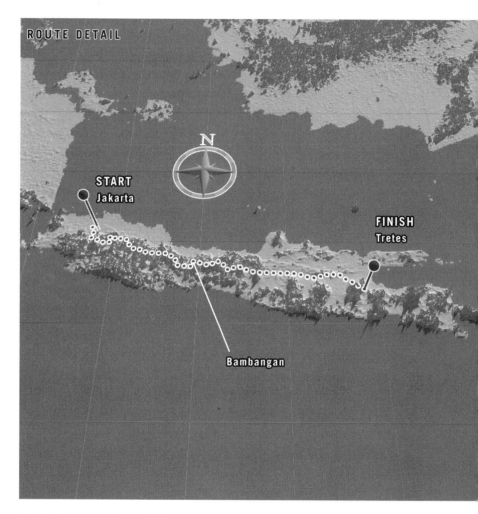

ROUTE DETAIL

START
Jakarta

N

FINISH
Tretes

Bambangan

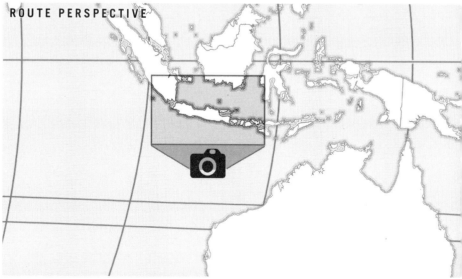

ROUTE PERSPECTIVE

Chasing the Dragon

A cycling and volcano-climbing odyssey across the most populous Muslim island on Earth in the wake of 9/11.

ORIGINALLY PUBLISHED IN AUGUST 2003 ISSUE OF *ACTION ASIA*

Sitting in Jakarta's swishy Cinnabar, Kevin and I sip beers with our friend Paul Dillon, a Canadian expat journalist. Minutes after we sit down, Paul's cellphone rings. He hustles outside to talk and then rushes back in to tell us suicide bombers have flown planes into buildings in New York and Washington. Here, in a bustling, poverty-stricken city of 17 million, we sit in disbelief amid the bar's brassy decor, white tablecloths and polished oak counters. A certain kind of world event affects people to such an extent that they remember exactly where and when they were when they first heard about it. These are always sudden, violent happenings like the space shuttle disaster, JFK's assassination and now this.

We head back to Paul's house and turn on the television to see for ourselves. The images are stunning, to say the least. Paul's fellow freelance journalists filter in and gather around to watch. Without a word, Paul coolly places half a dozen glasses and a bottle of whisky in the centre of the coffee table. Rather than expressing sympathy or shock, the journos murmur detached complaints about how this will suck the life out of their Indonesia gigs for at least three years and that they'll have to shift to reporting in the Middle East.

Java is the political and cultural centre of the Indonesian archipelago. Arising on September 12, we have to pull together and focus on what we've come here to do. After planning for months, Kevin Vallely and I brought our mountain bikes and running shoes from Canada to cycle 1200 kilometres across Java, east to west. En route, we plan to ascend all 11 of the 10,000-plus-foot volcanoes that stretch from end to end along the spine of the island. We call our trip "Chasing the Dragon."

Paul is a veteran of freelance adrenaline-junkie journalism in Indonesia. Two years ago, he covered the atrocities occurring in East Timor, and this year he reported on the civil war in northern Sumatra's Aceh Province and the headhunter bloodletting in Kalimantan. As much as anyone, he has witnessed the dark underbelly of this equatorial nation of 220 million people.

While we load our bikes that morning on his outer patio, Paul lounges on a nearby wicker chair, wearing nothing but his sarong and headband. He smokes a cigarette and, as always, his glistening, Buddha-like body sweats profusely. He's been living here for four years and still hasn't adapted to the thick 35-degree-Celsius heat. Blowing smoke rings, he reminds us we're biking across an island of 130 million Muslims in the wake of a disaster that will surely pit the Islamic world against the West. He further says that although the generally peaceful inhabitants of Java seem mellow, they can instantly be stirred into a frothing, angry mob. As evidence, Paul notes the riots in Jakarta three years earlier, during Indonesia's economic collapse, when the city burned and 1,200 people were killed.

Now that Paul has effectively stirred up the bogeyman of crazed Javanese locals jumping all over us with their machetes, we thank him, hop on our bikes and ride out of Jakarta.

*   *   *

Hell Highway

Java is a little over half the size of Great Britain, with over twice the population. It's an island of contrasts; the great sea of humanity there tends to be packed into the coastal areas, while the 50 active and 17 dormant volcanoes that rise out of lush central valleys remain sparsely populated. The main transport route is the *jalan raya*, or main highway, that runs the length of the coastline. It has one lane in either direction, jammed with emission-spewing trucks, buses and motorcycles filled to overflowing with people, livestock and produce. The vehicles hammer along at full speed, passing continuously into oncoming traffic with the smaller vehicles usually giving way by running off into ditches and paddies to avoid a brutal death. Our bicycles are invariably the smallest vehicles.

Both Kevin and I get headaches from the intense exhaust; breathing often means eating a lungful of unfiltered particulate. I feel like I'm smoking a lead cigarette while simultaneously exerting up the numerous steady grades that bring us to the base of our destination volcanoes. The exhaust and dirt from the road sticks to every inch of our sweat-soaked bodies, making us look as if we've been working down in a coal mine all day. We call the *jalan raya* simply "Hell Highway."

Whenever possible, we get off the *jalan raya* to take the more circuitous country roads, a welcome reprieve from the daily highway battle. A week in, we chance upon a winding side road. It takes us from small village to small village, connected by idyllic stepped paddies, tea plantations and banana groves.

The shiny greens and browns of the jungle crowd the edges of the road like cheering fans in the Tour de France, beckoning us onward. Small bridges cross steep valleys where trickling creeks slide and slip their way over glistening, smooth-hued rock to eventually divert into the rich agriculture of the valley plantations. In the villages, children and adults alike flash us ivory grins from their dark, gleaming faces and shout out the common "Hallo Mister! Where do you go?!" We reply with a smile and a *jalan, jalan* (just travelling around), inevitably drawing raucous laughter from the questioners. Everything we say seems to be funny to them.

Roadside stands, each usually tended by a woman and her children, are our sources of sustenance. *Air minum* (bottled water) pulls us through the muggy heat of day, and an assortment of packaged cookies and breads give us our energy. A midday stop for some *bakso* soup (boiled meatballs with noodles and veggies) from one of the many mobile push-stands provides us with more sustainable power. Bananas fresh from the field balance out our diet.

We get from town to town by asking locals "[insert town here] *di mana*," whereupon they point us in the proper direction. It is lovely, idyllic, tranquil soul-cycling.

In the town of Cikalong Wetan, our quiet country lane connects once again with the *jalan raya*. It is here that our peaceful path meets a WWE wrestling mat. As we look at our map for direction, a group of local men hanging around squatting in a circle on the corner took notice of us two *bules* (albinos, as we are affectionately referred to; pronounced "boo-lay"). Anyplace we go, we stick out like the dumb tourists we are and become the centre of attention. A discussion about us takes place among the squatting circle with laughter and pointing. Eventually, their appointed leader, a balding man with a thin black moustache, beige pants and a blue tank top approaches us with a smile.

"*Ke Mana?*" (Where are you going?)

"We're looking for a hotel here, people in the last town said there is a hotel here," I reply.

He shakes his head. "*Tidak* hotel." (No hotels.) "Darangdan hotel." (Darangdan being the next town.)

By this time, all seven of the men have gathered around us, putting in their two cents' worth. It's 5:45 p.m. and dusk is falling on Hell Highway. Kevin and I have to make it four kilometres along this battleground of a road in peak weekend traffic before we reach the relative comfort of a dingy cockroach- and mosquito-ridden hotel room.

After a quick *selamat tinggal* and *terima kasih* (goodbye and thanks), we roll onward. Slipping in along the edges of the madness with our lightless bikes, we begin the final stretch of the day. Our lights are buried deep in our packs, and we figure we're just about done for the day anyhow.

The mess of traffic shocks us into an immediate adrenaline rush, charged by the tonnes of hurtling steel and rubber ripping by our frail bikes and bodies, only inches away. Buses fire off piercing ship-whistle horn blasts at us; motor scooters whine past laden with two, three, sometimes four people; dump trucks swerve in and out of oncoming traffic, oblivious to any potential danger. The drivers seemed addicted to the buzz of the *jalan raya*.

As I hurtle down a steep, curving hill with Kevin about ten metres in front of me, a scene of carnage unfolds before us. A motor scooter with a family of three is clipped by a passing bus, sending it skidding sideways to the guardrail and scattering the passengers along the roadside. Two other scooters following close behind crash into the first. Obviously concerned, Kevin pulls up beside the casualties of the first scooter. The helmetless man who was driving lies motionless on the ground while his wife sits in wide-eyed shock and her child runs screaming to her. The stream of traffic flows along unabated; no one looks, no one stops — no one even flinches at the roadside distraction.

Kevin stands over them, assessing what to do, when I pull up to him. "Let's go Kev! Let's go! We can't get involved." I've been in this situation before. Once the police arrive, a couple of *bules* are easy pickings. We'd very likely be blamed for the accident and either fined or extorted heavily. Our perceived wealth (they assume all foreigners are wealthy, which, relative to the average Indonesian, is quite true) would be a hindrance. We hop back on our bikes and rejoin the inexorable *jalan raya* flow. A hundred metres down the road, we pass a police station. I have the impulse to go in and report the accident but catch myself. Good intent would be perceived as guilt. They would ask, "If you did not cause it, why did you stop?" My gut wrenches; I feel cruel.

With our hotel only 500 metres away, we stop and dig out our lights. A young Indonesian woman dolled up in heavy makeup and tight jeans walks up to me from a roadside stand. "I love you. You love me?" she asks. This is too much: injury and carnage just behind us, and a prostitute offering up her goods to me in the dark of Hell Highway. I am in no mood. "I don't even know you," I reply gruffly and turn away.

We climb up the final hill to the hotel. Our room is dingy, with a single dim bulb hanging from a wire in the ceiling. The water faucet pulls right out of the wall when I turn it, flooding the bathroom. Cockroaches scurry into dark crevices of faded yellow walls; mosquitoes drift in through cracks in the windows. Compared to Hell Highway, though, it's heaven.

*   *   *

Gunung Slamet

The people of Java have stories and myths associated with all their volcanoes. They offer rituals and pay homage to appease the volcanic spirits, a throwback to thousands of years of animist beliefs. The traditions still remain, intertwined neatly with their Muslim faith. With a population density of 800 people per square kilometre and close proximity to potential eruptions, it pays to be nice to the volcano gods here. Lying on the Pacific "Ring of Fire," where tectonic plates under the Indian and Pacific oceans descend beneath the Eurasian Plate, Java is the most volcanic island on Earth. There is no better place to explore and experience volcanoes.

Gunung Slamet, at 3432 metres, is Java's second-biggest peak. It's the target of our second ascent. With a six a.m. start on our fully loaded bikes, we work our way along a 17-kilometre jungle track from the mountain town of Baturaden to Bambangen, a small village at the base of Slamet on its eastern slope.

The first few kilometres are steep, rocky and washed out. Fat jungle palms crowd the edge of the road as we cross rickety bridges over steep, V-shaped creek valleys, with Slamet ever vigilant of our progress along its slopes.

The rough road subsides, becoming a smooth paved lane along which we bump into small groups of men with sickles and knives harvesting various plants from the forest. I nod at them with a cheery *salam* (peace, or hello), and they smile back enthusiastically.

The jungle eventually gives way to fields of lettuce, carrots, green onions and leeks before we hang a left to Bambangen, a village of perhaps 400. It's a classic, quaint Javanese community; very unhurried, with stepped-clay-tile-roofed Dutch colonial houses backing onto endless expanses of agricultural fields. The people look at us shyly yet curiously, seemingly happy and content with their lot in life. The road turns dirty, dusty, rough and steep. Kevin and I have to crank out of our seats in low gear just to get up it.

As we approach the top of the road, school lets out and Kevin, who's ahead of me, is suddenly besieged by 50 yellow-and-beige-uniformed schoolchildren with backpacks on. The squealing, laughing 5- and 6-year-olds must think he's a rock star, given the rabid fervour with which they chase him. All I can see is Kevin pumping along, his white helmet bobbing, as the beige-and-yellow swarm envelops him in a pulsing sea of joy.

At the trailhead, a man and his wife beckon us into their home. They grin incessantly, almost with disbelief that we are there. Mr. Mucheri is a diminutive man wearing a black Muslim skullcap, leather jacket and black pants. His wife wears a short sari and beams a cherubic smile at us as we sit down in her dining room, and she stuffs us with tea, cookies and *dodol* (chewy, gelatinous, chocolate sweets). Mr. Mucheri is the local guide and caretaker of this holy mountain.

"It will take you eight hours to get to the top, and then you'll have to sleep up there before coming down in the morning."

"Hmm, I think we can do it in six hours total, up and down."

Mr. Mucheri shakes his head and lets out a hearty laugh.

Kevin and I clip off at ten a.m., loaded down with four litres of water, coconut cookies and sweet bread. Speed-hiking through two kilometres of plantation grounds along the well-beaten trail, we pass local workers toiling in the fields, wearing peaked thatched headwear to keep the sun off. The two fast-moving *bules* seem to give them cause for pause from their labour — a reason to stand up, share a joke about us and then continue picking through their lettuce or carrot patches.

Once we get into the jungle, the trail steepens into a direct no-switchback line. Javan eagles fly overhead and the occasional monkey screeches as we huff up the red clay trenches worn into the mountainside by pilgrims over the years. The sides of the trenches rise higher than our heads; this would be an excellent place to be if a First World War skirmish broke out. We pass a few locals on their way down. Either barefoot or wearing thong sandals, they came up the day before to spend a freezing and starving night at base camp (2300 metres) before paying respects to their gods near, but not at, the *puncak* (peak).

As we pass 2500 metres, the forest thins out to a version of sub-alpine brush: thin, twisted trees, many burned out by lightning strikes, mixed with rough volcanic rock on the trail itself. At 3200 metres, we gaze up at a 230-metre volcanic scree slope to the peak. Stumbling and falling several times along our pick 'em route of black-and-red marble traction, we gain the summit.

The peak is located along a ridgeline overlooking an active crater, above the clouds. The crater centre steams with yellow and white gases shrouding shining grey stalagmite sentinels formed by the volcano's innards. Mile-high thunderheads have built up to the east and are moving our way, encouraging us to descend.

On our descent, we meet a group of four men we saw on our way up. They are moving slow as death, two of them barefoot, one in flip-flops and one in rubber boots. One man, hands out, speaks to me: "Aqua... Aqua." They've run out of water. I show him how to use my hydration tube, and he vigorously sucks down several gulps. The leader of the group holds up an empty oil can, their water container. Kev gives them a litre of water and we're off, having at least partially replenished the group of dehydrated men (and leaving some good karma back on the mountain as a result).

We arrive back in town and find that Mr. Mucheri has gathered a group of people to greet us. We've gone up and down in five hours, one minute — by far the new record, if such a thing even matters there. He feeds us endless tea, fried corn and peanuts and invites us to dinner. He says we are the first white people he's seen since a couple of Germans drove up to climb the mountain back in 1999. He's never heard of anyone who's biked to Bambangen before, much less from 600 kilometres away. The locals crowd around, following our every move. I smoke a courtesy clove cigarette with Mr. Mucheri and chat with him via our phrasebook.

Amid all the global turbulence involving Muslims, jihad etc., the people of Bambangen show us that in most of Java, people simply live their lives day to day. Their world exists inside the boundaries of their village or town, and they judge people as individuals, not by their connection to irrelevant geopolitical situations.

*   *   *

A Sudden Change

After three weeks into our journey over steep mountain passes and up narrow lava-rock trails, we've gotten into quite a groove. Having covered 1000 kilometres and climbed six peaks, we're quite satisfied with our progress. Five more peaks and 200 more kilometres of cycling and we'll be done.

Things in the world, though, have apparently changed. We've been obliviously travelling through Java without checking up on events since the WTC tragedy. Tensions have been rising, and the US is building up its forces on Afghanistan's borders. Once we cross into East Java, people are less friendly, colder. One day, things come to a head.

A palpable intensity is in the air as we cycle along with the busy Sunday traffic on the *jalan raya* for 15 kilometres before turning onto a quieter side road at Trowulan. Kevin feels bad today — stomach cramps, low energy. I even gap him going easy on the steep climbs, so I know he's hurting.

We spent last night in Jombang, a city of 250,000 that isn't even mentioned in our guidebook. The cute 19-year-old at the Warnet (internet spot) spoke decent English and said we were only the second and third Westerners she'd ever seen in the city. A Polish guy had popped up a couple of years ago, but that was it. Before leaving Jombang this morning, we noticed a significant police presence. One officer I asked directions from told me "Hati-Hati" — be careful. Hmm. So nice he was concerned.

The highway blasts three or four massive buses in a row by us on a regular basis. The "BOM, BOMMMMM!" of their horns gives us loud warning. We have to swing off the road a couple of times to avoid them as they pass at 150 kilometres an hour in the oncoming lane. Pretty standard stuff.

On the quiet side roads to the mountain town of Tretes, with perhaps 1300 metres of climbing, things begin to unravel. I stop to ask an older man chopping high grass with his machete if we're going the right way. He kindly points me down the road, and I turn to start, when Kevin says, "Did you see that?"

"What?"

"Guys in the van telling us to 'Fuck off, America.'"

"Were they joking or angry?"

"Seriously angry."

I head down the steep hill and catch up to the offending minivan stopped at an intersection. Immediately, three young men, mouths spraying bile, eyes wide and angry, poke their heads out of the windows. They flash me the finger, screaming "FUCK YOU AMERICA! FUCK

YOU! FUCK YOU AMERICA!" They emphasize their point by spitting at me viciously like caged cobras. I smile and wave at them, which just incenses them more.

A kilometre later, climbing up a steep pitch in the town of Prigen, a moustached man sitting crouched on the railing of a balcony locks eyes with me and follows my movement with the barrel of his semi-automatic rifle, no humour in his face. Fuck. Small mountain town; word gets around, and has gotten around from the city centres to the small towns. This is a particularly sensitive area we're in. East Java is the hotbed of Islamic fundamentalism in Java, with most of the major fundamentalist parties based here. We're white, therefore we're considered American. We're the Infidel, no questions asked.

Kevin's sick, with a rotten, gurgling gut. He passes out in our hotel. We've seen on the internet that there have been huge protests against the US in Jakarta; hundreds of Indonesian Muslims signing on for the jihad at established polling stations. In major cities, fundamentalist groups are conducting sweeps, looking for Americans. These groups have made a solemn vow that American interests will be destroyed and Americans driven from the country if Afghanistan is attacked. Do we want to be around when the shit hits the fan?

Kevin wakes up, and we discuss our options. There are perhaps four days left on our planned itinerary. Things are heating up, the Muslim population is getting poisoned with the rhetoric of the fundamentalists and we're the easy, and only, targets around. We've seen no foreigners over the past couple of weeks save a few in Solo, where they were being swept out. One pissed-off fundamentalist is all it takes. Only inches from us on the highway, a slight jerk of the steering wheel, and he takes us out. Kevin thinks we should abort. I lean toward agreement but am not fully convinced. We've cycled 1000 kilometres, with 75,000 feet of elevation change, and climbed six 10,000-foot volcanoes. Time to cut out while we still can? Perhaps a good decision.

Still torn, I go out to get water and beer; it's five p.m. and I haven't eaten since nine a.m. A friendly old man cooks me up fried tofu with spicy peanut sauce from the food cart that he carries on his shoulder with a bamboo pole. As I wait for the meal, I hear shouting from across the street. A stocky man with a paunch, balding pate and face twisted in fury is pointing at me and shouting "America! America! America! *Tidak* America!" like he wants to kill me right there and then. The vendor motions for me to ignore the angry man and waves him away. "No worry, no worry." After I've consumed the 50-cent feast, my decision is made.

Kevin and I have decided to give our bikes to a worthy candidate when the trip ends, and that moment is upon us. Where to find such a person among all this negativity? I go to the trailhead of Gunung Arjuna and am met with indifference. People brush me off and tell me to go away. Fine, no bike for you.

Descending back to the hotel, I stop at a roadside shop to buy my beer. I need a beer. The wooden frame structure is adorned with red-and-white wrapped cookies and bottles of water. Behind the counter, a woman in a sari smiles warmly and asks if I want *dingin* (cold) beer; her daughter runs back to get it. Her son, perhaps eight, sprays ants with a spritzer bottle by the roadside, happily engrossed in his play. I get my beer and the family sends me off with a warm *terima kasih.* Candidate #1.

I return to the hotel and ask the kind old food server where he lives; he says Tretes. "Do you have a bike?" I ask.

"*Tidak, curam, curam.*" (No, steep, steep.)

Too bad.

I gather up Kevin from his fetal position on the bed, and we go out to give away our steeds. First stop, the family at the store. I walk up to the doorway beside the stand and look through the screen door to see them sitting in their cramped, spartan living space. I knock and ask, "*Apakah kamu suka sepeda?*" (Do you like bikes?) The sari woman and her sister stand up and reply, "Ya."

I show them the bike through the door and say, "For your *keluarga* (family)," then point to the ant sprayer boy and say, "For him."

They ask, "*Berapa?*" (How much?)

I reply, "*Gratis.*" (Free.)

Stunned for a moment, they take it all in. The Norco Mountaineer bicycle — shocks, V-brakes, made in Canada. It was now theirs. They laugh and invite us in. We take a picture of the bike with the family around it, and the little boy, named Dimas, shakes my hand in a dumbfounded state of shock. They give us their address. Canada is good here. Westerners are good here. This Muslim family will always have a good image of the West. We didn't give them rhetoric. We gave them a bike to be used for years, for Dimas to grow up with and into, the envy of Tretes.

Kevin adjusts the seat for Dimas and he beams a bright, beautiful smile. The mother, sister, aunt, uncle and grandmother all beam. Such a day. A day to be remembered.

We roll down the street with one bike yet to give. Two boys sit on a block of concrete, gazing out at the empty road. I walk up and ask if they like bikes. They nod shyly. Tana and Iman are their names, one 10, the other maybe 11. I grab the bike and motion that they have to share. Leaning the bike toward them, I tell them to hop on. They immediately understand and both jump up and sit on their new bike, posing with it. Best friends with a bike for life. Soon they'll be cruising around Tretes with Dimas. Their families appear and surround the boys, gushing gratefulness. Their fathers get the boys to write down their names for us, to use their schooling; they're proud of their boys. The joy of the families gives Kevin and I so much more than we give them.

After warm farewells, we head into a restaurant. Kevin can't eat but wants some water. A few locals hang out in the back. The owner looks agitated as he speaks to another man, using abrupt hand gestures. He is friendly to me, and I order *nasi goreng* (stir-fried rice) and *kopi susu* (a coffee-and-milk drink). Three big men, all between six feet and six-foot-three, enter the restaurant and walk into the back like they own the place. They look Middle Eastern. One, with a moustache, coiffed hair and cargo pants, glances at us to size us up.

They order beer and sit down beside us. These guys definitely aren't Indonesian. Perhaps 20 to 24 years of age, they speak a different language and carry themselves with an intimidating swagger.

Kev leaves, tired and sick. I stay to finish my coffee. The biggest guy, the one who sized us up, is very tough looking. He turns to me. In excellent English he asks, "Where are you from?"

"Canada. And you?"

"Pakistan," he says, looking hard at me for a reaction.

"Oh, yeah," I comment, as casually as possible.

His friends stare at me silently, sipping their beer. He stands up and so do they. The owner of the place and the men who were chatting earlier at the back are quiet, stealing quick glances at us here and there. They're scared of these men.

"Come with me, we go for a walk."

I smile and say, "No, no... need to finish my coffee."

He accepts the excuse and they sit down beside me again. We chat. They're all from the same town in Pakistan and have been in Java for two weeks.

"What do you do?" I ask.

"We're in the Pakistani militia."

"Oh... What are you doing here?"

He pauses. "Selling carpets in Jakarta."

Right, militia guys selling carpet. Tretes is a popular getaway for wealthy Indonesians, infamous for its prostitutes.

"Where do you live?" he asks.

"Vancouver."

"No, no... here in Tretes."

I think for a split second then point down the street. "Kali... um... Kali..."

"Kalimas Hotel?"

"Yes, yes... Kalimas." No use hiding it; Kevin and I are the only Westerners in town.

They finish their beer and all stand up at once. Each of them pauses to give me a firm, sincere handshake on his way out. Phew. Pakistani militia in Java. Whose side are those guys on? Things are definitely getting weird.

We leave the next day at four a.m., headed to Surabaya to catch a ten-hour train back to Jakarta. No less than four different people tell me *"Hati, hati"* (be careful). A cabbie comes up to me and says, "Dari Mana?" (Where are you from?)

"Canada."

"Oh, America."

I shake my head, put up one hand, point at it and say, "North America." I point low and say, "Mexico," then point in the middle of my palm, "America." I finally point at the fingers, "Canada."

He looks at me blankly, then says, "America."

It doesn't matter. I'm a Westerner and therefore an American to them. People have stopped saying "Hallo Mister" to me and now just said "America." I'm branded.

"Ke mana?" he asks. (Where are you going?)

"Jakarta."

"Hati-hati."

The TV in the train station blares the Jakarta protests, showing foreigners leaving the city in droves and Muslim groups organizing to expel Americans. I just wanted to tour across this island, climb volcanoes and interact with its people in a positive exchange. Ninety-nine per cent of the people are the friendliest I've ever met, but the few extremists are poisoning the well.

In the darkened early-morning streets of Tretes, we board the minibus to Surabaya. Dark, hijab-framed faces are dimly lit by passing vehicle lights. The glow of cigarette embers are all we can see of the silent men who sit around us. On the taxi ride to the train station in Surabaya, a blood red sun rises over the skyline. Things are still and serene as we quietly slip away.

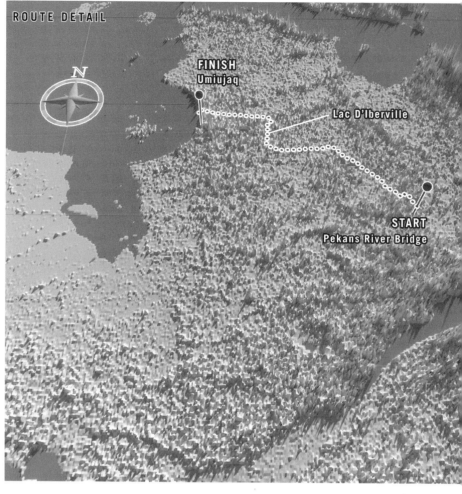

ROUTE DETAIL

N

FINISH
Umiujaq

Lac D'Iberville

START
Pekans River Bridge

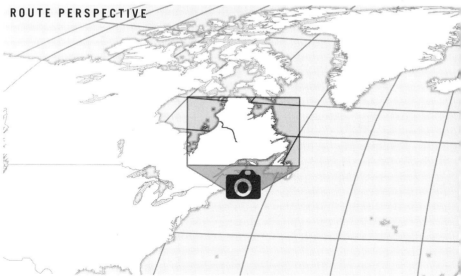

ROUTE PERSPECTIVE

Time

A meditation on time during a 1350-kilometre canoe journey through northern Quebec.

ORIGINALLY PUBLISHED IN SPRING 2018 ISSUE OF *EXPLORE MAGAZINE*

> *I've been standing right here listening to you*
> *But I can't seem to hear you at all*
> *To hell with this fear and the laziness too*
> *If we stay in this scene you know we're bound to fall*
> *It's about time*

—FROM THE SONG "TIME," BY PEIRSON ROSS

Dirt and rain streak the windshield of my mom's red Dodge Caravan. We're driving a winding ribbon of gravel on Quebec Highway 389, looking for our put-in. I'm at the wheel, with mom riding shotgun and Peirson Ross and his girlfriend, Sooj, in back. Two and a half days of driving from Toronto have brought us here. That's a lot of time spent sitting in a car and eating fast food. The sedentary days have me bursting to be out of this van and into the woods for the rest of the summer.

Sooj and my mother — saints that they are — volunteered for this arduous shuttle. For my 75-year-old widowed mom, it's an adventure.

She's never been up this way, and the journey has released her from the hollow creep of time alone in the city. I live on the other side of the country so only see her occasionally. Every moment of the trip for her has been a joy. I'm happy she's happy.

The GPS beeps and I pull to a stop at the Pekans River Bridge, about 45 minutes south of Labrador City. We quickly unload our canoe and gear, the ladies give us good-luck hugs, and before you know it Peirson and I are watching the mud-spattered van turn around and disappear into the mist, leaving us alone with our mission. One thousand three hundred fifty kilometres of hard tripping await us as we set off across the broad expanse of northern Quebec to the Inuit town of Umiujaq on the Hudson Bay coast.

Time off, time on the water, geological time, camp time, time well spent... this canoe trip is about time — and it's finally time to hop on the water and get going.

⋆　⋆　⋆

Whitewater

Peirson is a professional musician based in Toronto. The last canoe journey we did together was a 750-kilometre route through southern Ontario and Quebec, touring his last album. I played the role of canoe "roadie," navigator and tour manager. We stopped at various venues along the way, where Peirson performed to intimate audiences in cottages, lodges and bars during the course of a relatively relaxed, languid trip.

Now we're in the true North — a land of cold water, serious rapids, no resupply and no buffer. We need to move efficiently and pull long days with little rest. We have to be on our game.

Peirson and I drop down a boiling tongue and squirt out of a burly corner rapid on Quebec's upper Nastapoka River. We're clipping along perhaps too fast in the screaming current as we hit smooth water on the approach to the next rapid immediately around the bend. The outside line looks best to me, avoiding the holes and ledges in the middle.

The beautiful thing about running a rapid is that you are absolutely in the moment — the "before" and "after" don't matter, there is no time, there is only "now." If you drift off from the task at hand, you'll find yourself flipped and swimming in the blink of an eye.

As we come into the meat of the drop, I see there are three large boulders we'll have to shift through — a simple manoeuvre that requires but a couple of strokes. We're now well into the journey and should be a cohesive team in the boat, having run countless rapids to this point. We should be.

I call for Peirson to give me a pry stroke in the bow to straighten out the boat so we can slip easily through. Instead, he gives me a draw stroke — the exact opposite of what we need in this situation, and far worse than not paddling at all.

"No! No! A Pry! A PRY!" I shout again to Peirson, but it's as effective as a tourist repeating himself loudly in English to a local street vendor who does not, in fact, speak English.

In an instant we veer broadside into the biggest of the boulders, slamming hard against it and sticking. The water quickly builds up against the canoe and I lean hard into the rock to prevent us from capsizing. Pushing desperately off against the bottom of the river with my paddle, I manage to slide us off and back into the main current, free of the impediment.

I'm pissed off. Twenty-seven days in, and Peirson still can't do a bloody pry stroke. It's an ongoing thing that shouldn't be an ongoing thing.

As we drift in the calm water below, I lose my cool.

"What the hell was that Peirson?! You almost fucked us there! You have to give me the stroke I need when I need it or else we'll be wrapped around a rock here in the middle of the wilderness!"

He quietly responds with a "Sorry."

I'm not having any of it. "Sorry doesn't cut it. It should be automatic — this is *day 27!* Like the three chords of a song — you only need to know three strokes in the bow — forward, draw... and PRY!"

I catch myself and simmer down. I can be a hard-ass on these trips and need to take a breath sometimes. We only have a few more days to go, and I should expect these lapses by now. Peirson is, above all else, an artist. He's completely absorbed in an amazing ability and passion for music, sometimes to the point of distraction at inopportune moments. A chronic creator, he's already composed an album full of new songs in his head on this trip alone. For all I know he was in the midst of a new lyric when I called for that pry back there. I was existing in the timelessness of the rapid, while he was in a musical dimension far, far away.

*　　*　　*

Wolf

We paddle into the broad expanse of Petit Lac des Loups Marins. A movement catches my eye and I see a distant wolf trotting casually along the rocky, spruce-fringed shore. We stop to watch it amble along. Like all the wild animals up here, it has no schedule to keep, no clock to punch — it simply does what it's hard-wired to do in order to survive. It moves all day in the search for food, and when opportunity knocks, it fills its belly until the next opportunity arrives.

Life isn't easy for animals up here — but who said life should be easy? Living on the razor's edge of survival is certainly not comfortable, but I'd argue it's the most engaging way for mammals of all sorts — including humans — to live.

Our modern world makes happiness hard to find sometimes. Technology designed to make our lives convenient and comfortable has taken away our purpose. We fill the gap with time-killing measures like jobs, sports, games, the internet... pastimes that are amusing but fail to fulfill our hard-wired need for purposeful, physical struggle.

Canoe tripping is also at first glance another unnecessary pastime. Unlike most urban activities, though, a journey like this falls closer to the way of the wolves. Once you put yourself in the situation of needing to cover an average of 45 wilderness kilometres per day carrying only a 30-day supply of food, you quickly tap into the ancient pulse of the wild. We're in it, and there's no turning back. My mom's red minivan is long gone.

On this trip there's a perpetual scratching at my subconscious — something that drives me to move all day, every day in order to cover a lofty amount of landscape while still remaining safe and fed. It puts us in the head of that wolf — we're looking through its eyes. Like it, we're driven to purposeful movement, ignited by the ancient survival spark that exists in all of us.

*   *   *

Brook Trout

We're camped in a narrows at the south entrance to Lac D'Iberville, having just crossed into Tursujuq National Park. At 26,000 square kilometres, it's the largest park in Quebec. Created in 2013, it protects a vast, unique wilderness managed by the Kativik Regional Government that oversees the primarily Inuit region of Nunavik. Nunavik, meaning "great land," comprises the northern third of the province.

I cast my line into the channel and immediately hook a three-pound brook trout — a fine accompaniment to our evening ration of freeze-dried food. It's a beautiful creature, bejewelled with a bright orange belly and speckled silver back. I cast a few more times, and each produces another trout, but I throw them back. The first fish will be plenty for us.

The life of a brook trout is one I try to emulate. I drift in the current of existence until something interesting appears on the surface, and then I strike it with gusto. Unburdened by a regular schedule of commitments, I seize on projects and opportunities when they arise. The key is simplicity — as long as my heart is beating and I have a regular source of food, the basics are taken care of. Like the metaphorical trout, I'm free to follow the current where it takes me.

Self-employed, retired, between jobs, entrepreneur... it's difficult for me to categorize my career status. Needless to say, there's not much money living like this — it's more a lifestyle than a living — but having time to follow my passion is more fulfilling to me than spending it bumping up bank numbers. Peirson's music-immersed approach to life is similar, and here we are.

The river systems we move through on this journey — the Caniapiscau, Great Whale and Nastapoka — used to be travelled extensively by the Indigenous Inuit and Naskapi people up here. Change is inevitable, though, and the advent of bush planes and airlines has left these waterways virtually unused for half a century. Local people now fly over this wilderness from one town to another, disconnected from a land once as familiar to them as their present-day living rooms.

With the luxury of time but without the means to hire a bush plane to fly us over difficulty, Peirson and I are pushed into a millennia-old way of travel. Upstream, downstream, through the bush — we move at the pace of the land, taking what it gives us. It feels as natural as breathing. A van drop at the edge, a month-long window and a creative route through the wild are all we need to set it in motion.

Time itself is a funny thing, if you think about it — like money, it's something we've created. We manufacture clocks and dollar bills in an attempt to quantify time and money, but in nature these are ephemeral concepts. The brook trout swimming perpetually in front of our campsite are completely unaware of either time or money. These magnificent creatures, like the wilderness of northern Quebec, are timeless.

*   *   *

Pokey

"Peirson!"

A groan emanates from the tent.

"Coffee's ready in five minutes."

"Oooooh... okay."

I return to sipping my hot coffee and gaze across the lake at the thundering rapid we portaged around the evening before. Reflecting on the pulsing halo of green-and-pink aurora borealis that stretched above me when I stepped out for a pee last night, I slowly savour my oatmeal and get into a second cup of joe. A half hour passes. Peirson has yet to emerge.

"Peirson! Coffee and oatmeal are getting cold!"

Another groan. He fell back asleep. Again. It's the same pattern most mornings, and I'm used to it. Alas, he's the one who chokes down cold coffee and oats, not me. His well-earned nickname over the years is "Pokey," as in "slowpoke." It takes Peirson a long time to get anything done.

He came on this trip overweight and out of shape, just a few days after a month-long gig in Europe, producing a couple of albums for musicians over there. From late nights of drinking fine wine, eating schnitzel and sleeping 'til noon, he's been thrown abruptly into five a.m. mornings and chilled gruel.

I never know where our next camp will be. We paddle, portage and line steadily for about ten hours every day, starting after breakfast and finishing a couple of hours before sunset. I know from experience that this will average out to the right distance for the amount of food we have. I dubbed this trip the "Maze of the North" in homage to the crow's-view tangle of waterways that comprises the route. Peirson has renamed it the "Race of the North," due to the speed we move and the distance we cover. There are evidently two very different perspectives of trip happening in one canoe, but only my way will see us through before our food runs out.

In order to keep to our schedule, Peirson's "Pokey" ways have me getting up earlier and going to bed later than him every day. I can do in a few minutes what sometimes takes him an hour. In order to keep things moving along at the required pace, I end up doing the cooking and packing myself, leaving him to set up and take down the tent, and little else.

Though frustrating at times, Peirson is a great trip partner. There aren't many people willing or able to take on a journey like this, and he's always upbeat. His bright, sunny disposition shines through in the toughest of times. For me, attitude is everything in an expedition cohort, and Peirson has an excellent one. Besides, once in the canoe, he goes the same speed as me.

Peirson is a virtuoso player of multiple instruments; his hands are his life. A couple of days into the trip he asks me "Can you feel your hands?"

"What do you mean?"

"I don't have feeling in my hands... is that normal?"

"Uh, no."

I've never heard of such a thing before. Bad circulation? Nerve damage? Who knows.

On long-distance trips, being uncomfortable is part of the package — and it provides perspective like nothing else. All that matters on trip is the moment — we have to seize it and see it through. Peirson's hands will have all the time in the world to heal afterwards. And, to his credit, despite continued numbness throughout our journey, he doesn't complain, soldiering on admirably. Pokey or not, Peirson keeps on going. The "Race of the North" goes to the tortoise, not the hare.

*   *   *

Achikunipi

The Nastapoka River drops 373 metres over its 400-kilometre course in a series of thundering falls and rapids, spilling eventually into Hudson Bay. Its source is Lac des Loups Marins, which literally translated from French means "Lake of the Sea Wolves."

The "sea wolves" here are a rare species of harbour seal that live year-round in the Nastapoka. The exact number of this species — known by the inland Cree as *achikunipi* (freshwater seal) — is unknown, but there are thought to be only somewhere between 50 to 600 individuals in total.

Our first three weeks of the journey were spent in the spruce thickets of the boreal forest, but on the Nastapoka we've broken above treeline and will spend our final week in the open expanse of the tundra. At the end of one of countless rocky portages around waterfalls, I plop the canoe down at the edge of a pulsing eddy when something catches my eye. Thirty metres away, a seal is surfing one of the huge standing waves at the exit of this powerful rapid. Its black, torpedo-like body skips repeatedly like a stone, then submerges. A few seconds later, it pops up 50 metres downstream and then rides the recirculating current past me back onto the wave, where it repeats the fish-and-surf cycle — a simultaneous act of work and play.

This species of seal was locked inland during the deglaciation period of the last ice age thousands of years ago and has since adapted to the freshwater environment. They live their lives between thundering sets of falls, well fed by a bountiful supply of trout.

The *achikunipi* are relative newcomers to the landscape — merely a deep breath in the geological life of a land comprised of billions-year-old wind- and ice-scoured rock. If the seals are a deep breath in the timeline of this place, Peirson and I are not even a flash of sunlight on a swinging paddle blade. We are completely irrelevant — tourists that are not part of this world but are merely passing through it.

* * *

Umiujaq

We run with the ocean current on glassy Hudson Bay and make it the 46 kilometres from our site above Nastapoka Falls to the Inuit town of

Umiujaq in a day. It's lovely and warm as we glide over sandy-bottomed, crystal-clear water accented with waving seaweed. Fish jump on all sides of us, and the common cousins of the *achikunipi* track the glide of our red canoe.

We arrive in the evening and set up our tent on a broad, glacier-polished expanse of stone on the outskirts of town. The sun is setting. It is windless, warm and insect-free. With a scheduled flight out the next day, we enjoy one final evening in this timeless land.

ROUTE DETAIL

START / FINISH

Puffin Cove

N

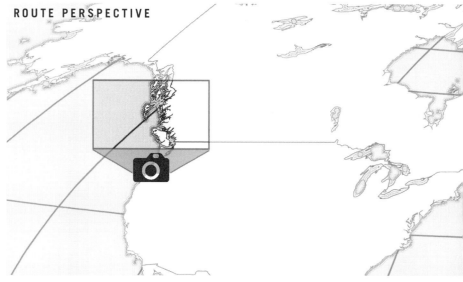

ROUTE PERSPECTIVE

A Day in the Life

**Finding refuge in the former homesteader haven
of Puffin Cove during a kayak circumnavigation of
the Haida Gwaii archipelago.**

ORIGINALLY PUBLISHED IN FEBRUARY 2006 ISSUE OF *ADVENTURE KAYAK MAGAZINE*

We hole up in Mike Inlet for the afternoon, hoping the building seas will
calm. The four p.m. forecast comes around on the VHF but doesn't bring
the news we want. A big nor'wester is coming. It's a tough decision. We're
only six kilometres from Puffin Cove, where local legends Neil and Betty
Carey built a cabin and homestead that they lived in from the 1960s to
the early 1980s. Keith had read Neil's book *Puffin Cove* and Todd had read
Bijaboji, Betty's account of her 1930s canoe trip up the Inside Passage.
During the course of his reading, Todd became somewhat smitten with
adventurous Betty. The blackflies were brutal in Mike Inlet, the camping
marginal at best, and love — well, a man in love cannot be denied.

We gather belongings that have been airing on the pebble beach,
stuff them into our kayaks and are ready to go in half an hour. When we
started our circumnavigation of Haida Gwaii 30 days ago, the process
lasted more than twice as long. Four hundred sixty kilometres around
Graham Island worked out all our packing kinks for this second leg.
Just six kilometres to Puffin Cove... a mere six kilometres. It turns out
to be the biggest water of our trip.

Mike Inlet is one of a handful of safe coves that cut into the 3,000-foot-high storm-scraped San Christoval Range. Dropping straight down to water level along the west coast of Moresby Island, the mountains are stark in their nakedness. Coined in 1774 by Captain Juan Perez, "San Christoval" is the first recorded name ever to be applied in British Columbia. Perez was unable to land due to stormy weather, but he holds the distinction of being the first white man to lay eyes on Haida Gwaii. St. Christopher was aptly chosen as the namesake since he was well known for his great height and protection of travellers. Today, we hope the peaks will cast some of that saintly cover over us.

Between bays, rolling buses of swell crash relentlessly against jagged rock, creating boomer zones and clapotis that test even the most skilled paddlers. Rounding Hippa Island two weeks ago, I was pounded over shallow reef by a hulking rogue wave that broke unexpectedly, jettisoning me from my boat. The experience instilled in me a respectful fear every time we ventured out along the perpetually exposed coast.

My hand curls comfortably around the paddle shaft, a month's worth of calluses finding their place for another evening's work. The blade bites into rippled water and my muscles fall into rhythm. As we move out from the safety of the cove, we know we're in for it. Dark sentries of swell march steadily across the exposed mouth, growing like anthills under time-lapse photography. The forecast calls for a huge northwest sea of three to four metres, with waves up to twice as big on the faces.

Breaking out from the shadow of the mountains, we join the big blue at its huffing, puffing best. Thirty-five-knot gusts drive the swell and begin to shove us inexorably toward Puffin Cove. The conditions are so strong that within a couple of minutes of leaving Mike, it's impossible to backtrack. We're committed. Six kilometres of huge water to cover or bust.

Ever seen the movie *Castaway*? There's a scene where Tom Hanks's plane has just crashed into the ocean during a storm. He's clinging onto a little yellow rubber raft, the camera pulls up and away, and all you see is this little speck bobbing up and disappearing behind mountains of water in the middle of the sea. That's what it felt like watching Todd and Keith, their kayaks reduced in scale to little paper boats made by children.

Trying to draw focus away from the growing knot of fear in my gut, I look ahead to the beehive-shaped island that indicates the entrance to Puffin Cove. Gripping the paddle shaft so tight I think it's going to shatter in my hands, I crush every stroke like it's my last. Time grinds to a halt, our destination only a dream. Though we're hauling ass, it feels like we're paddling on a treadmill, never getting closer. Every time I look up, the distant cove remains static. If I let the waves take me, I'd instantly surf seven metres down the face and pound into the trough at the bottom, submerging my kayak halfway. The best thing to do is back-paddle when a wave breaks behind me, let it wash over and then stroke like mad before the next one breaks. We all try to stay close, but not too close, as we might end up harpooning each other with our boats.

When I planned out this trip five months ago in a skid row diner in Vancouver, I envisioned a journey that would take me away from the crawling city and bring me face to face with raw nature, far from help or hindrance. I wanted to go to a place where I was a mere speck of dust, something that could be absorbed in an instant without the surrounding ecosystem missing a beat. A bleak thought squeezes into my brain as another wave rolls over my back: "Frank, you should be careful what you ask for…"

After 40 minutes that seem like 400, the biggest, baddest wave rears up just as we're about to turn into the lee of Puffin Cove. With Todd and Keith just behind me, a behemoth 20 metres wide and who knows how high passes underneath and then breaks only ten metres ahead of us in one simultaneous explosion that seems to turn the entire ocean white. A little bon-voyage kiss from the North Pacific. Moments later we're drifting gently into Puffin Cove.

Emotions on the outer coast swing between extremes that lead to the purest form of euphoria. One minute you're paddling for dear life, and the next you find yourself relaxed in a secluded nirvana, your mind bathed in endorphins. A narrow channel brings us into a placid lagoon encircled by perfect powder sand and protected by an amphitheatre of rock, and our jaws drop. It's like we've entered the set of the 1970s show *Fantasy Island*. I half expect a flock of bronzed women in hula skirts to run down to the beach, greet us with hugs and put leis around our necks. At any moment Ricardo Montalbán will appear in his white suit to welcome us while diminutive Tattoo cries out, "The Kayaks! The Kayaks!"

*   *   *

The Careys were Americans who sought out a life away from the hustle and bustle of California. After years of searching, they found Puffin Cove. Their cabin is still there, fully intact after 40 years, perched up on a bluff in the corner of the lagoon. They were incurable beachcombers, and there are still piles of fish floats, buoys, glass balls and other flotsam and jetsam stashed around the cabin's foundation.

A typhoon could be blowing full kilter on the outside, but you won't notice it in Puffin Cove. We really appreciate this; a bad storm in Haida Gwaii can stretch from one day into several. On the fourth day of our trip up Graham's east coast, we were pinned ten kilometres south of Rose Point by a hammering gale. A further four days later, going stir-crazy, we thought we'd never escape the bludgeoning, wind-driven sand. Here in Puffin Cove, with conditions building to gale outside, a forced layover wouldn't seem so bad in comparison.

We enter the cabin through a trap door via stairs underneath the greying 12-by-12-foot cedar structure. Seashells are displayed neatly on the left wall; rows of books and *Reader's Digest*s line a ring of shelves. A little wood stove sits in the corner across from the kitchen table, a double mattress and a kid's bed. Faded bottles of Off repellent, sewing kits, fishing hooks and other bric-a-brac sit around waiting to be used. Nothing in here postdates 1987, which was the time the Carey's lease ran out and Parks Canada took over the land to make it part of Gwaii Haanas National Park. For over two decades, the Careys fished, foraged and explored a forgotten coastline, pioneers in every sense of the word. The cabin is a bit musty, but for all we know, Neil and Betty might as well have stepped out a few minutes earlier. A logbook indicates we're only the 14th party to visit there in five years. Though we're in one of the world's great parks, the outer coast requires so much commitment that most kayakers instead explore the sheltered archipelago on the eastern shore of Moresby.

The Careys' haven is one of the few nooks along the West Coast where there wasn't once a Haida village. This is most likely because the whole lagoon dries out at low tide, making for poor water access for the Haida's 100-foot-long cedar canoes. At the height of their civilization, the Haida numbered 20,000, but dwindled to as low as 600 by the mid-20th century, victims of a smallpox epidemic introduced by Western traders. Weathered totems and remnant longhouses are the only evidence of their millennia-long habitation of a shoreline now patrolled only by black bear and whale. In the larger bay outside the lagoon there used to be a village called Sq'i'na, which provided free launch but must have been hammered when a southwester reared up — reminding us of how resourceful and tough the Haida were.

Even though they aren't physically visible to us on the outer part of the archipelago, we can feel the spirit of the original people flow strongly through every rock, tree and living being. On day 18, we cross paths with a super-pod of over 100 transient orca, their man-sized dorsal fins dropping and rising on all sides of us. Like an ancient tribal greeting party, they came out from a bay in front of the abandoned village of Tian, where archaic totems carved with clamshells and stone still stand. We bobbed breathlessly amid the procession, staring in wild awe as the creatures faded into the horizon.

The conditions outside Puffin Cove are good for paddling the next day, but we decide to linger. Ling cod and rockfish practically beg us to throw our lines out, there's endless reading to be done and we soberly realize we're only a couple of weeks from the end of our journey. That afternoon, Todd grins as he serves me up a fillet on the beach, fried over fire in one of Betty Carey's old pans. Keith slowly chews the white, flaky flesh, gazing quietly out at the breadth of the North Pacific. With most of the difficulty behind us, we want to savour the remaining time we have in this magical land.

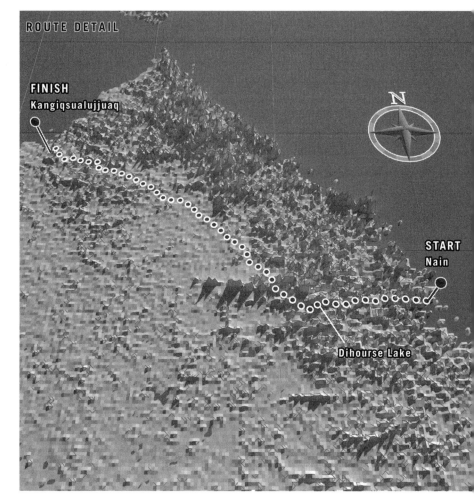

ROUTE DETAIL

FINISH
Kangiqsualujjuaq

START
Nain

Dihourse Lake

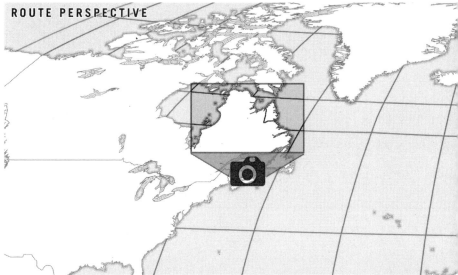

ROUTE PERSPECTIVE

The Third Person

An inside look at the filming of a gruelling 620-kilometre journey across the rugged Labrador Plateau.

ORIGINALLY PUBLISHED IN SPRING 2013 ISSUE OF *CANOEROOTS MAGAZINE*

July 22, 2012. I'm only halfway there, carrying the canoe up a three-kilometre-long, 1,500-foot-high portage. A sandstorm of blackflies keeps me company and has bludgeoned me to the point where the protective shirt wrapped around my head is soaked in blood. The temperature in the wind-less Poungasse Valley has crept to 30 degrees Celsius, and sweat mixes with blood, running in a pink stream down my chest. We're trying to crawl out of this chasm in order reach the expansive Labrador Plateau. "Shoot when it's hard," they say. It's showtime.

I drop the canoe on the tundra, pull the camera out of the case strapped to my chest and go to work. First, a close-up zoom and comment on my beaten face and the general situation. Next, run ahead 20 metres to set up the camera on a tripod for a third-person perspective of the carry. Finally, flip the canoe back on my head, grab my little point of view (POV) camera and turn the lens to my face before continuing to march uphill past the tripod. Drop the canoe again, pack up the camera gear, pop the canoe up and carry on with the journey.

On the double-back down the mountainside, I meet up with Todd. He's been seized with heatstroke and is on the verge of puking. Of course the camera comes out. I interview him about how he feels, then set up the tent so he can escape the blackflies, hydrate and sleep off his condition. He drops into the shelter and immediately conks out for three hours. I speak on camera about what's happening (I narrate my films with audio from the journey rather than scripted narration). Then, through the tent screen, I film his passed-out body from an aesthetically pleasing angle before shifting focus to a foreground of no-see-um mesh. I put away the electronics, grab a couple of bags and start back up to the canoe. So goes day three of a 620-kilometre, 21-day expedition and film production through Nunatsiavut and Nunavik with my friend Todd McGowan.

As an adventure filmmaker, I typically juggle the duties of director/videographer/editor/producer/expedition leader/camp cook/Sherpa. Working within this box, I try to create intimate, fun portraits of the landscapes I pass through. With CBC having nationally broadcast my past three productions, I've managed to keep scraping along from one project to the next.

To avoid burnout, I take an occasional break from the celluloid. So in 2011 I completed a canoe trip up to Hudson Bay without my cameras. It was bliss. I basked in the experiential simplicity of that adventure — just a friend, a canoe and the boreal. After that camera-less joy, I struggled with committing to filming the next journey.

I had an idea of what I wanted to achieve film-wise in Labrador, but the all-consuming process of shooting a layered, broadcast-worthy movie about a tough expedition is like adding the logistical complexity of a third person to the canoe. In terms of energy and effort, it's like bringing a toddler along. On the other hand, I'm most creative when I'm in difficulty, and the films I've made have always been deeply rewarding. The tug-of-war in my brain didn't end until the morning we left Vancouver for Goose Bay — with the third person barely making the roster.

Labrador is a vast region of 294,000 square kilometres with a population of only 26,000 that's largely concentrated in the southern towns of Goose Bay and Labrador City. North of Goose Bay there are no connecting roads, and the only way up is by plane or ferry.

With our canoe on board, we took the MV *Northern Ranger* on its two-day voyage up the Labrador coast to its terminus at the Inuit village of Nain, where I'd have my only chance to record Inuit perspectives on the land before we disappeared on our expedition. Nain is the capital of Nunatsiavut, the Inuit region that comprises northern Labrador and means "Our Beautiful Land" in Inuktitut.

For me, filmmaking is a journey that parallels the canoe trip — you have an idea of where you want to go but never know exactly what, or who, is around the next corner. The camera, like the canoe, is a powerful tool if you have a purpose and mission. It invites local populations to share ideas and stories they otherwise wouldn't tell. I didn't contact anyone in Nain in advance, so once we arrived I immediately began hunting for relevant interview subjects.

Sarah Leo is the recently elected president of Nunatsiavut. I asked her about the area we were about to canoe through. She laughed heartily and said, "That's not an area people go in the summertime — partly because of the difficult access, but mostly because of the flies." I used this quote in the narration for our buggy portage up the Poungasse a few days later. One interview down.

From Nain, it's 238 stiff kilometres to the George River in Nunavik. After speaking with Leo, I wanted to know if the rest of the locals thought what we're doing is rational, mad or somewhere in between. In a grassy field along the shoreline, I interviewed Johannes Lampe, an experienced local hunter and the minister of Culture, Recreation and Tourism. (Four years from now, in 2016, he will become Nunatsiavut's third president.) He encouraged and discouraged me at the same time. "It will be difficult... but if you are determined, I think you can make it." A nice bit of narration to lay over the portage footage, I think. In just a few hours, I had managed to grab the local commentary I needed to give context to the first leg of the film.

Films and expeditions need an element of mystery to be engaging. Reacting to unknown twists and turns is what adventure is and where inspiration arises. I look to explore remote regions that I'm interested in and about which little information exists. Nunatsiavut fits these criteria perfectly.

The Inuit and Innu have been roaming these lands for millennia, but a British explorer named Hesketh Prichard seems to be the only person to have crossed over the Labrador Plateau from Nain by canoe. He paddled and, after abandoning his canoe partway, hiked a route north of ours over 100 years ago. Looking at the maps, I crafted a route that I thought made more sense than Prichard's.

It's hard to find unexplored territory in this day and age, so our journey across the plateau was a great opportunity to travel unburdened by information. Prichard entered a land unknown to him, and our differing route ensured Todd and I had a similarly mysterious experience.

*   *   *

On July 29, Todd and I are huddled behind a monolith on the shore of a large, unnamed lake while we wait for a heavy head wind to ease off. That's the thing with the Labrador Plateau: it's either windy or it's buggy. Both conditions present their own challenges. Though it's pleasantly bug-free behind this hunk of rock, we're just sitting here, not moving.

Progress has been slow since we crested the Poungasse and gazed across the plateau's moonscape of rock and heather. Many of the rivers and lakes shown on our maps are severely shallow, boulder-choked and unnavigable. As a result, we've had to be content with dragging slowly over the tundra with short spurts of paddling across small lakes. Averaging only 12 kilometres or so per day, it's been a grind. We were looking forward to this big lake, 20 kilometres across, as our first stretch of consistent paddling. Then the gale blew in, and so we sit. Sigh.

The wind across the plateau doesn't make it practical to carry the canoe, so I've had to drag it overland with a line harnessed to my PFD. In the past week, I've shot every conceivable dragging angle possible, to the point where the leading candidate for the film's title is *Dragging My Canoe across Nunatsiavut: A Fool's Journey.*

Groping for a fresh perspective and something to do, I pull out the rubber mosquito mask I've made for this trip. I slip it over my head and strip down to my briefs. Having recently filmed a glut of super-close-ups of mosquitoes and their natural movements as they crawl over various parts of my body, I begin filming a sequence where I crawl mosquito-like around the tundra; the film will fade into a shot of a mosquito doing the same.

On a deeper level, I want this film to show the interconnectedness of all living things in the region, and this performance-art scene will bridge the gap between man, mosquito and everything in between.

The Inuit spoke of this connection during my interviews with them in Nain — though it's unlikely they foresaw it this way. The look on Todd's face as I repeat variations of the scene over and over makes me think that I may have buzzed over the proverbial edge — though "crazy" usually makes for good film.

We've finally been released by the plateau into the crystal-clear, brook-trout-laden Natikamaukau River. This waterway is a blast to paddle and a privilege for us to descend, as very few, if any, people have done so before. The 22-kilometre-long Natikamaukau drops 900 feet from its source at Dihourse Lake, snaking through water-smoothed rock slots down a deep valley framed by high, barren ridges roamed by caribou and black bear. It eventually spills into the oft-travelled George River, which we'll ride north to our finish in Ungava Bay.

Todd is waiting with the canoe at the top of a Class 3 rapid while I set up a fish-eye lens on a bluff to get an overhead view of the run. Mounted on the back of the canoe is the POV camera, set up on a three-link boom called a Magic Arm so both of us are in the shot as we run the rapid. Often used as a lighting mount in studio work, the arm is the perfect device for shooting canoe films, as it can be clamped anywhere and at any angle on the gunwales or thwarts. Having at least two unique perspectives (wide and POV) of the same rapid is key to making a dynamic sequence. I never portage and repeat the same rapids to redo shots — it's not authentic or true to the journey. This is a one-shot deal, so I try to set it up right.

I give Todd the hand signal, and he waves back. I press *record* and scramble over the rocks, bash through the shore alder, splash through the shallows and hop into the canoe. With the POV camera rolling, I tuck into the spray deck, and we're off.

The canoe slips into the current and we engage the river. I forget that I'm filming and enjoy the moment as a series of standing waves crashes over Todd in the bow. We side-slip a series of pillow rocks before peeling safely into an eddy behind a large boulder.

After a bit of euphoric hooting and hollering, I hop out, scramble up the embankment and run 100 metres back to the still-running camera. In my mind I can already see how I'll cut the scene when I get home. Surrounded by the barren splendour of Nunavik, it dawns on me that this is a pretty good office — and I'm glad the third person managed to come along with us on our journey. The run down the rapid was a success, and the footage looks great. The creative course of the film and the physical journey of the trip are moving ahead, side by side, toward a successful conclusion. As an adventure filmmaker, I couldn't ask for anything more.

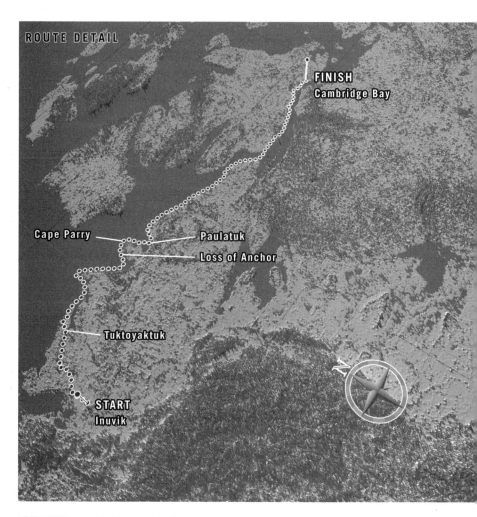

ROUTE DETAIL

FINISH
Cambridge Bay

Cape Parry

Paulatuk

Loss of Anchor

Tuktoyaktuk

START
Inuvik

N

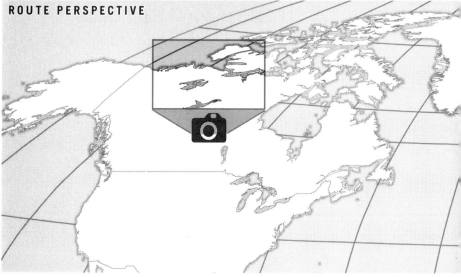

ROUTE PERSPECTIVE

The Anchor

Inuvialuit locals share their perspectives on climate change with a team of rowers on a perilous journey through the Northwest Passage.

All four of us are fast asleep, our sleeping-bag-enveloped bodies squeezed together inside the cabin of our rowboat like sardines in a can.

The previous couple of days have been good. We caught a nice current running down the west side of Franklin Bay and are beginning to catch up some of the distance we lost in the first couple of weeks. After an easy day out of Inuvik down the Mackenzie, we faced near-constant wind storms that kept us at anchor off and on for days, as we can barely row this one-tonne beast in even the slightest of headwinds, much less the northeast gales that have been lashing the Passage.

The good going is over again, as this northwest blow snapped in as we worked our way up the east side of Franklin Bay during a five-kilometre crossing of the mouth of a smaller bay. The wind came up fast, as it always seems to do, and blew us deep into the bay, forcing us to throw out the anchor and wait it out once more. We'd been going for 72 hours straight, Kevin and I taking a three-hour shift at the oars, followed by Paul and Denis for three hours, then back to us, then back to them, and so on.

We were all nicely tired as we covered some decent distance during our run. As we looked out over the whitecaps churning toward us across the open bay, it seemed like a good time to have a nap.

Our rowboat is 25 feet long, custom made with lots of storage throughout the vessel in hatches beneath the deck. There are two rowing stations with sliding seats and oars at each. A small fore-cabin is used for more storage, while a larger rear cabin is where we relax between shifts at the oars and post blogs and photos via satellite — and where, when the wind blows, as it does now, all four of us can sleep. It's only high enough to kneel inside, but there's enough length to stretch out and lie down.

My spot is against the wall of the cabin to the right. Next to me is Paul Gleeson, an Irishman from Limerick. Next to him is Kevin Vallely, a fellow Canadian and old friend of mine from North Vancouver. Finally, at the left wall, is Denis Barnett, another Irishman, who hails from Dublin. In my dream state, I'm half aware of a bumping rhythm to the ocean that wasn't there when we bedded down. Of course, it could just be part of a dream.

"Guys... guys! Get up! The ice is pushing against the boat!"

I wake quickly from my slumber and see that Kevin is kneeling, still half in his sleeping bag, peering out the cabin door. He looks back at me, eyes wide with concern, his voice stressed.

"There's a huge pan of ice that's pushed up against the bow! The wind must have blown it in!"

We all hop out of the cabin onto the deck and see that, indeed, a pan of ice the size of a hockey rink is jammed against our bow, with the driving wind trying to push it past the boat. The bow is tipped downward, and the anchor line is so taut it vibrates. While I pull out my camera to film the action, Paul and Kevin try with all their might to free the anchor, but it's no use. The ice pan is perhaps ten metres thick, and the anchor line runs straight down its underwater face and then 90 degrees along the bottom of it. The bow of our boat is slowly but surely tipping downward under the pressure. There are only a few possibilities here: the boat gets pulled under or flipped by the inexorable ice pan, our anchor line snaps or the eye that holds the anchor line gets pulled out and does significant damage to our boat. No scenario has us saving our anchor. Our only choice is to cut it.

Kevin slices the rope and sets us free. We drift quickly away from the ice as the wind grabs us and pushes us to the shore. We run the boat up to the shore edge but can't even inch the beast up the sandy shore. Our craft is based on an open-ocean design, but we pretty quickly found out it is ill-equipped to handle the shallow, wind-whipped waters of the Northwest Passage.

The waves hammer the boat broadside, and we decide we have to find shelter somewhere in the treeless landscape. We push out and see that several ice pans have become shore-fast in the shallows. We row up to one, hop out and Kevin inserts a couple of ice screws on the lee side of the ice and we tether the boat to it. For a half hour this provides relief, but the relentless pounding of the waves on the ice pan breaks it apart, and we are forced to unhook ourselves and search for more permanent shelter.

We rotate short 20-minute shifts of hard rowing for a couple of hours and work ourselves deep into the bay, eventually finding a lee in a far corner rimmed with ice. We go onshore, build a fire and set up a tent, seemingly further from our goal than ever before.

$$\star \quad \star \quad \star$$

We set out three weeks earlier, on July 5, 2013, from Inuvik with the aim of being the first people to travel self-propelled through the Northwest Passage. The journey was the brainchild of Kevin and Paul, while I was brought on in the later stages as one part of the four-person team to row and to film the journey. Kevin had long been obsessed with the Passage, while Paul had rowed across the Atlantic Ocean during a biannual race. They stuck to it, Paul brought Denis on board, and — after primary sponsorship was secured from an Irish renewable energy company called Mainstream — it all came together. The name of the boat is the *Arctic Joule* — named by our sponsor (that's what 150 grand will get you). The hook beyond the feat itself was that if we could complete the journey, it would raise awareness about climate change in the Arctic. The Northwest Passage had been ice-free by the end of the two previous summers — a very graphic indicator of a warming planet.

Objectives like the Northwest Passage, Everest, the North Pole, South Pole — the well-known geographic points of history have, on their own, never been a natural draw for me. People have summited and crossed all these geographies in the past in various ways, and new expeditions to achieve various arbitrary firsts — "one-season," "fastest," "without supplemental oxygen" — are really just bucket-list feats of ego. In my earlier days, those things meant something to me, but now I prefer exploring relatively obscure areas that require a bit of creativity to plan for and whose mysterious nature is half the draw. But here I am, ego and all, trying to row the Northwest Passage in a frickin' boat that's a proverbial fish out of water. But the extra layer of making a film about climate change from the perspective of the Inuvialuit and Inuit — great subject matter — made my decision for me.

Tuktoyaktuk was the last town we were in, and I spent part of the day running around grabbing interviews with the town's mayor and some of its Elders. The main issue they're facing is the loss of permafrost to the point where every summer the whole town — perched on a sandy peninsula — is steadily sloughing into the Beaufort Sea. During my walkabout there, I wandered up to Fred Wolki, a 74-year-old Elder who was hunched over, working on his ATV.

"Hi there," I called out as I approached.

Fred straightened up slowly and turned to look at me. His broad, craggy face was framed by a blue cotton hoodie and adorned with a pair of yellow-tinted sport glasses. Pretty hip for an old Inuvialuk, I must say.

"You know how to fix these things?" he asked, pointing to his ATV.

"Uh, no, sorry." I shrugged. "I'm mechanically inept."

He grunted in understanding, then looked more closely at me. "Where'd you come from?"

"I rowed here."

He laughed and I smiled — realizing what I said sounded ridiculous.

Fred and I chatted for a bit, and he told me about the town, how he'd grown up there since the 1930s, and how the ice out in the bay we'd just crossed used to stay all year round up until the 1970s. After that, things began to change, and the ice would clear for longer and longer periods of time each summer.

"See that island out there?" He pointed to the middle of the bay. "Used to be three times as big. Now it's almost gone because of the melting permafrost." He was very pragmatic about it, not wistful or sad. The older Inuit and Inuvialuit never seem too panicked about all the change. Things just are as they are, and they deal with them as they come. They are Zen masters.

Later in the afternoon, I had coffee with Mayor Darrel Nasogaluak, also an Inuvaluit who talked about all the damage to infrastructure caused by the permafrost melt, but most interestingly that beaver now live in this treeless area. The climate has become palatable enough for them that they're coming north to "Tuk" and damming up the rivers, which hinders the local people's ability to catch their traditional haul of whitefish. I asked, "How do they dam up the rivers in a place where there aren't any trees?"

"If you look around, you'll see there's lots of wood on shore. The Mackenzie River pushes it all out into the Beaufort Sea from the boreal forest to the south. Plenty of wood for beavers." Other atypical southern species moving up here with the warmer weather include venerable predators like the barren ground grizzly and orca, who are putting predatory pressure on local beluga and caribou populations.

*   *   *

The morning after losing our anchor, we awake to quiet. For this boat, the only good rowing conditions are either dead calm or a tailwind, and today we have the former in our favour. We spend several hours grinding away at our stations, get out of the bay and head north to Cape Parry. Our plan is to row to the bottom of Darnley Bay on the other side of the cape to the town of Paulatuk in order to acquire a replacement anchor.

Kevin and I are at the oars as we begin to round the cape, when a broad, heaving ocean swell greets us. There is still no wind, just this swell rolling in from the east. Minutes later, a thick fog wraps us tight so that we only have ten metres of visibility in any direction.

Capes have a way of being problematic for crafts — Cape Horn and the Cape of Good Hope at the southern tips of South America and Africa have scuttled many a seafaring ship, and the capes of Bathurst, Parry and Dalhousie up here in the Passage are no different.

We pass the tip of the cape and turn south into Darnley Bay when the boat starts to spin quite madly. We can't hold her direction, as we seem caught in a vortex of current and swell. Well aware we don't have our anchor to throw out anymore, we work our way closer to shore. A sudden wind picks up from the west, freshening quickly to a gale that we are powerless against. Like a beach ball cast upon the sea, this boat will blow wherever the wind goes. It is impossible to move its beamy mass against it. We are rapidly and helplessly pushed away from land.

Our satellite map shows there's an as-yet-unseen danger out there in the middle of Darnley Bay. In the very direction we're being blown is a large pack of ice that we don't want to be anywhere near in a windstorm. The frozen multi-tonne chunks, bashed together against each other like cubes in a stirred glass of water, will obliterate our boat if we get in the middle of it.

Our chart shows us that the only thing between us and the pack is a single small island. A crescent shape on the left side of it hints at the possibility of a beach.

"It's our only chance," I shout to Kevin over the rattling wind. "Hopefully there's a good place to land!"

We manage to get some semblance of control, ferrying sideways to the gale. We're able to traverse the wind and then allow it to push us to the island, still unseen in the thick fog. Denis and Paul are out on deck now too, helping us to spot a possible landing on the island. When you row, you move like a lobster — unfortunately always looking at where you've been rather than where you're going. It is the most regressive mode of self-propelled travel on Earth.

There's a reason the Inuit used kayaks to hunt and navigate these waters for millennia — it's because they work. Wind comes up? No problem — just keep paddling or go to shore and camp. We can't row into any kind of wind, can't pull the boat onshore, and now, without an anchor, are more exposed than ever. It's not a complaint, just an observation. I'm here as a documentarian as much as a rower. The one good thing about the rowboat is that it gets us into epic situations that make for interesting film fodder. Cutting the anchor after being pinned by a big pan of ice is the most interesting bit of footage so far. The situation we're currently in seems promising from this perspective as well.

"I see it!" Paul exclaims.

I crank my head around to see the island, awash in surf, appear from the mist. We steer the rowboat to the left side, and there is indeed a steep, rocky beach there. We run the boat up onto it. Kevin and Denis use slings to establish anchors around some large boulders onshore, and we manage to use a winch to haul the beast a few feet up onshore and then tether it to several boulders and some of our dry bags that we fill with gravel and bury in the beach.

For the next two days, the gale blows. A large mass of ice pushes into the bay and actually dampens the effect on our boat of the pounding surf from the nor'easter. We have to check regularly on the anchor points to make sure the boat won't be torn loose from the beach and maroon us there. If we had our anchor, it would be a simple thing to wait it out by the cliffs on the lee side.

We set up camp in the middle of the 200-metre-wide island, reading and wandering around. On one of my walks I spot a wooden object tucked in the heather. Reaching down, I pick it up and see it's the corner piece of an old sailing rig. Things don't decay up here in the Arctic, and this artifact is weathered but intact. It's likely quite old, perhaps from one of the old British expeditions a couple of centuries ago — maybe even from John Franklin's final, disastrous journey, the most notorious of the many disaster stories associated with colonial attempts to find a route through the Northwest Passage. We're lucky to have escaped a similar fate.

We wake up in the wee hours of the second night to a tent no longer flapping in the wind. The storm has passed, and the retreating water has left our boat high and dry on the rocky beach. We quickly pack up our tent and slide the *Joule* into the water. With Denis and Paul at the oars, we slip through docile water in golden morning light, headed back to the shore we were blown from.

A couple of hours later, we spot a cabin and a collection of aluminum motor boats nestled on the edge of a cove. As we approach, a figure onshore waves us in.

We pull up and are greeted by Steve Illisiak, an Inuvialuit man from Paulatuk. Steve is a hunting and fishing guide, but right now he and some friends are gathering their annual harvest of beluga in this spot they call Brown's Camp. He has the wiry, weathered look of a man who's spent most of his life on the land. His sharply slanted eyes constantly dart past me, scanning the watery horizon for surfacing beluga.

Beluga parts lie all along the shoreline. Tail flippers, fins, skinned carcasses and squared-up chunks of muktuk dry in the cool breeze coming off the bay. It's somewhat shocking to see but absolutely normal up here. I don't think Raffi's "Baby Beluga" song is as big a hit up here as in the south. The guys head into the cabin while I walk with Steve along the line of beluga parts, asking him about life up here.

"Life is really expensive in the North if you buy things in the stores. Food from the land is way healthier for us and far more affordable. We need to harvest these animals as we always have — it's about survival."

"What's your favourite part of the beluga?" I ask.

"Come with me." He stands up and I follow him to a beluga tail flipper.

"See this?" He points to the tail and makes slashing marks with his finger along it.

"We cut this into strips and dry it. It's really tasty... but you'd need to get used to it."

I ask him about the role of humans in the North.

"A hundred years ago, when the fox pelt trade was booming, there were foxes everywhere. Now we don't hunt them and you don't hardly see foxes at all anymore. We have a role to play in the health of wildlife populations by hunting them — just like any predatory animal."

We head back to the cabin to join the others when I pause by a large, human-like leg bone, seemingly still fresh.

"What's this from?"

Steve very casually says, "That's the hindquarters of a ten-and-a-half-foot polar bear I got this past winter. Lots of fat on him. We use all the parts — the fur, the meat, the organs. We even give the shot-up parts to our dogs. Nothing gets wasted."

I ask him if he's noticed any changes in the weather or the land in his time up here.

He says, "The prevailing wind always used to blow from the northwest — but the last four years it's been a northeast. Also, we used to hunt beluga on the other side of the bay, but their migratory pattern has changed, so now we hunt them here at Brown's."

Back inside their cabin, all four of us try a piece of raw beluga. The outer skin is tough and chewy but the inner blubber is quite tasty — I would describe the flavour as ham-like, but with a richer, more buttery texture. So I'd say it tastes like buttery ham.

We linger for an hour, chatting with the hunters about their life up here. Like the *Arctic Joule* and our anchor, their survival is tethered to the land. If you cut them off from it, they'll spin into an abyss of poverty and starvation.

We part Brown's Camp, and Steve gives us a dried char as a parting gift. Our new friends wave to us as we go, and we turn our attention to Paulatuk, where we'll replace our anchor and have a lifeline once more.

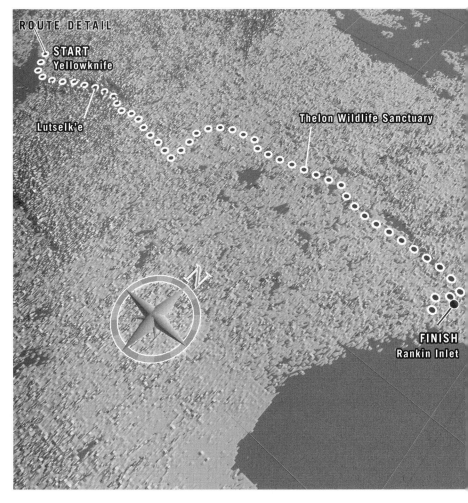

ROUTE DETAIL

START
Yellowknife

Lutselk'e

Thelon Wildlife Sanctuary

FINISH
Rankin Inlet

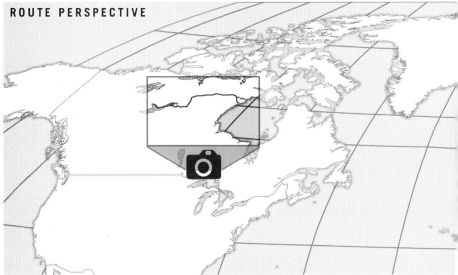

ROUTE PERSPECTIVE

Into the Land

**A 2000-kilometre canoe traverse across the
largest roadless wilderness in North America.**

"She cried."

We're sorting six weeks' worth of food in the room of our guest
house in Yellowknife. Eighty freeze-dried dinners. Two hundred
seventy-six packets of oatmeal. One hundred sixty tortillas. Seven
pounds of peanut butter. Eighty chocolate bars. Two bottles of Silk
Tassel rye. Forty clove cigarettes. All the items are spread out in neat
piles on the bed, the floor and into the hallway.

I pause from the task and look up at my partner Taku, who repeats,
"She cried for the first time yesterday morning." He stares at the
wall, blank eyes recalling the moment, then returns to cramming oats
into a storage bag. I nod in understanding.

Taku left his wife Ednoi at the door of their apartment in Vancouver to
join me on a 2000-kilometre canoe journey across the largest wilderness
area in North America. In her arms she held 7-week-old Ashitaka — their
first child. Taku has Ednoi's full blessing, and she has a big family support
network at home to help with the kid, but her emotions spilled over the
moment her husband stepped away for the summer.

Taku elaborates no further. He doesn't need to. He is fully committed to this trip, seeing it as an opportunity in part to learn about and

raise awareness of this vast Arctic region so that his son's generation and beyond may also benefit from its pristine nature.

The northeast quadrant of Canada spent several millennia being raked by multiple ice ages. As the glaciers retreated, remnant scars filled with ice melt. The resulting matrix of rivers and lakes form a world that is more water than land. It's a canoe tripper's paradise.

Our mission is to start here, the capital of Canada's Northwest Territories, and paddle to Rankin Inlet, Nunavut, a small town on the Hudson Bay coast. Our route will span two territories and bring us through the edge of the boreal into the vast, treeless tundra known as the "barren lands."

*　　*　　*

Waters of Life

The rollers are big this morning, swallowing our canoe in the troughs of waves before allowing us a summit view at each liquid peak. The sky is grey and the wind steady from the northeast. We're bundled in fleece and rain gear. The spray deck laid over our red Royalex Prospector acts as an additional security blanket, allowing errant waves to wash over us and harmlessly back into the big blue. The shoreline rises and falls in the distance, lined by stunted black spruce that give this region the nickname "land of little sticks." We are four days out of Yellowknife on our 270-kilometre crossing of the east arm of Great Slave Lake.

The sun comes out, illuminating the bright orange lichen covering the metamorphic slab that serves as our lunch stop. It's early July, but snow still rests in bungalow chunks along the shore. I plunge into the water for a dip and let out a primordial submarine scream as the chill sears my skin. Surfacing, I stroke hard for shore and drag myself out. I lie shivering and naked in the sun, warming myself like a snake on the ancient rock.

Great Slave Lake is the ninth-largest lake in the world and, at over 2,100 feet, the deepest in North America. It's the source of the mighty Mackenzie River and several other major water courses that flow to the Arctic ocean. The section we're crossing is dotted with hundreds of islands, and the water is clear as vodka. Besides Yellowknife, only a handful of small Dene (pronounced De-nay) First Nation villages occupy its shores.

This expansive body of water seems pure and untouched, but the broad stroke of dirty oil threatens it. With all water in the Northwest Territories originating in the south, the problem lies in Alberta's Mordor-like tar sands development.

Huge tracts of land in that province are being clear-cut to create enormous tailings ponds that hold the processing waste produced by the extraction of crude from the sand. Many of these tailings ponds are right up against the Athabasca River — which flows into the Slave River and then into Great Slave Lake. High levels of toxicity have been recorded downstream of the ponds, resulting in alarmingly increased cancer rates in downstream communities like Fort Chipewyan, Alberta.

As it stands, toxins from the tar sands will continue to flow steadily north until a cross-boundary agreement between the Northwest Territories and Alberta is reached. With the current pro-oil governments in Canada and in Alberta, the prospects for such an agreement taking place in the near future are quite grim. With every passing second, the Sauron shadow of the tar sands stretches deeper and deeper into the Arctic landscape.

*　　*　　*

Łutsel K'e

Taku and I are roaming the dirt roads of the Dene village of Łutsel K'e (loot-sel-kay), searching for the band office. The community is located on a proboscis of land that juts boldly out into Great Slave.

Whitewashed houses dot the hillside, giving the hamlet a quaint, idyllic feel. A pair of locals on an ATV wave at us and smile as they go by, kicking up a dust storm in their wake. A pair of stray pups tags along behind us, tumbling into random wrestling matches around our feet as we go.

Łutsel K'e is the easternmost community in the Northwest Territories and the last human enclave before Baker Lake — an Inuit town 1300 kilometres away by water on the far side of this boundless Arctic ecosystem. This will be our last opportunity to speak with local peoples about the land we'll be travelling through.

Chief Steven Nitah greets us. He's a big man, with a burly build and a round, olive face. He is reserved and somewhat suspicious about the two strangers in front of him with a camera. His community of 312 people oversees a traditional territory that covers an area twice the size of England. They are intimately connected with the land around them and familiar with people wanting a piece of it.

"We were hunters and gatherers just 25 years ago," Chief Nitah begins. "I, for example, grew up in the bush — on the traplines, in tents. I never spoke a word of English until I was 10 years old. The land means everything to us. So that's my society — that's my people."

Barely a generation separate the Dene from a subsistence lifestyle, and they have since been rapidly introduced to the ways of modern living. Included in that modernization is the lure of fast money from mining multinationals that covet the vast stores of diamonds and uranium contained within their territory. As Chief Nitah explains, it's a delicate and often controversial balancing act. "As First Nations, we have to ask ourselves: Do the benefits of this mining project outweigh the benefits that the land provides? To find that balance is always going to be a challenge."

Problems have already arisen with diamond mines run by multinational giants De Beers, BHP Billiton and Rio Tinto in the northern part of Łutsel K'e Dene Territory. Despite strict regulations that companies halt all operations when caribou migrate through their mine area, the herds have instead rerouted away from the mines completely, cutting the people of Łutsel K'e off from one of their traditional food sources.

Uranium is all the talk around town these days. With nuclear being promoted as clean energy, the resource is in demand to serve the anticipated influx of reactors around the globe. The area we'll disappear into for the next 30 days is a hot zone for the mineral, but so far the Dene have maintained a moratorium on exploration in their territory. They fear that the water and land that support the fish and wildlife they depend on will be compromised if they let things go ahead.

With our eyes opened to the past and present, we slip away from Łutsel K'e that evening, paddling upstream on the Stark River into the greatest expanse of wilderness in North America.

*   *   *

Little Friends

We're portaging by compass through a five-year-old burn. Somewhere ahead of us lies the Snowdrift River. I carry the canoe over a broken matrix of blackened, fallen spruce. The treacherous ground requires delicate footwork while at the same time calling for force as I bash my way with the point of the canoe through an endless thicket of seven-foot-tall birch saplings that have shot up in the rich, ash-laden soil. The bridge of Taku's nose is bloodied from repeated lashings at the hands of the springy young trees.

The canoe on my head protects me from the stinging whips — instead I'm assaulted by a cloud of hundreds of mosquitoes that have settled into the wind-less shelter of the hull to suck the lifeblood from my veins. I wear the sleeve of a T-shirt over my head so only my face is visible. A bug shirt protects my chest and arms. My hands and face are covered in DEET and soot, which mix with my sweat and stream like acid into my eyes as I toil forward.

Four hours and a couple of miles later, the glassy band of the Snowdrift appears. With a grunt, I throw off the canoe, and it lands with a thud on the grassy bank. Taku and I stand silent and exhausted beside the river, eyeing the sandy shore on the far side. It is 11 p.m. and still bright in this land, where sun and mosquitoes never go to bed. A cast of thousands escorts us across the river, playing little fiddles that harmonize into a droning lullaby as we collapse into the respite of our tent.

*　*　*

Grinding

The rock slams against his shin and he grimaces. He yanks himself out of the hole his foot is wedged into by pushing down on the gunwales of the canoe. A large, oozing wound smack-dab in the centre of his shin looks red and angry. He's probably been hit in that same spot about a dozen times in the past week as we make our way upstream to get to the headwaters of the mighty Thelon River. I bet he's wishing he could be chilling at home on the couch with his kid right about now. He never lets on, though — a stoic soldier to the end. Taku isn't a complainer and brings up his family only if prompted, and then reluctantly so.

We're camped alongside a rapid on the Eileen River. Taku has pulled in a fat grayling with our fly rod. The fishing is so easy here that if you don't have something on the line by cast number three, you move on to the next pool. After a quick fry-up, we lounge onshore, munching delicate white flesh while gazing at the hissing waters that for millennia served as a liquid highway for the Dene people.

I turn to Taku "So... you ever think about Ednoi and Ashitaka during the day?"

His brow creases, then relaxes. "I can't not think about them. I think about them every day and miss them more than I could have imagined. At the same time, though, it's worth it. The landscape we experience, the people we speak to — it's an education no university can teach. The lessons I learn out here will form and inform how I raise my kid."

On day 19, we portage over a rise, and Lynx Lake opens up before us. We've reached the headwaters of the Thelon River, which flows all the way to Hudson Bay. It has taken us 670 kilometres — including 400 kilometres of slogging up three river systems — to get to this point. Our feet are blistered and bludgeoned, and we're each ten pounds lighter from the effort. It was worth it. Moving through a wild landscape under our own power produces rewards that no bush plane ride can match. It puts us intimately in touch with the land and is as close as modern man can get to the primal life we are hard-wired for.

The boreal is behind us, and we're surrounded by rolling, treeless hills covered in lichen, moss and heather. From our perch, we can see forever.

*　　*　　*

Nature Gives, Nature Takes

The 900-kilometre-long Thelon River begins with a couple of days of fun Grade 3 whitewater before smoothing into a steady flow through the 56,000-square-kilometre Thelon Wildlife Sanctuary. The sanctuary was established on the recommendation of frontiersman John Hornby, who saw that the muskox population was dwindling drastically due to over-hunting driven by the demand for fur robes in Europe in the 1920s.

We pull up onto a willow-choked bank. I check a rough, hand-drawn map, scan up and down to confirm our position and then crash through the brush until it breaks into spruce forest. We're in the middle of the Thelon Oasis — a section of the valley distinctive for its thick stands of timber despite being above the latitudinal treeline. After walking for a couple of minutes, I come to a clearing and see the remains of a cabin. The roof is caved in, with only the lower four feet of the walls still standing.

In the fall of 1926, Hornby and his two friends Harold Adlard and Edgar Christian transported supplies by canoe to this point, taking several weeks to arrive. They wanted to build a cabin and then stockpile caribou meat to last them through the winter. The plan was based on Hornby's sighting of thousands of caribou the previous fall in the same spot.

Unfortunately for the trio, the caribou never passed through this neck of the woods that year. Winter came, the river froze and they were trapped in the cabin without food and — without a dog team — no way to hunt in the deep snow. Thus began the slow process of starvation. In a few months, despite desperate scrounging, all three died. A diary left behind by Christian detailed their plight. The wildlife sanctuary was created in 1927 — a year before their skeletal remains were discovered. Muskox, down to only a couple hundred at the time, now number in the thousands. The zone also supports large populations of moose, barren ground grizzly, Arctic wolf, Arctic fox and caribou.

The men are buried just downhill of the cabin. I kneel beside the three wooden crosses that mark their graves and read the initials carved into each one. John Hornby perished here, but his gift of preservation lives on.

* * *

The Migration

Out in the barren lands, you have two options when it comes to the general ambience of the place — wind or bugs. This morning there isn't a breath of breeze. Taku has held out as long as he can and darts over to a thicket of dwarf willows to relieve himself. Holding "it" until bursting is an old Inuit method for dealing with outdoor bathroom duties in the cold of winter. We've applied this technique to dealing with blackflies. Wait and wait and wait so that when your morning movement happens, it's like a rocket launch at Cape Canaveral. A minute later, Taku is dashing back, a horde of blackflies in tow. The little fellas have welted both of our behinds pretty good. Any seam or opening in your clothing is an invitation for these tiny winged flesh-eaters to crawl in and gnaw away. I have a circle of 20 bites on my leg where a hole the size of a pencil-head allowed the buggers a little feast. We pace back and forth speed-eating our oatmeal as the blackflies bounce off of our faces. They are used to going for the eyes of thickly furred mammals like caribou, wolf and grizzly, and treat my bearded head much the same. On the bright side, blackflies taste like blueberries and are a fine breakfast accompaniment.

Despite their vast numbers, mosquitoes and blackflies are not the creatures that form the backbone of all life in this region — that's the caribou. All animals in the North, humans and bugs included, depend on this species for food. Thirty days into our journey — and two weeks down the Thelon — Taku and I have glimpsed only two of these giant-antlered individuals, each of them swimming across the river. They move almost as quickly on water as they do land, with their hollow-fibre fur buoying them easily along the surface.

We come around a large bend a few kilometres before the Thelon fattens into the first of several large lakes approaching the Inuit community of Baker Lake. A great advantage of the treeless landscape is the ease in which we can spot animals. I've been "top spotter" so far — sighting several muskox, wolves, moose and a wolverine. This time, Taku makes the sighting — and it crushes anything I've seen up to this point.

I'm looking straight downstream, completely unaware, when Taku blurts, "Frank... are those caribou up there?"

I turn and look to the south. A ridge about a kilometre inland seems to pulse. A gaggle of antlers and bodies streams along the crest. It's the migration.

We power for shore, run the canoe onto a gravel beach and bolt up the soggy tundra hillside. After stumbling and bumbling for what seems like an eternity, we reach the top of the ridge and look down into the next valley. It contains a stream of life that extends as far as the eye can see — thousands of caribou moving smoothly through the rough landscape as if they were on a conveyor belt. They see us, and the band of life effortlessly shifts 100 metres farther away. Having been hunted for eons by humans, they treat us with caution. Among the herd is a hearty supply of calves. This must be the "Beverly Herd" — named after their birthing grounds in the area around Beverly Lake, just a few kilometres downstream. This group has bred and begun the long journey south to the boreal forest in the north of the provinces where it winters over.

It's a powerful moment. We hoped to see the migration but were losing faith as the trip wore on. We're both speechless, holding onto the moment, entrenching it in our souls. This display of life force will stay with us forever.

In the evening, we sit by a crackling driftwood fire on the sandy shores of Beverly Lake. A nice breeze keeps the bugs at bay. The freeze-dried food tastes exceptionally good. Taku lets on that our caribou moment will become part of the oral history he will pass on to his son. "It's a gift, a treasure," he says.

Despite the impressive display, worldwide caribou populations have declined by 60 per cent over the past three decades due to climate change and industrial development. The words of Dr. Robert Bromley rattle in my mind. He's a renowned biologist we met back in Yellowknife who worked in the field up here for 13 years and now is a member of the Territorial Legislature in the NWT. He ran for office on a platform of renewable energy and halting climate change. On climate change and the herds, he said, "The birth of calves has been synchronized for thousands of years with the flush of green growth that comes into the tundra in the summer. That growth creates protein and lipids that in turn provide the female caribou with rich milk to feed the calves. We are now seeing a one- to two-week shift in that flush, which reduces milk and milk nutrients and as a result is having a profound negative effect on the survival rates of caribou."

Climate change seems so subtle and intangible where I live in Vancouver — but up here the effects are being felt drastically. To make his point, Dr. Bromley mentioned that many three- and four-year-old buildings in Yellowknife are already being written off, as the ancient permafrost they were built on has melted away and collapsed the foundations.

*   *   *

Rankin Inlet

It is August 18, day 46 of our trip. We're working our way down the shallow rapids of the Meliadine River. The coastal Inuit town of Rankin Inlet is in the distance — a scattering of colourful Lego blocks on the windswept shores of Hudson Bay. The days of perpetual light are gone, and the sun is setting in layers of pink and orange behind us.

We paddle into town and pull into a small bay. The tide is way out, and I skate along a mud flat in the waning dusk to the first house I see. Forty sled dogs howl and yap in the next yard, pulling at their chains, wanting to run.

I walk up to three men talking in the gravel driveway of the house. One of them asks, "Where did you come from?"

I reply, "Canoed here from Yellowknife."

He asks, "Where you staying in town?"

"I'm not sure."

He points to the house beside us. "You're staying here, then."

The Inuit family inside greets us like we were one of their own. Harry Towtongie is the fellow in the driveway who invited us to stay with him. He also happens to be the town's deputy mayor. His wife, Cathy — a gregarious, jubilant woman — cooks us up a feast of caribou liver and potatoes. Harry shot the caribou only yesterday, and it is delicious — as free-range and organic as meat gets. He tells us he was raised on walrus, seal and caribou — food that still forms the base of his family's diet. The highly processed foods shipped up from the south tend to give the Inuit heartburn and other physical ailments.

The Towtongie clan speak to each other in Inuktitut — still the first tongue of most Inuit in Nunavut, Canada's newest territory. The stop sign on the street corner outside is in both English and Inuktitut. It truly is a different country up here, a place where the people have held onto their culture and traditions like few others on Earth.

Three days later, we depart for Vancouver. I give Harry our canoe in thanks for his hospitality, and he is gleeful, particularly when I say the capacity is 1,200 pounds — enough to transport a male caribou out of the tundra.

Home

We're waiting for our luggage by the carousel in the airport. A big grin is smeared across Taku's face as he cradles Ashitaka in his arms. He has missed over half of the boy's life and is eager to make up time. His wife chats happily with my girlfriend in the background, seemingly none the worse for wear despite her husband's long absence.

I ask, "So how does it feel to be back, Hoko?"

Taku smiles, "I'm happy to be back but also happy to have gone on the trip. Life is good when you have to choose between tough things."

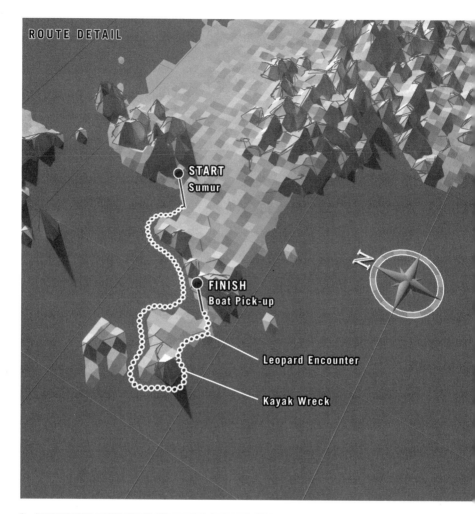

ROUTE DETAIL

START
Sumur

FINISH
Boat Pick-up

Leopard Encounter

Kayak Wreck

N

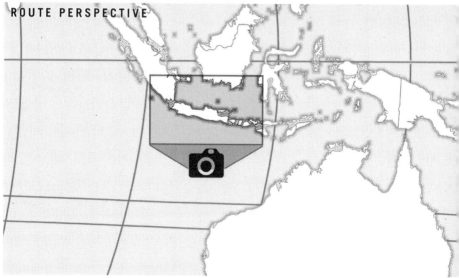

ROUTE PERSPECTIVE

Shipwrecked in Ujung Kulon

An epic tale of wrecking a kayak in a remote outer-coast beach in Indonesia, and a long walk out through the jungle.

ORIGINALLY PUBLISHED IN FEBRUARY 2001 ISSUE OF *SEA KAYAKER MAGAZINE*

In late January 2000, my friend Dave Stibbe and I set out on a paddling/ discovery adventure in Southeast Asia. Our starting point was Phuket, on the north end of Thailand's west coast, while our planned finish was Bali, Indonesia — 2800 kilometres away. We had a three-month window to complete our trip and agreed beforehand to just go with the flow; a free-form adventure, if you will. We were equipped with a Klepper Aerius Expedition Quattro and two cases of Spam, so we were feeling pretty confident. Both of us had a combined wealth of experience; I had paddled 8000 kilometres across Canada in 1995, while Dave had 18 years' experience as a guide in the outdoors. We both live on the West Coast of British Columbia, an incredible place for sea kayaking and other outdoor excursions.

Heading out on an adventure is always exciting. The possibilities — knowing that truly anything can happen — is why we do these trips. And so, our epic tale begins...

After successfully paddling the 300-kilometre Thai coast and whitewater paddling the Selangor River in Malaysia, we spent a couple of weeks in the Malay capital of Kuala Lumpur, waiting for me to get out of the hospital. I'd gotten a nasty systemic blood infection through a cut on my elbow while I was on the river; a bit of surgery and 24 hours a day of IV antibiotics were needed to clear it up. From there, we travelled inland through Sumatra and Java, eventually ending up in the city of Jakarta.

It only took a few days in that crazy, bustling city of 17 million (not to mention the several dry-land weeks before that) until we were ready to head out onto the water again for some peace, quiet and a little adventure. For the final leg of our trip, we planned to paddle 1200 kilometres of the Indian Ocean along the exposed south coast of Java to Bali.

Departing Jakarta, Dave and I travelled by bus and minibus to the town of Sumur on the west coast of Java. As in most of our travels in Indonesia, we were the only foreigners in town. We settled into a basic *losmen* (guest house) for the night. The next morning, we assembled the Klepper as 100 or so of the locals crowded in tight to see our craft come to life. Dave stashed our gear into dry bags while I put together the boat, accidentally poking some of the kids on occasion with Klepper frame parts since they gave me only inches of breathing room. The villagers just laughed. They followed, pointed and giggled at my every move as if they were watching a major sporting event. *Oohs* and *aahs* reverberated throughout the audience as our craft steadily came into shape. After sweating through that process in the 35-degree-Celsius heat, we packed the kayak, waved goodbye to the people and paddled toward Ujung Kulon.

Ujung Kulon National Park is 800 square kilometres of pristine roadless wilderness jutting out as a peninsula from the southwest tip of Java. It was declared a World Heritage Site in 1991 and achieved its park status in 1992. Bordered by wave-washed volcanic cliffs and jungle-covered volcanoes to the west; alligator- and crocodile-rich swamps and mangroves to the north; endless uninhabited stretches of surf-pounded beach to the south; and unique flora and fauna (including endangered Javan rhinos and leopards) in the jungle to the east, Ujung Kulon is a gem.

From Sumur, we followed the east coast of Selamat Datang (Welcome) Bay for 15 kilometres. Turquoise waters lapped gently onto the shiny, gold-sand shores of the bay. Local children played in the shallows, and fishermen casting hand-nets pulled in the shimmering, struggling bounty of the Indian Ocean. We had lunch beside a long-abandoned wooden fishing vessel on the beach and looked across to the park. The middle of the bay was far less protected than the shore, with whitecaps dancing on the water all the way across. We headed due east across the bay through one-metre chop, the ocean spray coating our boat and bodies as the sun sparkled off the ocean and the wind rippled across the water. With little incident, we arrived at Peucang Island, a 30-kilometre day. We camped there for the evening at the ranger station, the only spot clear of swamp and mangrove in this low-lying area of the park.

The following day, we paddled in heavy monsoon rain and wind in swells up to three metres high. There was no place to land on this northern-exposed rock-rimmed swamp for 20 kilometres. We ate a lunch of garlic, dry noodles and peanut butter on the boat. Continuing on, we eventually arrived, soaked to the bone, on sheltered Handeleum Island at six p.m.

Over a hearty Spam and noodle dinner, Dave and I expressed some of our reservations about the relatively slow speed of the Klepper and its open design (no bulkheads, canoe-style spray deck) on big Indian Ocean water. Our main concern was how the Klepper would handle during the really big surf landings that we would have to tackle.

On the morning of March 22, we tied all our gear into the Klepper and headed out of Handeleum. Our mission was to paddle 25 kilometres around the notorious Gedeh and Gehakalok points. Between these two points are 12 kilometres of 50- to 100-metre cliffs that drop off from the emerald-forest-covered volcanic peaks on the western tip of Ujung Kulon. This section is exposed to the full might of the open Indian Ocean and has laid claim to many a fishing boat. It did not disappoint. Around Gedeh Point we were greeted by massive, house-sized swells (five to eight metres) that crashed into the cliff faces with incredible force. The resulting similar-sized rebound-wave made for tricky paddling as we were being hit from both sides with these giant colliding waves. The ocean's colour had transformed from turquoise to a deep blue. Quiet, focused and a bit nervous, we ventured into the chaos. The Klepper's stability held true once more, and as we moved away from the point, we took in the rugged shoreline. The jagged islands and rock faces were constantly assaulted by explosions of whitewater from the gargantuan rollers. We spotted a tanker out on the open water as we crested a swell and then saw it disappear as we entered the canyon-like trough of the wave.

Around Gehakalok Point, we had lunch aboard the Klepper, already getting quite used to the water conditions. At one particular spot just around the point, a small rock island was being hammered by the ocean, resulting in huge ten-metre vertical sprays of water. I pulled out the camera from under the deck for a shot when both Dave and I heard a large roar coming from behind us. We turned to see a steep six- to seven-metre rogue wave breaking and heading for us. Up to this point the swells had been clean, but in this case there was a shallow reef I spotted in that instant in the trough of the wave that created the break. Dave shouted, "Put the camera away! Put the camera away! Paddle! Paddle! Paddle!" I said, "Fuck!" and hurriedly jammed the camera under and paddled like mad. We were both pumped full of adrenaline and made that Klepper move as never before, narrowly evading getting crushed against the lava cliffs by the oncoming wave. Oh, yeah! What a rush! We were buzzing after that one. We now pointed in toward Cibandowah Beach, a deserted 18-kilometre stretch of white sand rimmed by dark, low-lying jungle.

It was late afternoon, and we had to land somewhere along this shore. Beyond the beach was another long stretch of rocky cliffs, so

Cibandowah looked like our best bet. We were ushered into the shore by five- and six-metre swells, indicating that the shore break would be nothing to sneeze at. As we approached, the waves along the shore were popping straight up like rooster tails when they hit the beach. This meant it was a steep beach with a short, abrupt surf zone. Time to check out how the old Klepper, and we, would do in some serious trashy water.

Within 40 metres of shore, the break was big, steep, fast and powerful. Up and down the barren coastline, the story was the same everywhere. I was ready to go for it. However, as soon as we entered the surf zone, I knew we were screwed. The first couple of rollers steepened and broke just after passing under us. The next biggie approached and opened its gaping mouth at us. I said, "We're fucked." Dave replied, "Not yet!" It almost took us down — we stood precariously on its tip as it broke. I looked down the face of the wave and gauged its height to be roughly that of a two-story building. It didn't take us, and in the brief reprieve we glimpsed a stretch of flat water to the shore. We paddled hard for land, trying to work through the strong suck-back off the beach before the next wave hit — unfortunately to no avail. A six-metre beauty came quickly behind us, grabbed us and for a split second held the Klepper completely vertical before body-slamming us face first into the surf. We're talking a 600-pound kayak (counting us and our gear) tossed like a toothpick. I was jettisoned violently underwater by the sheer force of the blow. I popped up to be greeted by yet another wave, which shot me in toward shore. I swam after our capsized kayak, grabbed it and fought to get the water-filled craft to shore. I noticed immediately that its hull sank badly in the centre. After struggling with the strong ebb and flow of the surf zone, I got the boat partly onshore. Dave was okay; he thrashed around trying to collect the smaller yard-sale items that had not been tied into the boat. I helped him in this endeavour, and we eventually got everything high and dry. The casualties: two lost pairs of sunglasses, and, yes, our poor Klepper.

I inspected our craft and found the two main centre ribs, the side supports, the coaming, all the bow pieces, the metal rudder fitting and the rudder to be broken clean through. Eleven parts in all, completely trashed. Approximately half the frame was kaput and impossible for us to field-repair. It would be unthinkable to paddle the kayak in its present condition, especially on the Indian Ocean. It would act like a Slinky for a while until it broke apart due to stress on the unbroken frame parts. We were in the only uninhabited, roadless area of Java, in the farthest corner of Ujung Kulon. Our map had been destroyed by the water; we had only a macro map of Java to go by. From my memory of the ranger maps and our own map, we had at least 40 wilderness kilometres to cover with 300 pounds of gear. We were marooned. Frank and Dave. Gilligan and Skipper. Why couldn't Dave have been Ginger?

We packed our soaked gear into our two large duffel bags, Klepper skin bag, frame bag, rib bag, Dave's backpack and my large camera case. What a load. I felt pretty good, actually. This castaway gig was pretty cool. We were by ourselves in the wilderness and had a mission: get ourselves and our stuff out under our own power through unpredictable and unknown terrain. The true adventure never really starts until you mess up really badly. Hey, we fulfilled that criterion. Bring it on!

After shuffling the gear about ten minutes down the beach, we set up our tent on top of a sand dune. It was getting dark, a thin band of orange the only remaining light on the horizon. On one side of our perch, we peered down into the swampy, firefly-lit jungle; on the other we could see and hear the vastness and power of the surf that had crushed us. Our stove was soaked, but I dried it out and managed to get it going. It clogged up after a few minutes, so I took to cleaning it. With most everything still wet and us being on a sand dune, I super-clogged the stove even more. The more I fiddled, the worse it got. Spam time once more! After being gnawed on by no-see-ums during dinner, we went to bed tired, damp and full of spiced ham, knowing we had a big day ahead of us.

Thankfully the next day was overcast, with intermittent monsoon rains rolling off the ocean to cool us off. I shuffled 60- to 100-pound loads for ten minutes at a time eastward down the beach. I'd then run back for the second load and haul it to where the first one was. I wore sandals, while Dave trudged at his own pace barefoot. We needed to cover 15 kilometres along Cibandowah beach before we entered the jungle. Once in the bush, we needed to find a trail I had recalled from the ranger map that led back to Selamat Datang Bay. Once at the bay, we had to make our way back up its eastern shore until we reached the village of Taman Jaya — the first road out.

I cruised along in a Zen-like state, funnelled forward along the beach by the ocean on my right side and the waving trees and bushes of the jungle on my left. I thought of nothing much in particular except pushing forward. Black rain clouds would rise off the ocean and soak us, followed by brief blazes of equatorial sun that dried us off. We dodged driftwood, discarded sandals, fish nets, seaweed, shampoo bottles and anything else the sea had carried from far-off lands and deposited on the fine white sands of Ujung Kulon. I sang Village People and Abba songs to help keep me occupied.

We travelled for seven kilometres and four hours down the screw pine-lined beach to the Cikeusik River. Flowing out of the jungle, the 20-metre-wide river cut across the beach and out to the ocean. The tide rushing in up the river like a rip made for a tough crossing as we forded the armpit-deep river with our heavy loads. At one point, Dave was swept by the current into the lagoon behind the beach. He struggled in the deep water to swim his pack to shore, eventually sloshing onto the beach with a sheepish grin on his face. We tried to resupply our water here, but with the tide rushing in, all the water at the Cikeusik's mouth was brackish (a mix of sea and fresh water) — blah!

We decided to follow the Cikeusik upstream through the jungle for a ways to see if we could find some fresh water higher up. Grabbing our water container, we followed a crude trail that ran into the dark bamboo, ficus and fern jungle. Water dripped off the large tree ferns and cascaded like tiny waterfalls down to the muddy floor. The refreshing breeze off the ocean was replaced by the still, muggy air of the tropical forest. We slipped and slid our way along the path, in and out of the trees and vines, our senses bombarded by everything around us.

We came upon a small connector stream after about 15 minutes of tramping. I walked down to the murky, still water and gave it a taste. More fresh than salt — good enough. The rain became dense as I stood knee-deep in the small river, slowly filling up the ten-litre container. Beetle nut trees, bamboo, bushes and vines grew in a dense thicket along the shore, hanging out over the river's edge. Raindrops peppered the still water surface with millions of tiny explosions. Once the brown water had filled up our jug, I waded out of the stream and we made our way back to the beach along the slick trail. We later found out from some rangers that the Cikeusik is home to a good-sized population of saltwater crocodiles — some reaching up to three metres in length.

By four p.m., we had hauled our gear for ten hours and gotten to the end of the beach. We still had a couple more hours of light and planned to go through the jungle across the bottom of Tereleng Peninsula into Karong Ranjong Bay to camp. At this point, I had become well acquainted with my burden. For one load, I carried the Klepper knapsack-style skin bag, which also contained the spray deck, seats and PFDs. On top of this I threw the long, narrow frame bag that also contained our paddles, pumps and sail. The total was about 100 lbs. I walked in a crucifix position, with my hands spread out to the sides above my head to support the frame. My other burden was about 60 or 70 pounds, highlighted by a duffel bag that I carried backpack-style using its unpadded straps. Dave meanwhile had gimped his arches from walking barefoot in the sand all day with heavy weight. He hobbled around like a wounded animal. We followed the tracks of wild dogs, Javan rhinos, boars and wild buffalo that had blazed a trail along the beach before us.

We looked for some sort of trailhead at the end of Cibandowah Beach to take us through the jungle. A small brown patch stood out in the grasses on top of a rock shelf where beach ended and forest began.

Tired of trudging in sand, we welcomed the change of scenery and headed down the narrow, sloppy, three-kilometre jungle path. It led through ankle-deep mud and over and under fallen logs. Leaf monkeys and gibbons squawked and jumped in the canopy above as I passed in the approaching dusk. Biting flies and mosquitoes hammered me as I moved slowly along the trail. I lathered 95 per cent DEET Muskol onto my bare arms, legs, neck and face — it's the only thing that works against those bloodthirsty buggers. Unfortunately I was sweating so much the bug-dope never lasted long, and they'd come on back to feast again and again.

We came upon a bare patch of grass on top of a lava cliff overlooking the bay and decided to make camp there. Thoroughly sweaty and grimy, I clambered down the cliff to a small beach, where I took a dip in the ocean. My shoulders had become large, open wounds from the packs and stung when I submerged them. I was spent. I had pushed hard for 12 hours. My head ached and my stomach was queasy. My first bowel movement a few minutes later explained to me why. Hunched in a squat, I dropped my shorts, and a violent brown liquid spray blew out my backside like a firehose. I had picked up some sort of bug and had diarrhea.

I walked slowly back to the campsite where Dave, who had been coming along with his last load, was quite excited. He said, "Have I got a story for you!" It seemed he had been walking down the trail at dusk when he heard a loud rustling in the bushes. Before he could react, a good-sized leopard sprang onto the trail right in front of him, only two metres away. His eyes and the wide, focused eyes of the predator met for a moment, and then it sprang from his path and disappeared. He gathered himself together, trying to still his pounding heart. Dave moved on along, figuring the leopard had been more scared of him than he of it. Dusk was turning to dark, and everything went eerily quiet. Dave flicked on his headlamp and continued on, following the beam of his light through the inky blackness. With his injured feet and large pack, he hobbled along like a Quasimodo. After 15 minutes,

Dave approached a dip in the trail and was about to step over a log when he heard a sound that sent shivers up his spine and made his hair stand on end. It was a deep, guttural growl from just off the trail. Dave froze. The leopard was stalking him. In his hobbled state, he probably looked like a potential meal — the sick and the weak are always targeted by predators. Trying to control his panic, he walked the rest of the trail expecting the big cat to pounce on him at any moment. He arrived at camp relieved and a little shaken.

I listened to his story in disbelief, but felt so miserable I was relatively non-reactive. Adding a leopard to the mix was a bit too much for me to process, so I just discarded it. I'd had lots of bear encounters in my past and didn't worry about large mammals too much. I was more worried about severe dehydration, since I couldn't keep food and water in me for more than a few minutes before it wanted to do a backstage exit.

To top off the evening, we discovered I had inexplicably left the tent poles 18 kilometres back at our other site. Wonderful. With the mosquitoes out in full force in this renowned malaria zone, we couldn't risk sleeping out (the mosquito that carries the virus comes out to feed at night). We improvised and strung up the fly from some trees and suspended the tent body from the fly. I went off searching the jungle edge with my headlamp for some makeshift pegs when something caught my eye. There were hundreds of fireflies moving about like a pulsing galaxy in the blackness of the underbrush. Two of these flies were very large and still, only lighting up when I shone my headlamp at them. As I continued to look at them for a minute, I realized they weren't fireflies at all, but the eyes of the leopard. I could make out the outline of his large head as he crouched perfectly still, gazing intently at me only four metres away. In my tired, sickly state, though, I just shrugged, went back to the site and told Dave. He said something like "Great," and we both went to bed. What else was there to do?

I spent the night in the fetal position, squeezing my butt-cheeks together, trying not to redecorate the interior of the tent with my beige ass-paint. I popped Imodium like candy, but to no avail. By morning I had "gone off" ten times and was quite dehydrated. One positive effect was that I had unintentionally made a perfect circle of scent around our campsite, sure to ward off any potentially threatening wildlife (i.e., leopards). We had treated all our water and Dave was fine, so we figured I must have gotten sick testing for brackish water, even though I had always spit it out. I went to my emergency dose of Ciprofloxacin (for severe diarrhea) and within half an hour could take in water and food again. Phew!

Our day began with a six-kilometre jungle slog to the main beach in Karong Ranjong Bay. This time I suited up in long pants, long-sleeved shirt, socks and running shoes along with lots of bug-dope. We were both quite weak from the day before. Dave's feet were killing him (he had serious tendinitis in one arch), and I was still dehydrated. The trail was similar to the previous one, and we made the beach in relatively good time. After another two kilometres on the beach, we made it by mid-afternoon to the Karong Ranjong ranger station– the existence of which we'd had no idea of until we arrived. We were greeted by three rangers: Arnasan, Hutbi and Tegbuh — who offered us tea and also a much-needed lunch of *ikan goreng* (fried fish), rice and greens. A few days of pure Spam and oatmeal builds up your taste for other food, any other food. Arnasan spoke a bit of English and gave us excellent information on which trails would best get us to Taman Jaya.

The rangers get here on foot as well; Arnasan said boats don't usually land along this stretch of ocean. They take a day to hike in from Taman Jaya and spend a month at a stretch here, doing one seven-day walkabout during that time. All the rangers had contracted malaria at least once. They are armed with machetes and rifles, and their main job is to protect the wildlife — particularly the Javan rhino, of which only 60 remain in the world, all of them in Ujung Kulon — from poachers.

That evening, we had Spam that we fried over the rangers' fire, along with some rice and noodles they offered us. I also pumped the Klepper pack partway down our next day's trail to give us a head start for the morning. We chatted with the boys into the night. I was so dehydrated that I drank 15 glasses of water and 5 cups of tea and still couldn't pee. My diarrhea was thankfully gone. We went to bed feeling a hell of a lot better than the day before.

The next morning, the rangers offered to help us with our load, but after carrying a couple of our packs for about 20 metres, they decided we'd best do it ourselves. They were a diminutive trio (like most Indonesian men, they ranged in height between five feet and five-foot-six), and carrying packs close to their own body weight didn't sit well with them. Offering them a hearty *terima kasih* (goodbye and thanks), we set to our task.

Our day's trail took us four kilometres to Selamat Datang Bay. The route ran right through a swamp, so I prepared the battle gear. I wrapped my head in a smelly, Muskol- and dirt-soaked T-shirt, with only my face peering out of the shirt sleeve (old tree-planting trick). The only parts of my body exposed were my hands and face, liberally covered with Muskol. I sloshed through ankle- and knee-deep mud and water accompanied by a cloud of mosquitoes and biting flies in a monsoon downpour. My shoulder scabs were ripped open for a second straight day by the duffel-bag straps. My skin dissolved from the carcinogenic bug-dope. Birds were chattering, monkeys a-screeching; lush ferns and palms glistened with the new rain and humid jungle heat. It was real. A true wilderness experience.

Upon our arrival at the bay, we spotted a local fishing boat moored only 50 metres offshore. We walked out from the jungle into waist-deep water and flagged it down. Its old diesel engine fired up and smoked and sputtered its way to within ten metres of us. The rickety wooden boat's sole occupant was a young man, more than a little curious as to what we were up to. Having a better grasp of Bahasa Indonesia (the native tongue) than Dave, I negotiated a price of 50,000 rupiah (seven dollars US) for him to take us to Taman Jaya, a half-hour boat ride away. We waded our load of gear out to his boat, heaved it up, pulled ourselves onto the deck and were off. With that, our epic ended.

Ujung Kulon was not such a bad place to be. We explored it by kayak and by foot over six days and saw a total of five people — all locals or rangers. If our kayak hadn't broken upon its shores, we never would have gotten the full range of experience that, in retrospect, I'll cherish. Sometimes suffering is the only way to achieve such experience. If I get malaria because of it, I'm sure the suffering will continue.

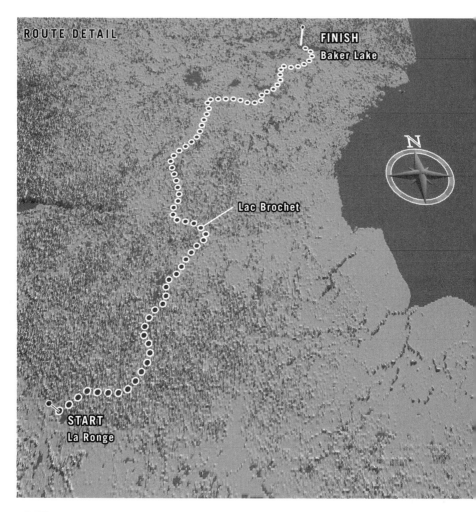

ROUTE DETAIL

FINISH
Baker Lake

N

Lac Brochet

START
La Ronge

ROUTE PERSPECTIVE

Loss

A reflection on loss during an 1800-kilometre canoe trip from Saskatchewan to the Arctic.

ORIGINALLY PUBLISHED IN SPRING 2017 ISSUE OF *EXPLORE MAGAZINE*

It eventually goes, the memory of her — of cuddling close in bed as she breathes softly in slumber; the pleasant, familiar scent of her hair inches away. That warmth, that security — it dissolves like sugar in the wilderness waters of this journey. I haven't seen or heard from my wife in weeks. Thoughts of her now rarely enter my mind. Bit by bit and day by day she slips deeper into my subconscious, until it's hard for me to fathom her existence. She is lost to me.

I awake in darkness on day 26, the tent fly flapping in the wind. It's not my wife beside me, but instead a huddled mound inside a sleeping bag, snoring away and smelling not so great.

I elbow my tent-mate. "Shawn... Shawn. Time to get up."

A groan acknowledges the nudge. It's 3:30 a.m. on Kasba Lake. Yesterday we were pinned in by a northwest gale — the first time, after 1,000 days of canoe tripping, that I've ever had to sacrifice a full day of progress due to wind.

The breeze has eased from gale to strong, and we're moving by five a.m. The more time I spend living wild in the North, the more I see similarities between us and the various creatures that make their home here. The land and the weather defines its inhabitants, not the other way around.

Take, for example, the simple mosquito. This wispy insect can't fly in any kind of wind, waiting for a lull to allow its vampiric work. Similarly, we avoid wind when we paddle, working the lee shore as much as possible, and sometimes, like yesterday, unable to work against its power at all. When the wind finally calms and gives us an opening, we strike full force and with gusto, tearing at the water with our paddles like mosquitoes at flesh.

Pulling hard out of our sheltered bay, we turn the canoe into the brunt of the blow for the final exposed 15-kilometre stretch of Kasba that leads to the Kazan River. The sky is slate-grey and the metre-high waves steep and black, coming at us like endless sentries fighting our forward progress.

It takes a half hour to get comfortable with the rhythm of the waves, angling the canoe just so in order to carry us high and dry over a crest, into the trough and then over the next crest. They come in ocean-like sets — building to a peak every seven waves or so and then easing off before building again. We groove to this rhythm for three hours until we hit the Kazan, its current sweetly pulling us away from the blustery lake and into its embrace.

Lengthy expeditions like this one are about loss — loss of comfort, loss of routine, loss of connection with those left behind. When every-day comforts are scuttled, life becomes exceedingly simple. A tent is home, a canoe is transportation and all food needed is on board. You immerse fully in the simple act of moving forward through space and time, without past or future to muddle the mind.

*   *   *

Job

Fields of canola pass by in a golden blur on arrow-straight Highway 2. Local paddle builder Mark Lafontaine agreed to drive us, our canoe and gear the four hours from Saskatoon. The time with Mark passes by in pleasant conversation as Shawn snoozes in the back. The expanse of the prairies transitions to a wall of deep boreal spruce, and we eventually arrive at the landing in La Ronge.

After unloading our gear, Mark snaps a couple of pictures, we shake hands in thanks, and then he peels away in his truck — a settling cloud of dust on the dirt road all that remains.

La Ronge is a small town that lies at the southern edge of Saskatchewan's portion of the Canadian Shield. Located on the shores of its namesake lake, this is the shoving off point for our 1800-kilometre journey to Baker Lake, Nunavut.

I quit my job to do this trip — another necessary loss. I had a choice between stability and passion. Passion won out, and now a summer of possibility awaits, future be damned.

$$\star \quad \star \quad \star$$

Body

On the morning of day three, we break camp and ready for the portage into the Churchill River system. We set up the evening before on a ledge perched above Nistowiak Falls — at ten metres, the highest in the province.

I'm untying our clothesline, and *pop* — the tendon that runs along the top of my thumb suddenly snaps and I can no longer flex the digit. The attachment point at the base of my wrist had been sore for months, and it suddenly gave way. I test my hand on a paddle and it works. Good enough.

When you put months of time and energy into a venture like this, the loss of partial hand function is a relatively small price to pay. A tendon can be repaired later, but these remote quests are once-in-a-lifetime.

✳   ✳   ✳

Culture

Two weeks in, we arrive in the town of Lac Brochet, a remote Dene First Nation community that is the only resupply point of the entire journey. From here, we'll carry 30 days' food with us to the finish.

We bring our freshly bought supplies down from the Northern Store to our canoe and begin to sort and pack it. A couple of kids — brothers Tyson and Dallas — tag along. Without a word, they settle into our canoe, sprawling comfortably on it as if it were a couch, and watch us work.

"Can I have some of your chocolate?" Tyson asks.

"No, we need it for our trip," I reply.

"What's that? Can I have that?" Dallas asks, pointing to a bag of energy bars.

"Uh, no," Shawn replies.

"Can you take us in your canoe to the bridge so we can go swimming?"

"How far is the bridge?" I ask. Both kids shrug in unknowing unison.

The boys seem so naturally drawn to our canoe, I assume it's one of their favourite activities. I ask them about it, but they say they've never actually gone canoeing before, their only boating experience being in the ubiquitous motorboats that line the shore. In light of the Dene history with canoes, it's a somewhat surprising revelation.

After packing, I head up the hill to devour one last ice cream sandwich before we go. Augustine Tssessaze, a member of the legendary Dene Drummers performing group, pauses to chat with me by the store entrance. A big man, he stretches one of his thick arms over the hood of his pickup as he leans against it.

"How'd you get to Lac Brochet?" he asks.

"By canoe," I reply.

He nods approvingly, yet with a hint of sadness in his eyes, "That's good... we've unfortunately lost that tradition. People in this community don't travel by canoe anymore — in fact, we barely travel on the river at all except for an annual gathering in Brochet (the next village downstream on the Cochrane River)."

The Dene — which simply means "the people" — were once masters of the canoe, using the craft to travel thousands of kilometres, following the migration routes of the caribou herds upon which they survived. The practicality of motorized boats is obvious — they'll zip someone quickly across a lake in no time. However, they'll also have to turn back at the first portage, where a canoeist will keep on going.

The canoe allowed the Dene an intimacy and access to their territory that modern convenience has taken away. To lose connection with this vessel that is such an integral part of their history is to lose connection with their land and traditions. It is akin to the disappearance of their native language. A culture adrift from its roots is no culture at all.

A major cause of language loss for all First Nations in Canada lies in the residential schools that, for decades, the Canadian government forced Indigenous children to attend. Similarly, the loss of the canoe in Dene culture began in the 1920s, with the introduction of the gas engine by white traders into these communities. In his book *Sleeping Island*, author P.G. Downes mentions this on a trip he took through the area in 1938: "It occurred to me that outboard engines are more of a curse than a benefit to the North. In a brief ten years' time they have swept the country like wildfire... no self-respecting Indian would think of going any distance without his motor and these were at one time the finest canoe men in the north."

*   *   *

True Adventure

The rain hammers down as I yank on the bow of the canoe with all my might, trying to force it through a tangle of spruce, birch and

Labrador tea. The branches tear at the spray deck as the boat painstakingly inches forward. Mosquitoes as thick as smoke complete the experience.

We're portaging around a log-jammed falls on an unnamed creek that eventually drains into Kasba Lake. There are no trails here, only a vein of water on a map. The Dene surely travelled this route on a regular basis throughout history, but no guidebook or internet post exists to suggest how to go about moving through. Sometimes we're able to run the rapids of this waterway and sometimes, like now, we have to work our way around obstructions. I call this six-day section our "mystery move" — and I like to include at least one such adventure in any journey I do.

The haiku poet Matsuo Bashō once said, "Do not follow in the footsteps of the wise men — seek what they sought." In this day and age, with a crush of information about any route or patch of dirt on this earth, you have to tread way off the grid to "not follow in the footsteps." And why not follow? There is comfort in information, comfort in knowing that there is indeed a way through. This reliance on information comes with a price, however. We lose our natural instinct to navigate strange landscapes — in fact, most of us have lost this ability already. Working through the unknown, seeing with your own eyes what few, if any, have seen, is true adventure. Everything else is just travel. And I love travel — but you have to throw in a bit of mystery from time to time to stoke the ancient fire inside.

*   *   *

People

Reminders of loss are everywhere along the 900-kilometre-long Kazan River — in particular, the disappearance of an entire group of people that used to thrive here. After feasting on a huge lake trout we hauled from the river, I walk back to a high point to get a view of the vast treeless surroundings to see if I can spot any large mammals that may still be about.

The river broke free of the boreal forest at Ennadai Lake a week ago, and we've since seen hundreds of caribou from the Qamanurjuaq Herd crossing at various narrows with their week-old calves in tow. Earlier today, a burly barren ground grizzly swam across the river in front of our canoe — so I'm excited to see what else may come our way.

I don't spot any big critters this evening, but I do find numerous tent rings — ancient circles of stone sunk into the tundra that once held down skin tents of the Ihalmiut people. The Ihalmiut were "Caribou Inuit," inland inhabitants whose lives were intertwined with the caribou herds and this river, which they named Inuit Ku (River of Men).

Starvation and disease decimated much of the population in the late 19th and early 20th centuries, eventually resulting in the relocation of the remaining Ihalmiut by the late 1950s from their traditional lands around the Kazan to centralized communities like Whale Cove on the Hudson Bay coast. So, ironically, men no longer inhabit the River of Men.

We come across dozens of these ancient tent rings along Inuit Ku, as well as numerous inukshuks, the silent rock sentinels of the North. They are lasting symbols that remind us of the ephemeral nature of life — both human and otherwise — in this beautiful, harsh and unforgiving landscape.

$$\star \quad \star \quad \star$$

Canoe

A herd of 25 muskoxen stare at us incomprehensibly as we drift by. They don't move, hesitant to leave the hearty patch of grass they are grazing on. One of the beasts flinches and begins to run, causing the whole herd to follow suit and stampede in a wide circle before ending up back where they started — standing like statues, gazing blankly at the big red canoe as it disappears from sight.

Around the corner, we hear the roar of a rapid. From my vantage point it looks benign... but the roar tells me something else is going on in there. The current is fast and powerful here, and brings us to the precipice of the rapid before we know it.

It has been a warm, sunny day, and we've been caught with our proverbial pants down — in this case with our PFDs off — and we're bobbing down the torrent before we know it. I spot a massive, recirculating hole that takes up the entire middle of the river.

I shout at Shawn, "Paddle as hard as you've ever paddled before!"

He puts his head down and we dig for all we're worth, just skirting the giant boat-eater and a certain, bitterly cold swim down the rest of the rapid.

A second set appears around the next bend. This time we're prepared and do a proper scout before snaking our way down. At the bottom of the rapid, we spot something on the far shore — a green object that is out of place in the environment. Paddling up to it, we discover a badly damaged canoe. It's one of those aluminum-framed folding boats — quite possibly meeting its miserable end in the hole that almost got us.

We later find out that a group of four canoes capsized here, losing much of their gear and two of the canoes. This is one of them. No one was hurt, and a rescue plane plucked them to safety. A century earlier, their error would have meant doom, but in this day and age the only loss beyond material was pride.

*   *   *

End

We arrive in Baker Lake, 44 days after leaving La Ronge. Though this was our goal, finishing is a letdown. For six weeks we moved through the wilderness... running rapids, dragging upstream, portaging through bush, crossing windy lakes... moving, always moving. And suddenly we stop. I think I should be doing something, be working out how to negotiate the next phase of the journey... but the movement is over. I am lost.

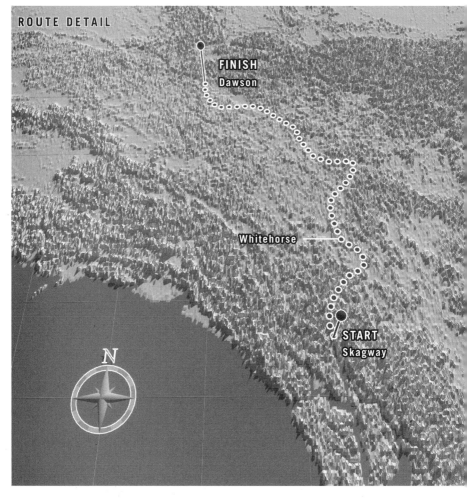

ROUTE DETAIL

FINISH
Dawson

Whitehorse

START
Skagway

N

ROUTE PERSPECTIVE

Kayaking the Gold Rush Trail

Discovering the past and present on a 900-kilometre hiking and kayaking journey from Skagway to Dawson.

ORIGINALLY PUBLISHED IN MAY 2002 ISSUE OF *ADVENTURE KAYAK MAGAZINE*

> *There are strange things done in the midnight sun*
>   *By the men who moil for gold*

–ROBERT SERVICE

Strange things to be sure. Our first night during solstice season in Whitehorse found us spending the wee hours at the 98 Hotel with Fish Lake Freddie, Lucky Lisa and Fireball Don McKenzie. An evening spent at the 98 is a step back to the wild days of the gold rush that brought similar characters up North over 100 years ago. The smell of beer, whiskey and cigarettes mingled with roaring laughter, shouts and music. Animal pelts lined the walls and an old brick fireplace sat at the back behind a table of wildly cackling patrons. Everyone, it seems, has a nickname in the Yukon. A hundred and four years ago, Siwash George, Skookum Jim and Tagish Charley discovered gold up on Bonanza Creek, which started the great gold rush. Although the gold is mostly gone, the spirit, beauty and tradition of that time is as strong as ever in the lands and people that remain.

In 1898, 100,000 people from all corners of the globe left their homes in search of their fortune. News of the Klondike gold strike spurred a feverish rush to the city of Dawson in Canada's Yukon Territory. Men, women and children endured incredible hardship as they travelled through one of the most rugged landscapes on Earth in order to fulfill their dreams.

Today, the 881 kilometres of waterways from the head of Bennett Lake to Dawson makes for one of the best inland sea kayak trips on the planet. The spectacular scenery, wildlife, local characters and history to be encountered along the route make it an all-time classic wilderness trip.

*　　*　　*

The Headwater Lakes

Your paddling adventure will begin on Bennett Lake, nestled in the Coast Mountain Range, 40 kilometres as the crow flies from the Pacific Ocean. The lake opens up as a wide navy-blue slash surrounded on all sides by 2000-metre rocky peaks. During the gold rush, the town of Bennett sprang up at the head of the lake — a tent city of thousands who waited for the ice to clear before they could commence their journey. Bennett gives way to Nares Lake, Tagish Lake and then Marsh Lake before the Yukon River gives you a tease of current that spills out into Lake Laberge before resuming all the way to Dawson.

Back in Bennett's heyday, much of the forest was cleared to build wooden flat-bottomed boats for the journey to Dawson. As many as 20,000 people waited in town that winter for the ice to clear, and Bennett became a full-facility settlement with butchers, bakeries, a newspaper and a church, St. Andrew's Presbyterian, which is the only structure still left today. With the passing of the gold rush and establishment of rail lines, Bennett, like most gold rush cities, was abandoned by 1900. Despite the disturbance over 100 years ago, only an occasional artifact here and there indicates you are not passing through a pristine environment.

There is no road access to Bennett Lake, so we arranged to have our kayaks, two singles and a double, put onto a flatbed car on the WP&YR train (White Pass & Yukon Route Railway). The train rolls into Bennett daily to pick up Chilkoot Pass hikers and return them to Skagway. I and my friends Andy, Kevin and Dave had chosen to hike the 53-kilometre Chilkoot Trail first before our paddle; you can choose to do the same or access Bennet on the train with your gear.

Our kayaks sat in the shallows with the Bennett Range as a backdrop. The prevailing winds come off the ocean and funnel over the Chilkoot and White passes, providing, as one local outfitter said, "tailwinds 90 per cent of the time." A paddler can't ask for much more than that.

We set off with a light breeze at our backs that built into a stellar wind, allowing us to literally surf the lightly breaking, two-foot waves for 43 kilometres all the way to the town of Carcross at the top of the lake. Puffy clouds sailed over our heads and danced over the peaks on either side of the lake. The wind was so favourable, I cursed myself for not having brought my sailing rig. Not that I had grounds to complain. We spotted a moose and calf drinking along the water's edge halfway up the lake on its eastern shore; giant eagles soared overhead and watched us from their perches at the tops of towering pines. Back on May 29, 1898, 7,000 boats loaded down with the eager stampeders made their way down this very same waterway. On this day, we were the only three vessels on the entire lake.

$$\star \quad \star \quad \star$$

Lake Laberge

"The Northern Lights have seen queer sights, / But the queerest they ever did see / Was that night on the marge of Lake Lebarge / I cremated Sam McGee." These famous lines from the Robert Service poem reverberated in my mind as we approached mighty Lake Laberge, 50 kilometres from Whitehorse. This 52-kilometre-long lake was the final bit of flatwater that we had to negotiate before we had the sweet push of the Yukon River all the way to Dawson. It was midnight at the south end of the lake when we arrived. The dead calm and silence of Laberge opened up before us like a big bowl of gravy. The wind had turned into our faces earlier in the evening before dying off, so we decided to make a go of it and do a night crossing. When the winds blow on Laberge, the waves kick up steep and deep, with sheer rock walls, particularly in the northern half, preventing any quick landings.

We sang songs to keep each other occupied as the sun dipped and rose before us, running in a circle around us for the entire day, always providing us with enough light. At 3:30 a.m., Andy and I were in the double kayak, bantering back and forth about obscure 1980s songs while our craft rippled the glassy surface of the water and the cirrus clouds blazed with orange above us. A headwind with two- and three-foot chop blew in at 4:30 and ground us to a slow plod for three hours until we pulled into a rocky beach and slept on mossy ground in the shelter of the black spruce forest, spent but content. We'd made it 34 kilometres up Laberge and all the way from Marsh lake, including our Whitehorse resupply, in less than a 24-hour day.

Laberge is a great example of nature's ability to heal itself. The lake's crystal-clear waters give no indication that mass amounts of crank case oil used to be poured on the ice by gold seekers in spring to quicken the breakup, so they could get a move on to Dawson.

*   *   *

Fast Flow the Rest of the Way

Once beyond Laberge, you'll experience a wonderful sensation not often associated with sea kayaking: moving water. Six hundred twenty-six kilometres to Dawson may seem like a long way, but with the Yukon humming along with a ten-kilometre-per-hour current, it's not hard to maintain a 15-kilometre-per-hour pace. Our biggest day over this stretch was 151 kilometres, achieved in about ten hours of paddling. Try doing that on the ocean! The water over this finishing stretch is completely flat save for one Grade 2 wave train at the Five Finger Rapids that is easily run just by pointing your craft down the centre of the right channel. The main problem stampeders and steamships had at the turn of the century was being hung up on sandbars, usually in the latter part of the summer, when the water level drops quite low. Remains of the SS *Klondike*, a steamer that ran aground in 1936, can be found at kilometre 320 (kilometres are measured from the start of our trip, at Lake Bennett).

The first stretch of the Yukon after Laberge is called the Thirty Mile, one of the prettiest sections of the river. You really begin to notice the "big sky" of the North up here. Blue skies with puffy cumulus clouds open up over sweeping emerald hillsides and bluffed mountains. This is the backdrop to your kayak-level view of spruced point bars and 200-foot yellow sand cutbanks as you wind along this narrowest section of the river (approximately 50 metres wide).

One constant companion you'll have in camp will be the famous Yukon mosquito. If you don't want to feed future "skitter" offspring, I suggest you offer your personal cloud of whining, flying friends a healthy dose of DEET-based repellant. On the river itself, the bugs are never a problem.

Campsites are easy to find, with several flat areas popping up here and there in the forest along the river's edge. There is usually always a sand or gravel bar on which you can easily beach and unload your kayak, as well. On our campsite halfway down the Thirty Mile section, we noticed an old telegraph wire in the woods behind our camp. This wire was put through from Dawson to Bennett in 1899, and its remnants can be seen here and there along the entire route.

We passed the mighty Teslin River, which empties into the Yukon, doubling its size. The mid-afternoon sun beat down upon us while the black spruce and aspen forest passed slowly by, with the rolling green of the Pelly Mountains as background. The river was moving our kayaks inexorably northward, and all was good.

*   *   *

Coffee John

At the 711-kilometre mark of our tour down the Yukon River, our kayaks hit the muddy sand embankment of Coffee Creek campground with a *hisssss*. Two canoes sat in the shallows, lashed to an aspen, bobbing in the current. We had a ways to go before another good campsite would show. We were travelling in spring flood, and many of the usual gravel bar campsites on the islands of this braided river were still underwater.

We walked up a narrow dirt trail through an emerald-green meadow, its two-foot high grasses waving in the wind. About 15 metres up on the right, a camp had been flattened out, with two blue pup tents filling the space. Just beyond the tents, three people sat around a fire, waving at the cloud of mosquitoes and blackflies that danced around their heads. I introduced myself, and one of the men, Wolf, stood up and said hi. He wore round John Lennon–esque glasses and had a mat of black, curly hair and matching beard. His cherubic face held blue eyes that sparkled whenever he spoke of the Yukon.

Wolf, short for Wolf-Dieter, was a German expat who'd lived in the Yukon since 1993 and had set up a business of his own guiding fellow Germans through the area. His two clients were from Stuttgart and spoke nary a word of English. I mumbled off a couple of polite sentences but definitely didn't possess the polished German tongue of my relatives.

Wolf said we were welcome to camp there as well; the meadow was a baseball-field-sized area cleared out in front of the forest by earlier homesteaders — an American family in the 1970s, Wolf told us, who were subsequently kicked off a decade later, when Canadian authorities found them out.

An odd man called Coffee John moved into the vacated space and began living year-round there. His nickname arose not only from his home on Coffee Creek but also from the fact that he drank about 20 cups of coffee per day. Wolf said a typical sight was Coffee John cruising the dirt trails around the meadow on his bicycle with a smoke in his mouth and a coffee in his free hand. He'd greet people coming to camp and then cycle away, looping around and around until well past their bedtime.

Coffee John had taken over the elaborate log cabin of the previous homesteaders but never kept it very clean. On his road-less homestead, 180 kilometres as the crow flies from the nearest town, coffee, smokes and mowing the meadow were his passions.

One day, some campers noticed Coffee wasn't looking so good; he was on his deathbed, in fact. A helicopter came in and evacuated him. He died in the Whitehorse Hospital, of cancer. That had been two years ago. Since then, the Coffee Creek homestead had been abandoned. The interesting thing, Wolf said, was that not a thing in the cabin had been touched or disturbed since Coffee John's death.

My curiosity was piqued, and later that evening I headed past a thicket of aspens to check out the log cabin. Everyone else had gone to bed, and I wanted a nice, inspirational spot to lay down some journal entries, away from the horde of skitters that were harassing me.

The log cabin sat low and sprawling among weeds and old garden implements. A meadow of wildflowers grew out of the roof, and wires were strung out from the corners to spots in the ground. I entered via a screen door into an eight-by-eight-foot entrance room, where I was greeted by a big set of moose antlers on the ground and an empty fridge in the corner. A faded note on the wall read, "Be back in an hour."

A heavy wooden door was the way into the main cabin, and I had to give it a hard push with my shoulder to get it open — the door had sunk into the floor a bit and was quite sticky. Once inside, I felt a rush of cool, dank air roll over me, literally chilling the temperature by ten or so degrees. The cabin was partially underground, creating a basement effect. I felt calm and comfortable, almost like Coffee John was saying, "Hey, bro, welcome to my abode. Coffee's on, help yerself." An oil drum stove was tucked into the corner on my right, and a pile of musty old mattresses sat in the far corner. A neat dark-wood table and chair sat in the centre of the room. The ceiling, stained black, was perhaps six inches above my head, making me stoop a little as I walked through. I headed for a ramp through a door beside the mattresses and stepped in, finding myself in a brighter, open room, perhaps the size of a good-sized high school classroom.

In the far corner sat a massive oil drum stove, perhaps used as a furnace. Children's toys were scattered about the room, probably left by the original homesteaders' kids. Coffee John had no reason or way to remove them. Three dim double-plastic bay windows threw light into a kitchen with unwashed dishes from two years ago still sitting in the sink and on the counter, with black, oozy mould streaked and chunked all over them. A couple of unopened cans of Coke sat by the white-tiled prep counter along with an assortment of cookbooks, children's games and dried and canned goods lying about with no particular sense of order. The roof sagged over the furnace, held by two steady timbers but still forcing me to crouch as I inspected the furnace. The wall by the entrance contained five large framed photos of sailboats on the ocean; one of the frames was cracked. Some pots of dirt that once held plants stood on a small shelf below a corrugated see-through plastic patch in the ceiling. On a long shelf below the sailing pictures lay a row of books in a half-fallen domino stance. I scanned through them: *Jaws*... *Papillon*... more pulp fiction... *Coming into the Country*... a few survivalist books about edible plants and hunting... then, last in the row, the biography of Ted Kaczinski, simply titled *Unabomber*.

On the other side of the entrance was another shelf of books, these ones all Christian and self-help books (examples: the 1970s classic *I'm O.K., You're O.K.,* and *Prison to Praise*). Below this shelf was a desk with his notes strewn all about. Lots of lists of stuff, notes to himself, that sort of thing. A pile of religious pamphlets and notes sat below the desk. I tried to imagine a man living here by himself all these years, only seeing the occasional person coming off the river during the summertime. Was he a hermit? A genius? Who knows. To each their own. The feeling was good for me in there. I sat in the old musty chair at his desk and wrote in my journal for half an hour, the thick dampness of the place being a welcome relief from the outside heat and bugs.

I left without disturbing or moving anything and made my way back to the tent. The log cabin was a snapshot in time of a man's life, held in limbo with his passing. A small placard at the turn-off to my tent had a small eulogy to Coffee John. It read: "Home is the Sailor. Home from the seas. And the Hunter has come home from the hills."

*   *   *

Fire's Burning

On our second-last day, we ran into a haze of smoke from a fire burning somewhere in our vicinity. The forests get extremely dry in summertime, and it doesn't take much for fires to spread over vast areas in a short period of time. Fires are a natural part of the northern boreal environment, and charred forests quickly give way to a blanket of bright pink fireweed, the territorial flower.

The smoke blocked out the blazing sun, reducing our previously unlimited visibility to a kilometre. I could taste and smell the smoke as it thickened throughout the afternoon. Pulling steadily on our paddles, we were unsure of what we were heading into; it seemed as if we were drawing nearer and nearer to the source of the blaze. Camping in the woods with a fire burning nearby wasn't necessarily a prospect I relished. To shore ourselves up, we lightheartedly sang that old campfire classic, "Fire's burn-ing, fire's burn-ing, draw near-er draw near-er, in the glow-ing, in the glow-ing, let's sing and be mer-ry."

As we arrived at our campsite at Mechem Creek, 838 kilometres into our journey, the smoke began to clear. Within half an hour, the wind changed and the smoke completely cleared out. We later found out the fire was burning hundreds of kilometres east of us and on the opposite side of the now three-kilometre-wide river. All we had to keep an eye out for now was the grizzly bear and cub who'd left some very fresh tracks on the landing to our campsite. Needless to say, all of our food was hung high, dry and far away from our camp and our kayaks. A grizzly can tear open a kayak like a can of sardines.

*　　*　　*

Dawson

We rolled into Dawson around noon the next day. We'd travelled halfway up the Yukon Territory by kayak and were in a mood to celebrate in the town that was the ultimate goal of all the stampeders who started off at the head of the Chilkoot so many years ago. It's a grand old place that has retained the flavour of its raucous past. The streets are still dirt — not to retain the authenticity of old Dawson for tourists, but because frost heaves wreak havoc on paved roads this far north. Wooden boardwalks serve as sidewalks, and over two dozen of the original buildings from 1898 still stand. During the gold rush, instant millionaires like Big Alex McDonald and Clarence Berry bought rounds for the boys in the "Snake Pit," now the oldest tavern in the Yukon. Its stamped-tin ceiling and original wood-beam walls remain as a tribute to the original builders of the town.

Most of the original gold-seekers arrived at Dawson after their arduous journey only to find all the gold claims already staked. Their riches were gained from the experience of their journey, travelling through the wilderness in chase of a dream. Most of them stayed awhile and made do as entrepreneurs, providing the services for booming Dawson. The population swelled to 30,000 people, which in 1898 made it the biggest city west of Winnipeg and north of San Francisco.

As part of our celebration, we went to the Downtown Hotel to enjoy a "Sourtoe Cocktail." To become a member of the Sourtoe Club, you drink down a glass of gin or whiskey with a black, mummified human toe in the beverage. While you drink, the toe must touch your lips in order for you to enter into the honour roll. Every year, toes are accidentally swallowed but are replaced by donations from Yukoners who lose their toes or feet through frostbite, amputation, etc. I'm not kidding. It's a must-do when you get to Dawson.

*   *   *

Grizzly Tale

I spoke with a man that evening who'd been on the river a day before us. Near our site at Mechem Creek, where we'd seen the grizzly tracks, he and his friend had witnessed something amazing. They were paddling down the main channel of the river when he heard a crash in the woods off to his left. Turning to see what the commotion was, he saw a moose and two calves swimming vigorously toward their boat. They drifted past the animals and watched as they continued across the river to an island in the centre channel. He remarked to his friend: "Wasn't it strange that they swam right at us? Usually the moose are quite shy."

They pulled over to the side to continue to watch the swimming moose when a chilling scene unfolded before them. A huge grizzly burst out of the woods and barrelled into the water. The mammoth bear steamrolled its way across the river "faster than we could ever paddle our kayaks," making a beeline for the calf farthest back. Just as the calf stumbled up on the bank, the bear was upon it and took it down right in front of the two frozen men. From only 40 metres away, they heard the wailing calf struggle in its last throes of life while the grizzly threw it around like a rag doll before ripping it to shreds. The adult moose and other calf escaped by crossing the island and swimming to the far shore. The two men sat rigid with shock, finally heading down the river long after the bear had gone.

As we saw, heard and experienced, the Yukon is never a dull place for a kayak trip. Like most of the stampeders, kayakers won't find gold, but they'll experience the adventure of a lifetime.

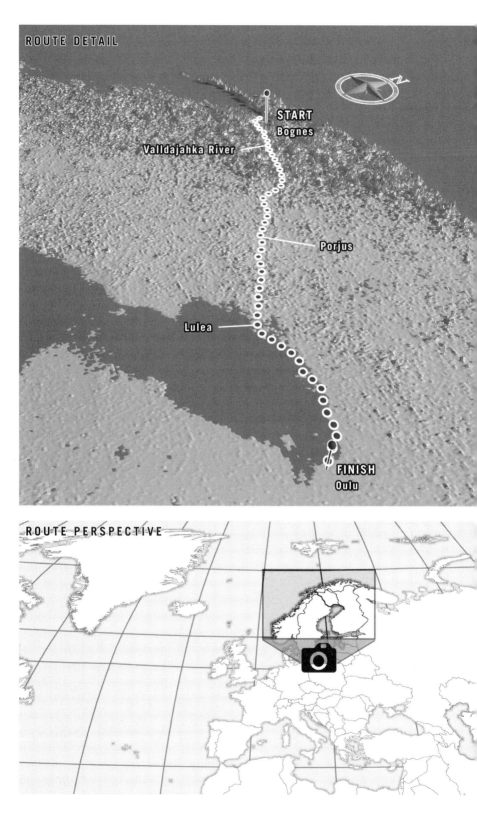

ROUTE DETAIL

START
Bognes

Valldajahka River

Porjus

Lulea

FINISH
Oulu

ROUTE PERSPECTIVE

Across Asgaard

Following an inland Viking trade route for 800 kilometres across the Scandinavian hinterland by canoe.

ORIGINALLY PUBLISHED IN JANUARY/FEBRUARY 2007 ISSUE OF *PADDLER MAGAZINE*

Thousand-metre-high granite walls dwarfed the shepherd as he counted his flock of sheep in a forest opening along the edge of Norway's Tys Fjord. Todd and I landed our canoe on the shoreline to say hello and ask the man a few questions. After we all exchanged pleasantries and Todd and I explained why we were there, he flashed his bright blue, inquisitive eyes down at our heavily loaded craft and asked, "You're going to carry all of that over the mountains?" We nodded. He then stated, matter-of-factly, "It will be hard."

It was June 27, and we were nearing the end of our second day of who-knew-how-many in our attempt to canoe across Scandinavia from the Norwegian coast to Finland. The 800–kilometre journey had begun the day before, in the tiny village of Bognes, 200 kilometres north of the Arctic Circle on the Norwegian Sea. Our plan was to go up Tys Fjord, over the border mountains into Sweden, then down the Lule River system to the northern terminus of the Gulf of Bothnia. Once in the gulf, we would paddle around into Finland, ultimately finishing in Oulu, the largest town in Finland's north.

The shepherd's name was Egil. He was an Indigenous Sami man, short and stocky with brown, wispy hair that fell in a line just above his eyes. His ancestors had been the first people to populate Scandinavia, 10,000 years earlier. Our route followed one of the dozens of trade routes that the Sami, and later Vikings, once utilized to transport goods by foot and by boat across the North. When the Vikings came to the region in approximately AD 900, they subjugated the Sami in Tys Fjord and in the Lule Valley, forcing them to pay a tax of fur, fish and reindeer. As Egil eloquently described to us, the Vikings gave his people a simple choice in this regard: "Pay the tax, or die."

Egil spoke perfect English and worked at the Sami cultural centre in Drag, the largest village in the 70-kilometre-long fjord. I wondered why his flock was so far away from the village, which was located ten kilometres across the water, on the opposite side of the fjord. "Well," he replied, "there are many bobcats by the town, and they attack the sheep; there are no bobcats on this side." For millennia the Samis have been travelling back and forth with reindeer along the rough trail that goes through the pass to the Lule River. Bobcats followed the herds over from Sweden and have populated the southern shores of Tys Fjord ever since.

*　　*　　*

The Portage

The pass through the Scandinavian Mountains loomed above us as we set off from the end of the fjord in search of Sweden and the Lule River system. I'd been told of this pass several years earlier by a travelling Swede I'd met in Vancouver. The existence of the trail awoke in me the possibility of actually canoeing west to east across Scandinavia. Joining Todd and I for the first week of the trip was Kevin Shepit, a cameraman who would help us film the initial portion of the trip. Each of us carried almost 45 kilograms of gear. Todd was loaded down with a jam-packed 115-litre pack he wore on his back, in addition to a 35-litre gallon pack on his front. I shouldered our canoe, a 65-litre pack and a video camera. Kevin lugged his camera bag and a folding kayak.

We spent 12 hours that day hauling our gear for 15 kilometres while gaining 700 metres of elevation along a root-strewn, rocky trail. The track took us up through a pine forest surrounded by granite spires that spewed thousands of tonnes of water from the dozens of thundering waterfalls cascading down their sides from the peaks. We eventually reached the tree-less alpine, where we travelled over grey slab around stunning Avzi Canyon, which cuts a jagged 300-metre-deep, five-kilometre-long scar into the otherwise unbroken massif. As midnight approached in a land where the sun never sets, a low point between two round-topped mountains represented our goal for the day: Sweden.

We put our boats into one end of a small tarn and paddled a half mile across to the other side. From there, a short 50-metre portage brought us into another lake and the farthest source of the Lule River. We had crossed the divide. Everything behind us flowed into the Norwegian Sea while everything in front of us now flowed to the Baltic. A GPS reading told us we had arrived at the border. Todd sat in the bow of the canoe, happy to be in Sweden, while I languished in the stern seat a dozen feet behind him, still in Norway.

*   *   *

The Valldajahka

A thousand mosquitoes hovered in a cloud under the canoe as I sloshed through soggy, knee-high sphagnum moss in a rainstorm. The canoe over my head kept me dry but also doubled as a party tent for the skitters as they drew a pint or two of my blood. We were on our second five-kilometre-long bush portage in as many days.

The previous morning, we'd started out on the Valldajahka River, which drains from the lakes at the divide. The river was gentle at first, meandering for eight kilometres through fields of tundra along banks of snow. It slowly evolved however, giving us bony Grade 2 and 3 rapids that forced us to scout and plan out precise lines. One wrong move and our folding canoe would be wrapped around a boulder or at least severely damaged. Days from any sort of village, this was not a prospect we relished.

On one particular rapid, we had a good scare as our cameraman, Kevin, broached his kayak sideways on a rock and went for an unwelcome swim in the frigid waters. Todd reacted quickly, managing to pull Kevin and his craft into the safety of an eddy. The rapids became more difficult and dangerous as the river wore on, eventually dropping into a Grade 4 or 5 canyon that forced us to do our first portage. Using a map and compass, we bashed our gear for a couple of miles in the driving rain through dense, swampy birch forests, eventually camping on a small, lonely outcropping of granite that rose mercifully above the swamp.

*   *   *

Angry Mother

The Valldajahka spit us out into the Lule River system, which is in essence a series of dam-created lakes that run for 400 kilometres from the Swedish side of the Scandinavian Mountains, through the foothills and then flatlands, ultimately terminating in the city of Luleå on the Gulf of Bothnia. A total of nine dams have been built since the 1920s to provide hydro power for the region — a once-raging river tamed by the Swedes to satisfy their power needs. It's a shame for certain, but the subsequent lake system that was created allowed us to attempt our canoe trip where back in the early 1900s it would have been impossible. The river had at one time been similar to the drainage that lay 60 miles to the south, the Pite River. The Pite still flows free but requires portaging at least 120 kilometres of Grade 6 to 7 water, 80 kilometres of which have never been run, even in a whitewater kayak.

Dam-created lakes always seem to be rather angry at being all bottled up. Instead of developing slowly through thousands of years of melting, erosion, etc., dammed lakes are created instantly and react to weather in violent, unpredictable ways. The first lake of the system, Akkajaure, kicked up steep waves and headwinds so strong that we literally couldn't move an inch forward one afternoon and had to wait until the evening came before we could paddle onward. *Akka* means "mother" in the Sami language, and it was one angry mother indeed. The area from the Norwegian border to the end of Akkajaure is part of Stora Sjöfallet National Park, which forms part of Laponia, a 9400-square-kilometre area that was placed on the World Heritage List in 1996. It is the heartland of the Swedish Sami, who still herd reindeer there, though now they do the herding in ATVs and snowmobiles instead of by traditional means.

*   *   *

Swedish Sunshine

Following our sunny day of portaging through the mountains in Norway, it stormed and rained continuously for a week. After crossing Akkajaure, we found ourselves dumbstruck on Langas Jaure (Long Lake) as we sat in dead-calm waters, watching a wall of solid white whip across the lake toward us. We'd been hit off and on by small squalls all day, but this was a big one and it was coming right at us, and coming fast. It was perhaps three kilometres away when we realized what it was. Because it obscured the trees on both shores of the lake, we estimated the squall to be approximately seven kilometres wide. Shortly after seeing it, we heard it: a loud hissing sound — like a million cats baring their fangs in unison. I felt a puff of wind introduce the squall as it neared us, only 100 metres away. Within seconds it hit us like a sledgehammer, battering us with so much rain it felt like we'd paddled into a giant waterfall. The lake around us turned into a frothy mess, and the force of the wind spun our canoe broadside and began pushing us back to where we'd come from. We powered hard with all we had through the building whitecaps, hit shore, dragged the boat up and ducked into the knotty pine forest for shelter.

Looking around, we spotted a cabin through the trees and walked up to it to see if anyone was around. To that point we'd seen a few cabins, but they were unoccupied. This one was the same — no one home, and all locked up. We did, however, find their smokehouse... and it was open. The pyramid-like, shed-sized structure was perfect for us to hole up in during the storm and have a dry spot to eat our lunch of Wasa bread, sweet cheese and corned beef. The style of shelter was a traditional Sami design called a *kota*. The original *kota* was similar to a teepee, built of birch poles and reindeer hides. As little as 50 years ago, the Sami were still a nomadic people and the traditional *kotas* could be quickly rolled up and loaded when it came time to move the community.

By the time we'd eaten, the storm had passed, though not for long. The squalls rolled in and out all day, giving us liberal doses of "Swedish sunshine" that had us looking like a pair of saturated muskrats by the time we pulled into our campsite that evening. The bad weather trend continued through most of Sweden, as 14 of the first 17 days of the expedition were cold and rainy. It seems our timing for the trip was less than impeccable: we chose to undertake it during Sweden's coldest, wettest summer in 80 years.

*   *   *

Coffee Grandma

There is an old law in Sweden known as "Everyman's Rule" that says you can camp anywhere you like on public land as long as your tent is a minimum of 50 metres away from any structure or road. Europe is renowned for large, crowded, expensive camping areas where tents and RVs are crammed in side by side on a large patch of turf. We'd come to this trip with the expectation of having to fork out some bucks to camp along the way, envisioning playing volleyball here and there with the Swedish bikini team to unwind after a long day's paddle. Lapland, however, is a vast remote area where camping in the bush is easily done anywhere. In fact, we never once had to pay for accommodation during our entire trip, and the bikini-clad women of legend were nowhere to be found.

Using the public access law to our benefit, we arrived on the outskirts of the village of Porjus and set up our tent on a soggy pebble beach between two cabins. I walked over to two women and a girl who were fishing in front of their cabin to ask if I could plug my rechargeable camera battery into one of their outlets. At that moment, the girl caught a fish and all hell broke loose. The women screamed and shouted that this was the first fish the girl had ever caught. One of them, a gregarious grandmother with fire in her pale blue eyes, unhooked the two-foot-long pike, exclaiming, "Her first fish! Her first fish!" after which she proceeded to smash its skull on a rock while carrying on a completely unrelated conversation with me about where I might plug in the battery. The grandmother's name was Harriet; the other woman was her daughter, and the girl her granddaughter.

The following morning, Harriet invited us in for breakfast. Over a meal of bread, cheese and pike she told us about her life growing up in the rough northern woods above the Arctic Circle. As she spoke, it became apparent that she had a particularly strong affinity for coffee. The elixir kept her warm and happy during dark winter ski trips and long summer days of fishing. At one point, she looked at me with wild eyes and exclaimed, "I couldn't live without drinking at least ten cups of coffee per day!"

Harriet had a young grandson there named Rasmus, only 18 months old but live as a firecracker. He drank voraciously from a little baby cup, which Harriet kept refilling with coffee. Within minutes, he was running around the room madly, eventually bumping his head, crying and soiling his diapers all at the same time. I asked Harriet how long Rasmus had been drinking coffee. She piped up excitedly, "Oh, he started when he was eight months old. It's good for him!" Sweden is known to have the highest per capita coffee consumption in the world, and after meeting Harriet and Rasmus, neither Todd nor I can dispute this claim.

* * *

Meissaure

A couple of days out of Porjus, we pulled up by the riverbank and set up camp. We were low on food and expecting to resupply in the nearby village of Meissaure. It looked like a fair-sized village according to our map and was listed on the major road signs leading out of Porjus. We walked along the road that led to the town for about half an hour — far longer than it should have taken. We doubled back to see if we'd missed something, and sure enough, we had. A small sign by the roadside indicated that the town had been moved decades earlier when the dam by our campsite had been built. The funny thing was, all the streets and street signs still remained. They simply put all the buildings on trucks and drove them off to a new location. The Swedish government, though, never bothered to alter their maps or road signs. For all intents and purposes, Meissaure still existed on paper. Unfortunately, if you walked into town hungry for food after a long day on the water, it didn't exist. We shook our heads and grumbled a bit, then turned tail and headed back to our campsite, deflated by the reality of soup and crackers for dinner.

* * *

The Gulf of Bothnia

The final leg of our trip began in the town of Luleå, where the Lule River terminates into the Gulf of Bothnia. Despite its large size and connection to the Atlantic, the gulf is mostly freshwater and only slightly brackish to taste, due to the numerous large rivers that drain into it. It also has no tide whatsoever, so when you paddle it, it seems more like one of the Great Lakes than part of the ocean.

The 120-kilometre stretch on the Swedish side of the gulf consists of an archipelago of pebble beach and pine-dotted islands. The wildlife is rich through the islands; aggressive terns continuously dive-bombed us when we came too close to their territory, and one evening a moose swam in front of our canoe as we paddled through a narrow channel.

Like any large body of water, the Gulf of Bothnia has its own particular challenges. Chief among them is a consistent south wind that creates a swell that is tricky and at times treacherous. The northern gulf is also home to several large bays and long distances between islands. A typical day would see us doing three or four crossings of up to six kilometres, with one-metre choppy swell coming at us from the side. No matter what trim we set the boat at, it always wanted to weathervane to the south as we headed east across the top of the gulf. Waves continuously came over the side of the canoe, washed over the spray deck by the wind.

Some of the islands were sprinkled with summer cabins. Due to the brackish water, most island residents drew their water from wells, which we sought out and utilized for our own water supply.

To our surprise, people we met along the way actually knew about us in advance. Before we left Luleå, we'd befriended some reporters who worked for the northern Swedish *Kuriren* newspaper. They did a story on our journey that ended up on the cover of their paper. During our three-day paddle to the Finnish border, we were met warmly, with some folks even bringing out a copy of the paper for us to see. Gladly answering their queries, we basked in our 15 minutes of Swedish fame.

*　　*　　*

Finland Finish

In Finland, the islands melted away, leaving us a five-day paddle down a flat, swampy, featureless coastline. On our way, we passed by the mouths of several large rivers that flow into the gulf through Finland from Russia. These waterways were once used by the Vikings to transport Russian slaves to their territories in Scandinavia. Canoeing along, attached to our paddles during ten-hour days, we related somewhat to those Russian slaves of yore, shackled to the oars of Viking ships as they toiled their way from faraway homes toward lives of servitude.

We saw few people over our final days, and those that we did see stood silent and still on the distant shore, greeting our waves with blank stares. The southerly winds continued giving us headwinds and side-winds galore. One afternoon, a sudden squall blew over our canoe and a simultaneous burst of thunder and lightning struck so close that our hands tingled from the supercharged air around us.

Finally, after waiting out a morning windstorm, we paddled into the town of Oulu, Finland, on July 21, at 11:40 p.m. Our 26-day expedition had taken us through the three countries of northern Scandinavia, following in the footsteps and paddle-strokes of the Vikings and Sami.

The following evening, we were sitting in the sauna of some Finns we'd befriended, celebrating our success and telling them about the trip. After hearing our story, a man named Mikka turned to me, smiled, whirled his finger around his temple and said, "Only crazy people carry canoes over mountains." We took it as a compliment.

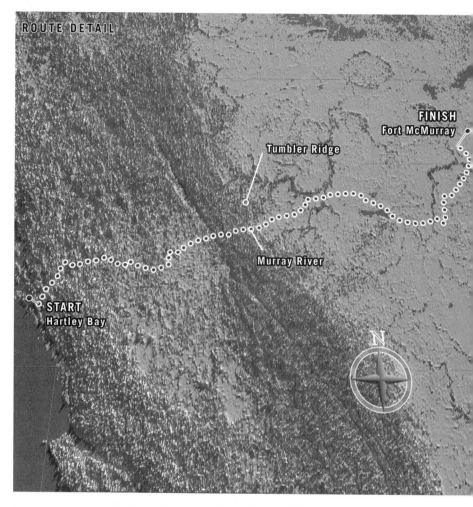

ROUTE DETAIL

FINISH
Fort McMurray

Tumbler Ridge

Murray River

START
Hartley Bay

N

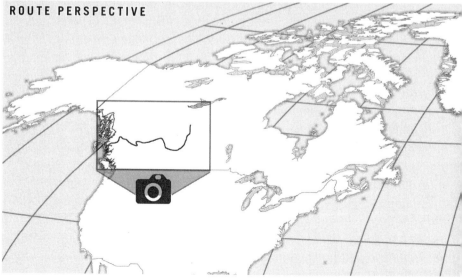

ROUTE PERSPECTIVE

On the Line

Exploring the nature and politics of a multi-billion-dollar pipeline in northern BC via a self-propelled journey along the GPS track of the proposed project route, from the tar sands to the British Columbia coast.

Tanker trucks whiz by a metre away from Todd and I as we spin along the shoulder of Highway 63. A sharp sun glints off the drifting sand of a landscape that looks more like the desert of Iraq than Alberta's boreal forest. The smell is what hits you first — a sulphurous stench that emanates from the industrial landscape. A huge smokestack in the centre of the operation is the likely culprit.

We're cycling around the Syncrude oil sands development north of Fort McMurray, at the start of a 2400-kilometre journey by bike, foot, pack raft and kayak along the GPS track of the proposed Enbridge Northern Gateway Pipeline route. The controversial $5.5 billion project would ship oil sands (or tar sands) bitumen from this place to a port in Kitimat, BC, for delivery to Asian markets. Our mission is to follow the route and provide an intimate, ground-level view of the pipeline through our journey and the voices of people who live along its path.

We pass by vast man-made tailings ponds dotted with scarecrow-like dummies wearing safety vests. Every minute or so, the pop,

pop, pop of noise cannons accentuates the war-zone ambience of the place. A couple of years ago, thousands of ducks perished after landing on what they thought was a lake; since then, measures have been put in place so they don't land on the toxic cesspools, where waste water from the extraction process is stored. Ten barrels of water are required to produce a single barrel of tar sands crude — and this is where all that water ends up.

The scarecrows and cannons may keep birds off, but these reservoirs bump up against the Athabasca River, where their contents leach through earthen banks and are transported downstream. The result is high levels of toxins in the water and in the fish of the river, exhibited in an alarming number of deformed and tumour-ridden fish, and a drastic spike in cancer rates in downstream communities like Fort McKay and Fort Chipewyan that depend on the river for food and drinking water.

The actual starting point for this particular pipeline is 400 kilometres to the south of us, at a place called Bruderheim, which will connect to existing pipelines already running from Fort Mac to there. However, no documentation of such a project can be complete without witnessing its source and getting a feel for why people live in such an eradicated landscape. The answer, as with any project of this nature, is simple and predictable: money — lots of money.

* * *

After breakfast at a diner in Fort Mac that morning, I chat outside with James Garriock, a heavy machine operator who's been up here for ten years. He's got a baseball cap pulled tight over dark curls of hair, his mouth framed by a thin goatee. He is brash, confident, opinionated — and an extremely nice guy to boot. He makes over $150,000 per year driving big machinery in the oil patch.

When I interview people for my films, I don't challenge their opinions or box them in, I merely want to hear their whole and honest opinion. At the end of a chat, if they don't like my line of questioning, they don't have to sign the release waiver I present to them. James is happy to oblige.

"And what do you do here in Fort McMurray?" I ask him.

"I run big equipment... it takes a certain kind of person to do mine work, a lot of people only last here doing mine work for three, four or five years, and then they move on. I've been doing it now for 15 years."

"So you enjoy the work?"

"Oh, yeah. I like it. It's my kind of work. It's rusty, dirty — it's my kind of thing."

"What do you think about the new pipeline proposed to run to the northern BC coast?"

"I think a pipeline's gonna be good. I think it's very good — I'd rather not sit at home and do nothing. And if you can make good money at it, why not?" James pauses for a moment and looked skyward before continuing: "Although it is, I'll be honest with you, it does look, like, kinda shitty. Excuse my language."

"What do you think of the possibility of a Deepwater Horizon or *Exxon Valdez* type spill on the coast as a result?"

"No, what happened with BP that's just a — it's a bad, bad serious accident. But I don't think it'll happen here." Again a pause and skyward look. "Then again, I'm not an engineer, so, you know... but I don't think that'll happen. It's just the hype, the hype, it was an accident. You know, like we had *Exxon Valdez* — that was a disaster, yeah. You know, like, it's bad. It's bad it's happened, but I don't think it'll happen again."

Through his self-argument, I see even someone like James, whose livelihood depends on the oil patch, is conflicted. Ultimately, though, I do understand why James wants the pipeline to go ahead. Everyone fights for their own patch of dirt on this earth. What happens in your own backyard means a lot more to you than what happens in your neighbour's. Albertans want pipelines, British Columbians don't.

*   *   *

We near the finish of the Syncrude loop and pull into a roadside parking lot that advertises itself as a spot for "Bison Viewing." We roll up to a fence that overlooks a grassy, sandy area with a few scrub spruce trees scattered about. Apparently this spot has been rehabilitated from tar sands extraction, and they placed a herd of bison here to show that everything is A-okay now. Today, the bison are nowhere to be found.

One other fellow is here. He's a young guy, maybe 24, with a strong build. His name is Aaron, and he's been working up here for not quite two years. He's a welder, and he helps to maintain the myriad pipelines that criss-cross the area and emanate like an octopus's tentacles from here to all corners of the country. A nice, bashful fellow, he agrees to chat with us.

He agrees we can learn a lot from the disaster down in the gulf — but his work is here, the money's too good. Like most of us, it's difficult for him to see how an individual can impact global issues — either good or bad, no matter which side of the fence you stand on.

We cycle away toward the heartland, leaving Aaron to his peering search for the elusive tar sands bison.

A few days later, and we're cycling along the actual proposed pipeline route through the rural community of Bon Accord. Passing by bright fields of canola and thick stands of corn, we're lured in by a sign that advertises the "Prairie Gardens Adventure Farm."

The place is basically a berry-picking farm, with the added bonus of a petting zoo, corn maze and various sculpted pirates and other colourful characters scattered about the property.

We locate the owner — and, in her own words, the "Director of Fun" — Tam Anderson, to talk about her business and the seeming juxtaposition of a major pipeline running through her property.

A friendly, portly woman with big glasses and a perpetual smile, she's eager to talk about her business.

"So what goes on here on your farm, Tam?"

"You know, on a busy day on a festival weekend, we might have 3,000 or 5,000 people on site here, shooting pumpkins and making scarecrows and getting lost out there in the corn maze — so, huge fun."

"There's this Enbridge pipeline, have you heard of the Northern Gateway Pipeline?"

Her mood becomes suddenly serious. "Yes, it's coming right past our maze here..."

"So as a farmer, connected to and dependant on the health of the land, how do you feel about that?"

"In Alberta, I must say, there are lots of pipelines all through our lands. And being farmers, we're always aware that as stewards of the land, it's important to take care. And, you know — it's kind of a thing, you know — the world demands oil, and we're certainly not prepared to give up driving. We're not prepared to live without heat in our homes. So I think just to take the right care and the right time and not rush through these projects and make sure that the answers are there before the problems arise is key to making these things work."

She takes me to a raised platform that looks over the corn maze. "The corn maze has five kilometres of trails through it, and the theme is 'Alice in Cornland' this year."

"And where would the Enbridge line run here, in terms of the location?"

Not losing a beat, she points across the pastoral landscape. "If it comes in, it'll be just halfway through the canola field."

*　　*　　*

After riding 1000 kilometres from Fort Mac through the pipeline-laced and pumpjack-dotted fields of northern Alberta, we finally arrive at the Starlite Motel in Grande Prairie. It's time for us to ditch our bikes and embark on our biggest hiking section of the journey. We stick them out front with a "free" sign leaned up against them. Not soon after, our neighbour knocks on our door. He says, "I'll take those bikes off your hands, fellas."

His name is Kai Mortenson, and he works in oil spill remediation — as he says in his own words, "Cleaning up all the shit people spill all over the place."

It's our first opportunity to speak with someone who deals with oil spills on a daily basis. He's perhaps 30, well-built and handsome — but has the tired look of someone perpetually dealing with problems.

"Have you heard of the Northern Gateway Pipeline that's being proposed, the one that's running from just north of Edmonton to Kitimat, BC?" I ask.

"I heard about it, just a small bit about it. But, you know, Alberta — it's all oil-and-gas-run here, so pipelines are all over the place."

"And have you ever had to clean up leaks from pipelines that may occasionally happen?"

"Yeah, pipeline breaks, lots of different breaks."

"And how do you deal with it if it gets into a river?"

"If it gets in the soil beside the river, we try to take out that contamination, but once it's in the actual river, it's pretty much lost."

"So if it's leaking around the river and you're called to clean it up, what can do?"

"You can set out different kinds of booms and try to capture it, but you gotta be as fast as you can if that happens. We try to protect our environment — that's what I want to do — but it's a pretty hard thing to do once it's in that water."

Four days after we speak with Kai, an Enbridge pipeline ruptures, spilling four million litres into Michigan's Kalamazoo River. The rupture occurs by a small tributary creek and isn't discovered until 17 hours later. It's the worst oil spill in Michigan's history. From what Kai told us about spills into rivers, there's not much they'll be able to do beyond the cosmetic — the river has been irrevocably damaged.

*　　*　　*

The Rocky Mountains poke up over the horizon, beckoning us forward. We've hiked 300 kilometres from Grande Prairie over the past week in the hot sun, along dusty roads through endless canola fields, so we're looking forward to some nature therapy. Earlier today we crossed into British Columbia, which lifted our spirits after the drudgery of self-propelled travel in this very bleak part of northern Alberta.

Another large tanker truck rumbles by, kicking up a cloud of fine particulate that adds to the layers already caked on our bodies. The dust permeates everything, including my nose — from which I blow black boogers every hour or so. Todd has two egg-sized blisters on his heels, his penance for not having properly broken in his heavy leather boots before the journey.

We make it to the juncture where the road turns north toward Tumbler Ridge, 25 kilometres away. An ATV track in front of us is our route into the mountains, but we have to head into town for supplies, after which we'll return to this point to carry on following "the line." We stick our thumbs out, and it's not long before we get a ride.

When we arrive, we find that there's a big music festival happening, with classic rock acts like Chilliwack and Loverboy mixing with modern fare like Marianas Trench. One of the main sponsors of the "Grizfest" is Enbridge. As part of its PR campaign for the pipeline, the company sponsors as many events as possible in communities along the route. It has deep pockets and shells out dough freely in an attempt to purchase public licence for the project.

We walk up to the desk where they're selling tickets and, under the guise of shooting a film about a biking and hiking trip through Alberta and BC (which is technically true), see if we can get some complimentary passes. After a few minutes, the manager of the festival shows up, and I give her my pitch. I lay out my background as a broadcast filmmaker and present her with a location agreement for the shoot, and she happily goes for it. "Anything to promote the festival," she says gratefully. Both Todd and I get press passes for the weekend, which gives us free access to wander anywhere on the grounds, including backstage.

The afternoon set features the band Chilliwack. The members are all in their late 50s now, I'd guess, but I recognize each and every one of the songs they sing: an amazing array of 1970s and '80s AM radio hits like "Fly at Night," "Lonesome Mary," and "My Girl (Gone, Gone, Gone)," to name a few.

The band's lead singer and songwriter is Bill Henderson. I catch him backstage after his set and ask if he has a few minutes to chat about the Northern Gateway Pipeline. He looks at me suspiciously at first, eyeing my press pass and most likely taking me for the local paper reporter. I quickly describe our journey to him, which intrigues him enough to submit to the interview.

Bill and I sit cross-legged on a grassy field 50 metres behind the stage, facing each other. He has wavy grey hair and is fit and relaxed, hanging out barefoot in jeans and a T-shirt. Total 1970s dude. No wonder I immediately like him — that's my favourite decade. He lives on Salt Spring Island in the Gulf Islands chain, off of Vancouver. Salt Spring is known as a progressive enclave, and he's well aware of the proposed pipeline and it takes little prompting for him to speak about it.

"I really believe, along with millions of other people, that we have to move away from oil and we gotta move to other things. I think part of it too is we have to learn to find the joy in life that is not necessarily created by having things, or travelling, or those kinds of things.

"For example, I've spent my life making music, and the reason I did it was because it made me feel so great. Music was a way of kind of easing the pain, at first, of youth — of growing up and not knowing what the hell is going on — a time when nobody seems to understand you and you feel like an outsider. Music was great for that. I started playing my guitar and it just made me feel better, right?

"And I learned something from that: that you can have a good life with very little. Really, you can have a good life with what you and the people around you — your family or whatever — can create for fun. And hell, that's not new. That's been going on for a long time. We don't need all the stuff that we got. Life is not about all that stuff, and really, that pipeline is about all that stuff. We don't need it, and it's really dangerous. So why don't we do something else?"

Bill's right, we don't need all that stuff — in fact we're better off without it. Experience, knowledge, friendship and adventure are what life is all about. All that "stuff" just gets in the way of actual living, and it's slowly but surely killing us.

Bill and I part ways but keep in contact. Despite some wrangling with his record label, I use one of his songs in the film to come — and he links me to his friend and legendary Canadian artist Terry Jacks, who gives me a whole bunch more songs for the film. It's one serendipitous meeting of many on this journey. If you stay open to the moment, it will come.

$$\star \quad \star \quad \star$$

After a day's walk, our double-track dirt trail suddenly ends, and we step into ancient nirvana. This is the beginning of our 25-kilometre bushwhack through the Rocky Mountains. The pipeline is proposed to run through here, so we follow.

It's a warm, humid day. An initial dense wall of trees gives way to fields of devil's club. We thrash our way through, with Todd continually slipping and falling on the greasy matt of thorny branches. At one point he's trapped like a turtle on his back, and I have to go back and take his pack from him so he can get up and make it through.

As we gain elevation, the devil's club disappears and the wonder of this place is revealed. Old-growth spruce tower over us in broadly spaced forest carpeted with glistening ferns and moss. A rushing creek runs through a small canyon that we cross and follow up to a saddle between towering peaks. Steady movement brings us to an alpine meadow by a small lake, where we camp for the night. Setting up the tent, I spot movement up on a distant ridge, high in the alpine. My binoculars reveal a grizzly ambling along in no particular hurry. As darkness falls, a lone wolf howls.

On day two, we see another grizzly, this one much closer. We're walking side by side through open forest when we hear a woofing sound from behind a bush only 50 metres away. A brown face pops up and then disappears behind the bush. "Woof! Woof! Woof!" The big bear ramps up its protest, telling us not to come any closer — or else. My first instinct is to get out the camera; Todd's is to grab the bear spray. More woofing from the bear. We look at each other. I say, "We should go."

"Uh, Yup," Todd nods.

We walk quickly and steadily away, leaving the big fella to his grazing.

Camping under the stars up at the pass that evening on another beautiful wildflower meadow, it hits me hard that Enbridge wants to blow a hole through this pristine wilderness. In the industrialized oil and canola fields of Alberta, a pipeline doesn't seem like such a big deal. The people there are ambivalent about another pipeline and, looking at where they live, I honestly was too.

Over the next month I'll hear from First Nations and other citizens of British Columbia who are unanimously opposed to the pipeline. They'll talk about how their culture and way of life are threatened by the project. Before I even get a chance to speak with them, in this very moment, I already understand. Breathing in the fresh air, the quiet, the beauty, the wildlife — the *wilderness* — I can touch and feel what's being threatened. These pristine, millennia-old, intact, ancient ecosystems are finite. Once we've stomped over them, they'll be forever altered — the world pushed closer to the precipice.

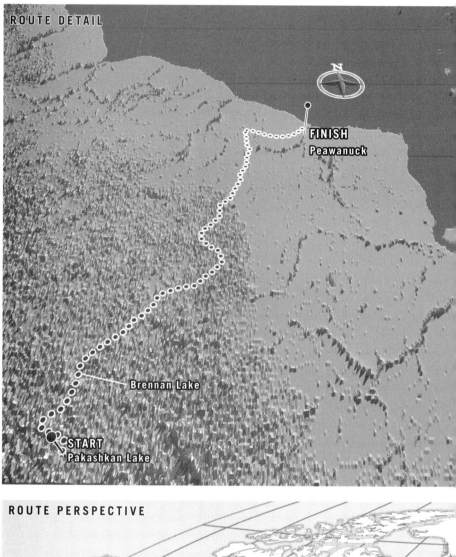

ROUTE DETAIL

N

FINISH
Peawanuck

Brennan Lake

START
Pakashkan Lake

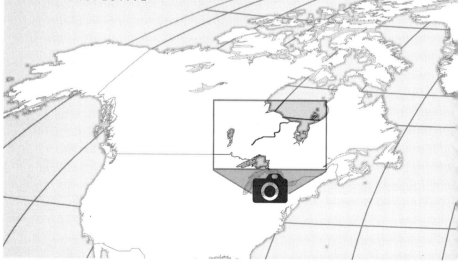

ROUTE PERSPECTIVE

The Art of Trip

A look at the creative elements that inspire and propel an 1100-kilometre journey by canoe from Thunder Bay to Hudson Bay.

ORIGINALLY PUBLISHED IN SPRING 2012 ISSUE OF *CANOEROOTS MAGAZINE*

Going through my gear stash this past spring, my eyes eventually settled on the protective case that contains my video camera. As an outdoor filmmaker, I feel a certain obligation to bring it along on any extended trip and attempt to craft an enaging work of celluloid. Creating art from the wilderness experience is a Canadian tradition made internationally famous by emissaries like Emily Carr and Bill Mason. Inspired by these icons, I've done my small part through the medium of film by sharing stories and themes set within the context of remote self-propelled expeditions.

Like many who read this magazine, I sweep out the winter cobwebs in my mind by heading out on a summer adventure. More often than not, I bring my canoe.

This time around, the plan was for my friend Todd and I to paddle through the deepest heart of the boreal forest of Ontario via a 1120-kilometre route that would span the length of Wabakimi Provincial Park and then continue north, eventually ending up at the mouth of the Winisk River. We were all set to go, but this time with one major difference: for only the second year in about a decade, I said no to filming.

Once I've committed to making a film, any situation in a trip that is hard, beautiful, interesting or relevant demands that I pull out the camera and start recording — an all-encompassing task that inevitably changes the personal experience within the journey. After making back-to-back documentaries, it was time to let my artistic outlet lie fallow and rejuvenate. This would be the summer where the canoe trip itself — not the filming of it — would be front and centre.

*   *   *

Jump In

Day five of our journey is a scorcher, with temperatures in the mid-30s Celsius cooking the already tinder-dry boreal. Ontario has literally been on fire all summer long, with 500,000 hectares of the northwest part of the province burned or burning by the time we began our journey in August. The smell of smoke comes and goes depending on the wind, and already we've been close to a few plumes rising from the shoreline forest. The best cure for fire, of course, is water — and I've been diving out of the canoe every hour or so. There's something severely satisfying — like scratching an itch — about launching yourself haphazardly and stark naked from a canoe into the depths of a warm, clear wilderness lake. It's a spontaneous, immersive moment that seems to happen more often than if I had to pause and think, *Should I film this scene?*

Rising from the depths of Brennan Lake, I claw myself back into the stern of the canoe, comfortably cool and content. Todd is lying back on the pack behind the bow seat, catching some rays. He's not much of a swimmer but is an awesome napper. We get back in our groove and cruise the calm waters until we reach a narrows where rock walls rise sharply on one side... and then I see it. A perfect overhanging cliff. I can't paddle past it. I need to jump off of it. I'm compelled to.

While I grovel up a side gully to get to the top, Todd positions himself to take a photo for posterity's sake. As I peer over the edge, the looming gap between me and the water takes my breath away. I inhale, let out a hoot and step into space for a moment before exploding into the liquid below. Under the surface, I look up through rising bubbles at the cliff as it bends in the expanding ripples like something in a Dalí painting. Experiences like this, stacked one on top of the other over the course of this canoe trip, strip away the dull sheen of a modern, vicarious iPhone life to reveal a basic animal core that exists in each of us. It is pure freedom.

$*$ $\quad$ $*$ $\quad$ $*$

The Shark

Everyone approaches canoe tripping differently. Some like to paddle to an island and chill out for a week. Others like to linger in camp, put in a couple of hours on the water and then linger in camp again. The beauty of canoe tripping is that it reflects the style of the individual — and no matter how you go about it, the rewards are rich. I approach the daily challenge of canoe tripping kind of like a shark — a creature in constant motion that rarely rests and is able to cover long distances.

A typical day on this journey is ten hours long, with perhaps a half hour break for lunch. We end up averaging almost 47 kilometres daily for the 24-day trip — including upstream, downstream, portages, dragging, you name it. I only sleep about five hours a night because I'm so energized by every paddle-stroke and aspect of this fresh environment that I want to jam as much action as possible into each moment.

We're done for the day, and Todd is setting up camp while I double back along a rough 1100-metre portage on the Witchwood River. I hop fallen logs and zigzag through the forest as fast as I possibly can to get the last pack. As I turn a corner, a knobby spruce branch wedges perfectly between my front and back leg, catapulting me headfirst into the moss. I curse the branch and look down to see a long, deep laceration on the calf of my left leg and a nice gouge on the shin of my right. Blood pours instantly from both wounds. I get up and continue to run, first at a hobble and then at a steady, rhythmic clip. My clenched teeth relax into a smile and everything clarifies. Blood, moss, spruce and movement in the heart of the Little North. Life is simple and I am extremely happy. I've been affected by a strain of madness, perhaps, but in reflection it makes perfect sense. People are hard-wired for this — to physically struggle and push our bodies in nature for long, extended periods of time. Our ancestors ran down prey and travelled under their own power for days at a time for most of the million years or so of human existence. If time is a gauge, we are only a blip away from that way of living (a blip filled with La-Z-Boy chairs and cheesecake, but a blip nonetheless), and our genetics retain that need to move. The canoe trip is a portal that allows us to tap into that tribal call and be whole once more.

*   *   *

Blank Canvas

Todd and I are in the Cree village of Peawanuck, waiting for our plane to come and return us to civilization. In the meantime, we're hanging out at the house of the manager of the local Northern Store, who has generously offered us accommodation. I'm in the dining room, hunched over a detailed map of Ontario, tracing a line over the blue veins and blotches of our completed route. I step back and admire the curves of the fresh line with a visual picture of every campsite, lake and river entrenched in my mind.

I love making films about canoe journeys, but I realize now that making a film is simply another artistic layer added to a thing that in itself is already so original and creative. Like an artist who is compelled to produce a painting on a blank canvas, the canoe tripper is similarly compelled to step into a blank landscape and then emerge at the end with the ultimate experience of a vision realized. If a film or painting is considered to be art, then canoe tripping is, in every sense, art.

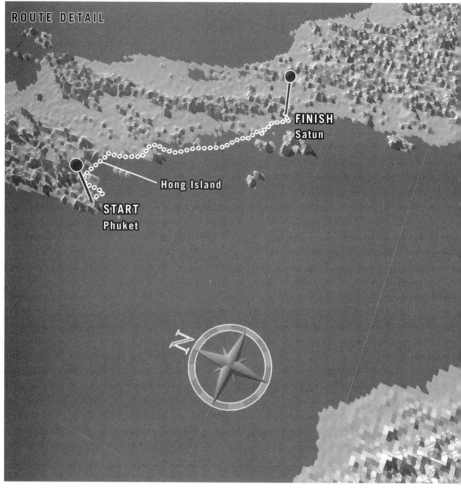

ROUTE DETAIL

FINISH
Satun

Hong Island

START
Phuket

N

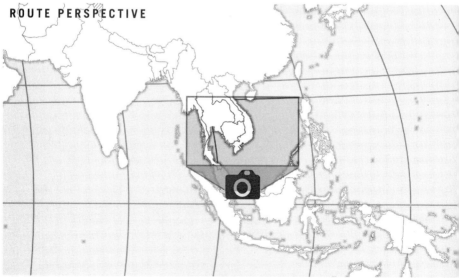

ROUTE PERSPECTIVE

Bird Nests and Bang Bang

Lost your wallet on a dangerous, heavily guarded island? That's just the start as one thing leads to another during a kayaking misadventure along the east coast of Thailand.

ORIGINALLY PUBLISHED IN NOVEMBER 2001 ISSUE OF *ADVENTURE KAYAK MAGAZINE*

Since the first humans shuffled barefoot around the dusty earth a million years ago, we have sought out adventure. Clubbing woolly mammoths that were stuck in tar pits eventually became tedious, so we looked elsewhere for inspiration. We looked to the oceans. What lay out there beyond the big blue? There was only one way to find out, of course. Build yourself a floating structure of skin stretched over bone, and strike out for the unknown. That sweet sensation we sought, the not knowing what could happen, was adventure. We needed it then, and we need it now.

As a group, people toiled through various evolutions and found themselves in the 21st century at the top of the food chain, the world no longer such a mystery. The oceans and their extent could be seen in a second via a quick spin of the classroom globe. However, we do still maintain a primeval lust for adventure — that urge to strike out for places unknown and experience whatever or whomever we may find. To further this end, to satisfy this urge, we have the sea kayak. What better vessel with which to disappear into the big blue? What better way to explore the infinite possibilities that lie within every square inch of that patch of turquoise covering two-thirds of the papier mâché sphere that sat on the corner of your Grade 4 teacher's desk? Trusty sea kayak, let me point you in a direction where the destination is unknown. Take me out of my predictable everyday life and make me whole.

*   *   *

Dave Stibbe and I sat on the pier, staring out through the haze over the emerald waters of the Straits of Malacca. Escaping the confines of our Canadian routines, we had packed up our double folding kayak and boarded a plane, and now found ourselves in Phuket, Thailand.

We had our safety gear, some food, and, yes, we had maps. Glorious black-and-white maps showing a maze of islands that were completely foreign to us. We were grinning to ourselves and staring at the glinting, tantalizing, dancing Indian Ocean, wondering where to begin our journey.

"Where to, Dave?"

"Anywhere, it all looks great, it all looks good! Who knows what we'll see out there; it's gonna be mind-blowing, Frank! We're in Thailand! Siam of old! Country of kings, elephants and opium! Let's go! Let's go! Let's just go!"

With that, our Siamese adventure began. I could tell you we saw lots of sand beaches, paddled some rough water, covered some kilometres, and that would be all fair and square. In fact, we ended up covering 300 kilometres of the west coast of Thailand all the way down to the Malaysian border. All the statistics are in my logbook, every last fumbling detail. What stands out in my mind, though, what released the ancient adventure spirit in me, was a day and night of losses and triumphs in the middle of those shimmering straits.

We pick up the tale 12 kilometres up the east coast of Yao Yo, the largest island in the Thai portion of the Straits of Malacca. It was our second day of paddling...

*   *   *

Working our way steadily against a headwind blowing out of the north from Phang Nga Bay, Dave and I take in the rugged Yao Yo coastline. The rolling hills of the island are covered with a dense foliage of low-lying palm trees, teak trees and bushes that cascade down the slopes and crowd the shores. Rocky beaches dampened by ocean waves look like mounds of smooth, shiny gemstones piled up intermittently amid the dark, bursting green of the coastline.

A dim lump of an island has been staring us down from the northeast for most of the morning, getting closer with each paddle-stroke. Our efforts eventually bring us due east of the island, now only a kilometre away. From our vantage point, we see a green tuft of trees sitting like dishevelled hair on top of sheer limestone cliffs that drop straight into the ocean. We are irresistibly drawn to the island. We are also off the top of our last map — paddling blind, so to speak — with no idea what the name of the island is or where it exists in relation to anything north of it. It is the one map we weren't able to obtain and, as fate would have it, the one area our adventure is to take place. Off the map; just like our ancestors. We pick up our tempo, and adrenaline surges as the island takes shape in front of our eyes.

Within 100 metres of the island, we're greeted by 400-foot cliffs that rise straight out of the ocean and stand like pillars on either side of a two-bus-long white beach, which tapers back into a jungle valley. The overhanging cliffs have three-metre-long stalactites and vines hanging from them. Dark caves dot the rock faces, giving them a lunar texture. Entering the cove of the beach, we stop paddling and let our craft drift in with the momentum of our final, strong pulls at the water. We float over crystal-clear shallows that reveal corals and small multicoloured fish below. The bow of our kayak hits the sand shore with a *hissss*. We step out and pull our boat onto the beach, securing it with a line to a fallen tree. Gazing up at the cliffs, I feel like I'm in an ancient amphitheatre and the beach is centre stage. A continuous, high-pitched bird call reverberates from somewhere up on the cliffs and seems to be all around us. The heavy tropical stink of the jungle mixes with the warm saltwater air, providing an exotic smell so thick I can taste it. This is the place. Livingstone, Shipton, Indiana Jones: this is the kind of place where they pursued their adventures. The pit of my stomach gurgles with excitement.

At the top of the beach, we find a white sandy path that runs through some low crabgrasses and disappears into the jungle valley between the limestone monoliths. Dave and I glance at each other knowingly and head up the trail. The path winds lazily along around palm trees and tree ferns until it ends up in a small clearing at the other side of the island. Three open-air huts with thatched roofs are arranged in a triangle in the centre of the area. A small dock runs off between the two huts closest to the shore. Some machetes rest on the stoop of the nearest hut, and a chicken walks jerkily by us as if we don't exist. In one of the huts, a lightly swinging hammock with a leg and an arm hanging off the side show us we're not alone.

Not wanting to wake the locals, we turn and begin walking back toward the beach when something catches my eye. Off to my left I see a rickety bamboo ladder lashed together with cordage and propped up against the base of the vine-covered wall. It calls to our primal selves, and we answer. I make my way up first, taking each rung of the seven-metre ladder gingerly as it flexes under my weight. Reaching the top of the ladder, I find a boardwalk made of bamboo tree trunks that lead over a black chasm in the rock to another seven-metre ladder that goes deeper up into a hole in the wall. A third ladder awaits us, and finally a fourth that tops out at the base of a cave.

This is no ordinary cave, though — it's the mother of all caves. Cathedral-like in size, it has 30-metre-high ceilings and runs back for 100 metres until it peters off into darkness. It's 40 metres wide where we stand, illuminated by an opening that looks out over the jungle valley to the ocean beyond. The bright sunlight from outside mixes with the inky blackness from within to form an eerie green light in the area of the cave we stand in. The cool, damp inside smells like rotting fungus in autumn; I feel as if we've just stepped into a different world.

In the centre of the cavern, a swimming-pool-sized pit is sunk into the limestone floor, filled partway with a tangle of cut bamboo. In several places around the cave, bamboo stalks are propped upright and run up into smaller openings that pock-mark the ceiling and sides of the caves. Bird droppings coat much of the floor with a black-and-white slime. Dave and I are quiet as we observe our surroundings. There's a palpable feeling of foreboding.

"Pretty cool, eh, Dave?"

"Yeah."

"Do you want to go back into the cave and explore a little deeper?"

"I do and I don't."

"What do you mean?"

"I feel like we shouldn't be in here. My gut tells me we should just leave. Let's get off this island."

His thoughts are similar to mine, so I agree. We make our way down the ladders, along the trail and back to our kayak. The tide is rising and laps against the rudder of the kayak. I untie the bow while Dave fiddles with the foot pedals. Shoving off, we take a last look at the island before paddling on.

*　　*　　*

It's mid-afternoon by now. We head east through a series of rocky islands that show little promise for camping. After an hour, Dave spots white sand out of the corner of his eye, signalling us like a beacon from five kilometres off. We steer toward our potential camping site and discover another paradise. A perfect crescent beach opens up before us, ringing a protected bay with a small island in the middle of it. The beach is surrounded by more palm trees, crawling vines and exotic fruit plants backed by 500-foot cliffs.

We congratulate ourselves on our luck and hammer in toward the shore. Behind the fringe of trees, we discover a simple thatched roof bar and food stand run by some local Thai. They tell us we're on Hong Island. A group of four travellers have been boated to the island and are camping there as well. Perfectly relaxed, I grab my snorkelling gear from one of our dry bags and saunter up to the edge of the bay. Sitting down, I slip my fins on and pull my mask and snorkel over my face. Submerging beneath the water's surface, I'm greeted by a school of clown fish and bright coral fans and sponges.

After 20 minutes of exploring the reef that wraps around the small island in the middle of the bay, I get out and walk toward Dave. He's busy unpacking camping gear from the kayak. Or so I thought. As I near him, I see his movements are frantic. I jog up to him.

"What's wrong?"

"My waterproof money belt. My credit cards, money, traveller's cheques, passport... everything! It's all gone!"

My heart drops into my stomach.

"Are you sure?! Have you looked everywhere?!"

"Yes. Everywhere. Three times over."

"Where could you have lost it?"

"I don't know. I could have left it at our campsite last night. Maybe at that village we stopped at to resupply our food. Or...I may have left it at the cave island. It may have fallen onto the beach when I was making some adjustments on our way out."

I quickly run the situation through my mind. Here's Dave, with no money or means of identification, in a foreign country thousands of kilometres from home. The only thing I can do is go back to the cave island and hope it might be there. The island is now about ten kilometres away. In addition, the tide has come up at least a couple of feet since then; if he dropped it on the beach, the money belt's probably been taken by the tide. Damn. I can't just sit around and do nothing. While Dave rummages for a fourth time through the kayak, I go over to a lone long-tail boat operator who shuttles people to Hong

Island on day trips. Unable to speak Thai, I point in the direction of the cave island and say, "I need to go there."

He smiles, nods and motions for me to hop in.

I shout back to Dave, "I'm going back to the island to look for the money belt!"

Before he can turn around, I'm off.

At first, the owner of the boat, Tutu, and his two brothers take me 50 metres to the point of the bay. They think I'm just a curious tourist wanting to explore the far side of the cove. I shake my head vigorously and point to the cluster of islands Dave and I paddled from, far off in the distance. Tutu, a small, dark, wiry man of perhaps 30, observes me thoughtfully. It's dusk now, and the tropical sun is sinking quickly. Time is of the essence. Tutu finally agrees to take me there, albeit with a bit of hesitation.

And so, wearing only surf shorts, I make my way over with Tutu and his brothers. The long-tail has a large upswept bow powered by a propeller attached to the end of a long motor drive shaft at the back of the boat. It's slow and jackhammer loud. After about 30 minutes, we near the islands. I point to the cave island, and Tutu, who does speak a little English, exclaims, "Kalat?! No, no! *Bang Bang! Bang Bang!*" and motions with his hands like he's holding a gun.

I speak with him slowly and get the whole story. He tells me the people on Kalat Island are highly protective of their bird's nests, which they collect from caves and sell to China and Japan as a delicacy for use in bird's nest soup. The nests are very valuable and bring in large amounts of money. Certain Thai families have occupied bird nest islands like Kalat for generations. As a result, they've built up organized Mafia-like protection around the islands to guard their interests. According to Tutu, many people have been shot and killed by the keepers of the nests for invading their secret collection spots. Like other primal instincts, gut instinct had certainly come in handy for Dave and I in that cathedral cave on Kalat. I later learn the nests are made by swiftlets, and the combination of their saliva and the grasses and twigs they collect makes up the ingredients of this Far East delicacy. The bamboo poles we saw in the cave are used to climb up into the nesting areas for collection purposes.

I convince Tutu to at least take me close to the island. He reluctantly nods. It's now pitch black as we putt-putt slowly around the corner until we're in sight of the beach. For obvious reasons, Tutu doesn't want to land, so I slip out of the boat into the calm, black water and begin swimming the last 30 metres to shore. The limestone monoliths stand like giant pale ghosts, lit up by the gathering starlight. The water around me looks like rippling oil as I steadily breaststroke my way to shore. My eyes are wide and alert, scanning the beach for any movement or sign of life. My hand touches sand and I stop for a moment on the shore. All is quiet, no sign of trouble. I heave myself up and scurry in a low crouch along the strand to the spot by the fallen tree where our boat was.

The tide has indeed come up and all signs of the boat are gone. Straining my eyes, I helplessly search the water for Dave's black money belt. A needle in a haystack... make that a needle in the ocean. What hope is there now? I exhale in defeat and turn my head slowly to the half-sunken tree. I blink twice, thinking I'm seeing things, but, no! There it is! Dave's money belt is hanging in the bare branches of that marvellous tree, dangling only an inch above the rising tide! I've come just in the nick of time to retrieve it.

Losing myself in the moment, I let out a loud "Whoop!" I found it, I found it, I found it! A successful and worthwhile hunt, to say the least. The ancient gods have tested us, and we've passed. I clip the waterproof money belt to my waist and swim quickly back to the dim silhouette of Tutu's boat.

Grabbing the oiled wood gunwales, I pull myself in, euphoria pulsing through my entire body. I thought our trip was going to be stopped dead, but we've gained a new lease on life. Tutu revs up his engine and sputters away, relieved to be away from Kalat. His two brothers sing in Thai and smoke at the stern, the embers from their cigarettes glowing like fireflies. Tutu and I move to the front and laugh about our little venture. As we banter back and forth, he teaches me how to say "stars" and "water" in Thai. We ride the long-tail back, grinning from ear to ear under the spectacular starlit sky as phosphorescent wake splashes over the edge of the boat and a warm breeze flows over us like gravy.

We pull up to Hong Island, where Tutu beaches his vessel and lets me hop out. Dave is sitting by himself in the dark, as grim and bitter a soul as I've ever seen. I think of playing him along for a bit and not telling him I've found his money belt, but I don't have the heart. He looks up at me, obviously expecting the worst. I smile and produce it.

"Oh, my god! You found it! I can't believe it!"

We high-five each other and laugh.

"Thank Tutu, he was the driver." Tutu waits patiently by his boat.

Dave walks over to him and gives him a big hug and 20 US dollars. Tutu isn't sure about the value of the money we've given him, as he only thinks in terms of the local currency, the baht. We assure him he's been paid well, about twice what he usually makes in an entire day. With a big grin, Tutu wishes us well and leaves us to our impending celebration — he has to go back to his family on the mainland.

Dave turns with a grin, "Frank, the beers are on me tonight."

We drink several beers amid much banter that night at Hong's thatch-hut drinking hole with a group of about ten Thais, three New Zealanders and one Scotsman. A pair of Thais, Ti and Ling, who run the establishment, bring out some *poi-pois* (flaming balls on strings) and spin them around in dazzling circular sequences all around their bodies. Eventually, an arm-wrestling contest breaks out. The sounds of our celebration float out into the hot, sticky equatorial night until the wee hours.

When everyone else has gone to bed, I walk down the beach, beer swimming pleasantly in my head. Lying down on the sand, I have a fish-eye view of the big cliffs, stars and ocean that surround me. I am content to the core. Our sea kayak led us on an off-the-map, see-saw journey to Kalat, and then here to Hong Island. My primal adventure urge has been more than satisfied. I close my eyes and drift into the warm, dark embrace of sleep.

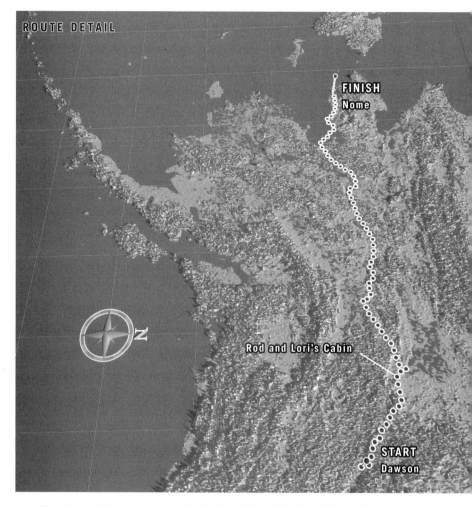

ROUTE DETAIL

FINISH
Nome

N

Rod and Lori's Cabin

START
Dawson

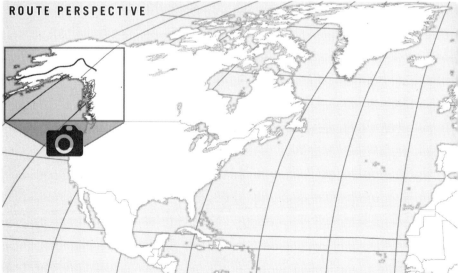

ROUTE PERSPECTIVE

Yukon Fringe

A peek into the characters and trail life of a 2000-kilometre cycling journey along the frozen Yukon River, following in the tracks of two gold miners of a century ago.

In 2003, Kevin Vallely, Andy Sterns and I cycled 2000 kilometres in 49 days from Dawson City to Nome. We carried with us the journals of Ed Jesson and Max Hirschberg — a couple of gold miners who'd done the same route by bicycle in 1901. It may sound preposterous that these two fellas completed this journey around the dawn of cycling, but they did. In fact, their journey was more feasible than ours. Back in 1901, about 10,000 people travelled from Dawson when a new strike sent the world buzzing toward Nome. With ocean ice preventing ships from accessing the rich fields, a frenzy of people used any mode of overland travel possible to get there.

Using mostly dog teams, those who'd lost out on the 1898 gold rush in Dawson packed a virtual ice road along the whole route. Cookhouses that provided food and lodging popped up everywhere to serve the migration. The two cyclists therefore had a firm route and provisions available as they made their way to Nome in only a month. Jesson and Hirschberg never found any gold, but their journey lives on in the annals of history, interwoven with the historic characters the Yukon is so famous for. Our slow grind through drifts, melting ice and team dynamics never revealed any gold either — our reward was the experience of self-discovery and unearthing of the present-day characters of the Yukon.

*　　*　　*

March 8:
15 kilometres to Cor Guimond's Cassiar Creek cabin

I wake with a ring of hoarfrost exploding all around the circle of sight from inside my sleeping bag. It dropped to around minus 45 Celsius overnight, but I was cozy in my bag. Andy slips out a few minutes before us to melt some water and get breakfast on. Shortly after, we hear a sharp yelp and rush outside the tent to see what's up.

Andy is bent over, yammering and shaking burning gloves off his hands. The piercing cold has shrunk the O-rings of the stove pump so that it's no longer sealed. When Andy pumped the MSR stove to pressurize it, fuel leaked onto his gloves, so when he lit the fuel cup to prime the stove, he also ignited his hands.

Two burned plastic shards in the snow are all that remain of his gloves, but his hands are luckily fine. When I try to open the pump mechanism to check it out, the brittle latch that holds it together snaps, and a duct tape sling has to be applied to keep it together.

We all laugh afterwards about the possibility of Andy falling back into the tent with his burning hands, igniting the tent, and the three of us burning to death in the middle of the snowy Yukon River during a cold snap.

It's still bloody cold in the a.m. by the time we get going, but the upside is that the track has firmed up nicely. Me and Kev have no problems, but Andy is having trouble stabilizing on the crunchy track. You have to keep to the centre of the snowmobile/dogsled track, where the snow is most consolidated. It's like riding a North Shore–style mountain bike boardwalk forever — except less smooth and with give. Dogsled runners test your balance like nothing else — the degree of difficulty is maximized by an unwieldy, loaded bike. Though Andy is a veteran of 24-hour mountain bike races, he has a lot of trouble with this technical style of riding and perpetually drops out of sight behind us.

We work through fields of jumbled ice. The landscape resembles thick shattered glass that's fallen from the sky and lodged vertically into endless white flesh — all jagged and haphazard, sticking up in all directions.

We cross a couple of glazed, frozen overflows from side creeks, falling and sliding several times before making it across. It's a beautiful, bright, clear, minus-15-Celsius day. We roll along the river beneath towering spruce, poplar and alder — sprinkled slopes where no one lives. In any urban centre, these would be covered with condos so everyone could have a view of the river, and all the trees would be destroyed for said view. Here, it's just trees looking over a ribbon of white that stretches inexorably toward the Bering Sea.

We finish the day early at the cabin of Cor Guimond, one of three structures in a bend of the river on the top of a bank, looking across a spectacular snow-blasted rock face soaring 1,000 feet high. Inside there's a smoker of a woodstove, a little balcony up front, lots of mags (most notably German *Men's Health*, with loads of naked women inside — many long, lonely nights satisfied by them, no doubt), a table in back with candles and a bed beside it; a nice loft up top too. Tomorrow we hope to get to the former town of Forty Mile, 30 kilometres away.

Andy wanted to quit again today — at one point his speed was literally 50 per cent of ours. The issue will arise again and again, I'm sure. We want him to finish with us — he's got great spirit and has lots of northern experience (or so we think). Kevin skied the Iditarod Trail with him a few years earlier and assured me of his strength. It's become quickly evident, though, that riding a loaded bike on tricky snow is a far different story for him than pulling a sled on skis. We all enjoy the cabin life, though — a great way to finish a day on the trail — with the bonus of finding a meal of frozen burritos here, wrapped in tin foil. They were probably left by a musher during the Yukon Quest dogsled race a few weeks ago and kept in state by the natural freezer known as the Yukon winter.

This evening there's a brilliant, crisp crescent moon and stars, with aurora borealis shooting up the river in green and pink streaks, pulsing to and fro. Kevin and I stand outside for a while, having a toke and taking it all in.

$$* \quad * \quad *$$

March 9:
25 kilometres to Seb and Shelly's place
at the mouth of the Fortymile River

Today is a great day of riding — in fact, we ride it all. Andy gets into a better groove and lags just a bit. Lots of jumbled ice to work through, big 20-foot-high piles that we meander in and out of for ten kilometres or so — lots of fun up-and-down whoop-de-dos too. Funnelled through walls rising up on both sides of the river, brisk wind at times puts the bite on my face.

We stop to check an abandoned cabin set just atop a bank along the way, 20 feet above the hard-packed river trail. People's insignias from as far back as 1967 are still there on the back wall — pretty much all summer folks, though; not much travel through in the winters, it seems. One person wrote of teleportation: "Got drunk in Chicken, then woke up here. — Bill, 1997." For us, I add: "Kevin Vallely, Andy Sterns, Frank Wolf -35 Celsius last night, high of -15 today. Biking on the frozen, ice-jumbled river from Dawson to Nome. Yes, we are fools."

We arrive at the home of Sebastian and Shelly — the only inhabitants of Forty Mile, the former mining boom town that quickly died with the Dawson strike. The old RNWMP detachment with telegraph office is still there. Seb and Shelly live in the former general store (original wood walls, roof and floor). Seb reputes it to be the oldest inhabited building in the Yukon.

Our hosts are kind and generous. Seb's been in the Yukon since 1979 and has lived at Forty Mile for ten years. A Brit originally, he fishes and tends the provincial campground in Dawson in the summer and mushes dogs in the winter. Shelly is from New Brunswick and has lived here with Seb since the beginning; she also mushes.

Seb has a solid beard, crazy long straw hair and a gleaming dome. Smart and well versed in current affairs, he warms up to strangers slowly, like me. Shelly's an outgoing, bubbly brunette; she whips us up a great spaghetti with moose meat sauce, homemade buns and even some wine to finish. The cabin is small; we sleep on the floor, with our hosts only a couple of feet away on their bed. A highlight here is the outhouse, spectacularly situated with a view of the big bend of the Yukon where the Fortymile River empties into it.

*　　*　　*

March 10:
24 kilometres to Jonathan's wall tent at Sandy Slough

After a hearty breakfast of pancakes and bacon, and helping to bring in chopped ice from the river for drinking water, Seb rides my bike around a bit and then says to me, "Hmm, maybe you guys will make it." The idea of cycling through the environment is foreign because such things aren't done too often — apparently a French team with massive support attempted it years back and, for whatever reason, never made it. We've also heard of two Germans who tried to do it, starting in the darkness of December — one of them eventually losing body parts to frostbite after falling through overflow. These mysteries, rumours and forbidding tales that creep around my mind, especially before departing, make me wonder about the sanity of the undertaking.

Seb and Shelly tell us a great story about Helmut, a Dawson dentist who landed his ultralight beside us to say hi a few days ago. Apparently, he makes his girlfriends — usually attractive younger women — legally change their names. He named one Aedes — a common species of northern mosquito — and another Merlin, as in King Arthur's wizard. He hasn't yet changed the name of his current girlfriend because, Shelly says, she has a cool one already.

Anyhow, Seb and Shelly are good folks, salt of the earth, in touch with nature and what's important in life. They give us a whack of homemade cookies, granola bars and leftover spaghetti on our way out. Andy's eyes shine.

Good travel today: we leave at noon and arrive at a Unabomber-style wall tent by 6:15 p.m. Set back in the woods about 50 metres, it's ten feet by ten, with a wood stove, elevated bed on the left with storage underneath and a prep table in the far right corner — which is just a foot past the door. It's fully insulated, with pink fibreglass inside a wood frame and canvas outer skin. We start out by chopping wood on a big round block 40 metres past the tent, breaking down big blocks with a splitter into quarters and then into smaller kindling. Starting a fire in the barrel stove, we get the hut smoking hot and fry up Seb and Shelly's spaghetti on the DragonFly stove.

Jonathan, who owns the cabin, ain't here. He likes Victoria's Secret catalogues — which seems to be a recurring theme in these lonely outposts (don't blame the inhabitants) — and science fiction books. We sit around in this unintentional sauna, shirtless, talking maps and distances. We're moving slowly, but we're still moving.

I imagine that I could move up here, live the northern life and find me a young lady who shares my interests, to keep me warm at night... But then, I'm sure that was the dream of Jonathan here — and this is the kind of stuff he writes:

I want to get drunk. And smoke. Falling on my face drunk
with a lit cigarette falling out the side of my mouth and

a bottle of booze teetering precariously in my grasp. In
12 days this shall be me (perhaps minus the cigarette
but I could actually care less today. The faster my body
decays the better). Well, this is not improving my spirits
and it's probably not inspiring to read so I'll sign off now.

Take care sweetheart,

Jonathan — the depressed bush guy beginning his descent into madness.

This quote was taken from one of a series of unsent letters to his
girlfriend that are piled in the corner of the wall tent. Loneliness and
isolation do strange things to people's minds, almost like a voluntary
imprisonment. They lust for and relish the independence of living free
in the bush — but are conversely imprisoned by their decision to live
outside of society. Jonathan would be a lot happier and more stable
with a woman by his side — but that's the trick, isn't it? Where to find
such a creature? Shellys are hard to come by.

*   *   *

March 11:
Wall tent to Gaetan Beaudet's cabin
at Poppy Creek, 34 kilometres

Good day today, plenty of riding on hand with a wind-packed and
blown trail with occasional pushing through drifts. There's lots of
grinding through headwind, so we use our goggles and balaclavas,
which work well. There's a constant hiss of chalky snow as it skims
over the crusty base, propelled by a blasting wind from the north,
all the while under a brilliant, sharp Yukon sun. The distant Ogilvie
Mountains look down at us all day, their white-domed peaks brilliant
in the light.

Andy was slow but toughs it out all the way. Neil Young's "Helpless" and Kansas's "Dust in the Wind" repeat in my head as I grind along, moving delicately on the ice and then balancing that with power in the drifts, lifting my ass off the seat and pumping hard on the pedals whenever I sense my wheel drop into a soft spot that threatens to stop the bike dead. The crisp, cold, endless wilderness; the deafening din of the elements; me, sober as a stone — I feel energized and alive.

Gaetan is another loner who Seb and Shelly mentioned lives along the river. He is very, very quiet answering the door. After we knock, he opens the door a crack and says a soft hello, then nothing. I blurt out an account of our day, dropping Seb and Shelly's names and how they said we should stop by. I can feel the warmth from inside creeping around him and teasing us. Oh, the comfort of a cabin after a long day on the frozen trail — there's nothing like it. He finally, gently invites us to come in.

Gaetan built this place in 1980 and has lived here ever since. He has an exceptional collection of books (Pirsig, Hesse, London, Michener, lots of other travel and philosophy). On the right is an opening that leads to his workshop. Up some spiral stairs to his room is a TV with rows of videos to watch. Beside a wood-fired cooking stove, a big heater stove sits near the front.

Gaetan stays very quiet for the first hour, a very hard man tap into — not at all surprising, as he lives on his own up here, Wall Tent Jonathan being his closest neighbour, 34 kilometres away. Over the evening, his visage melts, and words drip out like water from an ice cube.

He's a fisheries worker in the summer (tagging), wood carver in the winter (ducks, chickadees — he once did a life-size bald eagle that sold for six grand). He's also building a monster two-story log home beside this one — all by himself, an unfathomable undertaking.

The structure sits half-built, 100 feet away, seemingly far too big for a man who lives alone. He later tells us his longtime girlfriend left him earlier this year. Looking back at the house, you can see it was for the both of them... perhaps a family was on his mind. It now sits there unfinished, probably a painful reminder of life plans gone terribly awry. She left for Vancouver. He stayed, alone with his dog in the bush, the only life he's known for 23 years. For dinner, he served us up a veggie and moose stew to start, then cubed moose meat with green peppers and sauce over ice. He shoots a moose every fall, and the meat lasts him the entire winter.

Gaetan's about six feet tall, with a trim grey moustache, thick curly shock of salt-and-pepper hair, French nose, medium build. His dog is sweet, named Mushka, the runt of a sled dog litter from legendary musher Jeff King. Mushka, who loves attention, is very mellow at 14 years old. Gaetan mentions a few times that Mushka won't last too much longer. Once that happens, he'll be absolutely alone. It's too bad. He's a good man.

*   *   *

March 12:
34 kilometres to Eagle

Gaetan feeds us a heaping breakfast consisting of moose patty, hash browns, bacon, scrambled eggs and cup upon cup of hot coffee. Kevin is a strict vegetarian and — though he does his best to be a carnivore on trips like this, where every bit of fuel you can stuff into you is crucial — can't bring himself to finish the rare ground meat of the patty.

He pushes it to Andy, who happily devours it into his bottomless black hole of a stomach. I found out this morning that our host is a world champion wood carver, having won the Worlds in Maryland back in 1998 in the "raptor" category.

This morning, I get some good marten and whisky jack coverage on video. The marten is gnawing at the frozen meat of the haunch of Gaetan's moose, which Gaetan stores by hanging it suspended in a cargo net on a tree outside, kept fresh by nature's freezer.

I like Gaetan immensely — he is understated and dignified to the core. His girlfriend is gone; soon his dog will be gone too. His only love left will be the Yukon. Here's to hoping he finds a new companion in the future to share his unique lifestyle and passions.

*   *   *

March 19:
Slaven's cabin to Rod and Lori's cabin

Our first taste of Alaskan cabin hospitality isn't exactly heartwarming. Kevin knocks on the door of a reputedly friendly cabin, and Rod answers. He gruffly says that Kevin should have called out hello as he approached. "Knocking on the door'll just get you shot." Kev asks if we can camp on the property. Rod doesn't bother to invite us in, instead pointing to a spot by an old shed in front of a snow machine. Kev says it's the unfriendliest Alaskan welcome he's ever had.

A few minutes later, Rod steps out, a little more at ease, and invites us to come help ourselves to some leftover food.

There's no sign of Andy yet. He will come in at nine p.m., a full two hours after us. Kevin and I rode casually and steadily today, but Andy dawdled more than ever. While he fell way back, Kev and I waited and tried to look around for any remnant of the Woodchopper roadhouse that Jesson and Hirschberg reportedly used, but there was no sign of it. Kev napped in his down in the sun for an hour while I checked our GPS coordinates. Finally we'd had enough of waiting and beelined it for this place.

Kevin and I are carrying most of Andy's gear on our bikes by now to lighten his load, but he still can't keep up. In the unstable snow, he keeps falling off of his bike, then tries to ride again, then falls off again. All this stop-and-go explains his speed. We tell him repeatedly that until we get to firmer snow, it would be easier and faster for him just to push his bike all day for some consistent movement rather than riding. He refuses, though, always trying to ride. It's a stubbornness that is admirable in some ways but is also selfish in that it's negatively affecting the daily distance required to succeed in our mission. At this pace, the ice on the Bering Sea at the end of our route will break up before we can cross it, and the trip will be doomed. When he finally arrives at the cabin tonight, he looks grim and reserved. I think he gets broken every day on trail.

Inside the cabin, Rod and his lady, Lori, are quietly watching *American Idol* with two other rough-around-the-edges fellows (one might describe them as rednecks). They pretty much ignore us and keep on watching, with the occasional music critique followed by a "yep" or light chuckling. Lori eventually turns and points us to the leftovers. We are like wolves on a carcass, feasting on moose ribs (good), moose stew, cake (blueberry surprise), fresh homemade bread and pepperoni sticks with Ritz crackers. After *Idol*, we watch a bit of *MacGyver* and *Sanford and Son* with our reluctant hosts before calling it a night.

*　　*　　*

March 20:
34 miles to Twenty Mile Cabin

It was bloody cold in the tent last night (minus 40?). Andy slept inside his minus-40 suit inside his minus-50 bag and snored like a chainsaw all night. He was on his back and unable or unwilling to turn because of the load of down he was wrapped in. I must've kicked him about 50 times.

This morning he says, "I must've been snoring, 'cause I think you were kicking me last night, but I just kept falling asleep again — then you'd kick me, I'd wake up and fall asleep right away. I was too tired to turn over." Poor Andy — being beaten during the day on the bike and then at night in the tent. Amazing how he keeps so cheery. Despite the negatives of his riding speed and eating habits, he has a spectacular attitude.

Rod stops by the tent and invites us in for breakfast. We were just about to cook up some oatmeal, when — bang! Next thing you know, we're sitting around with Rod, David and Richard (the rednecks from the night before, now transformed into actual human beings) and Lori, watching Fox News Channel.

The war in Iraq started 12 hours ago. George W. Bush (or should I say Dick Cheney) got his way. Richard, with his Chevy hat, goatee and squinting steel-blue eyes, is doing dishes and keeps throwing in comments like "Saddam better be fuckin' scared." Nicest guy of the bunch, though. His family built a cabin on this land in 1971. In 1991, a flood from an ice jam carried it away, so they built a new one.

In 1978, Jimmy Carter's regime created Yukon–Charley Rivers National Preserve, which includes this piece of land. Rod and Lori don't officially own the land, but the Park lets them stay. "Carter decided to make about 18 parks on his way out," says Rod. "He screwed us."

"Does the Park give you trouble?" I ask.

"Nope. Not yet," he replies, deadpan. These guys are definitely hair-trigger about the land; it's a topic to tiptoe around. They have a "This is my land, get the fuck off" kind of attitude. The mere possibility of the Park somehow affecting them 25 years after they took over irks them to no end. They hate the government impinging on them in any way, but they love the rah-rah cowboy war their government is waging on the TV in front of them — and they seem ready for a war of their own. No wonder the Park leaves them alone — they're armed to the teeth.

Medium-length 1970s dirty-blonde-haired, goateed, Carhart-overalled, tough-lookin' sumbitch Dave is quietly drinking a can of MGD in his chair along the far wall.

I comment, "Beer for breakfast?"

"Better 'n coffee," he replies.

A holster with a .45 handgun hangs from the rafter above him. I point to it and ask, "You use that for hunting?"

He looks up and says, "Yep, caribou, moose, whatever. Hit 'em from 100, 150 yards, no problem. After 100 yards, the bullet starts to drop, but I adjust the trajectory fer that. Otherwise I also got my 30-ought-six on my snow machine." The .30-06 is the most popular

30-calibre rifle in the US; the ought-six part designates when it was first made — 1906.

I munch into the creamy sausage gravy and wipe it up with one of Lori's homemade biscuits.

"Thet's caribou sausage," Rod informs me.

"It's great... deeelicious, Rod."

"Yep — trophy hunters come up from the lower 48 and just want a 'rack' to take home with 'em. Got two carcasses that way this year beyond my limit. I turn 'em into sausages, pepperoni, you name it."

"You headin' out to check your trapline on the Charley?" Dave asks Rod.

"Yeah, today. Got some beaver traps set under the ice. Almost hope I don't get one. Them's hard buggers to clean."

"Why are they so hard?" I ask.

"Lotsa fat. Thick fat everywhere you got to cut through and take out in order to skin it. Takes me over three hours." Rod stuffs a piece of sausage beneath his black moustache.

"How do you get in and set up and remove your traplines?"

"Snow machine and sled... used to mush in with a dog team, but they got too noisy so I got rid of 'em."

"Yeah, and gave 'em to my kid," Dave quickly remarks.

"He wanted 'em," Rod retorts.

"Sure, he was a kid! You gave 'im dog food, dogs, harnesses and a sled... what'd you think he'd say? He was a kid! Kept those dogs in the backyard for two months. They'd start yappin' at night and I'd have to waste a bunch of ammunition gettin' them to shut up. Firin' shots into the air to scare them quiet. Couldn't take no more, so I loaded 'em all in my kid's truck and said, 'Take 'em away — don't you bring a one of 'em back.' And he did. Nothin' left in the truck but a few collars. Never did know what he did with 'em."

After breakfast, we bid farewell to our armed friends, ride the north shore of the river and then push the south shore. At one point, Rod flies low over us with his ultralight aircraft, just metres overhead, and gives us a wing-tip wave by tilting the plane side to side. It took awhile, but he took a liking to us eventually.

As the light wanes, the evening sun casts long shadows of spruce, jumbled ice and mountains on the open river and in the twisty beaver sloughs before we arrive at the Twenty Mile cabin. It's nicely built, with separate beds at opposite ends of the house. Andy was slow, but the day has been better than usual. We get in at 7:30 p.m. after a 10:45 start.

It's another night of perfect stars. (Last night's aurora borealis was amazing. Huge, arcing streaks, pulsing back and forth over the cabin like a live Dalí painting.) I lie in the kitchen bed, listening to Andy and Kev chat about cabins down the road. Warm propane lights cast a cozy glow to the soothing hiss of the wood stove.

Today we met Ramona, an older woman with a canvas backpack being towed on her skis by her dog. It took her just three hours to get from this cabin to the point where we met her — a stretch that took us eight hours. Her support team of Mike and Mike are hauling gas and supplies behind her in their snow machines. They're going to Eagle, then back to Circle, in the matter of a day.

As Ramona and the snow machines disappeared into the distance, I watched with some envy, realizing we may just be travelling via the least efficient mode of travel possible in this environment. I thought at first of blaming Hirschberg and Jesson for sending us on this mission, but paused in that conviction as I gazed about the beauty of this place. A slow, bumbling travel by bike was the only way for us to synchronize with the glacial, meandering pace of the Yukon and its sparse inhabitants — and for that, we give thanks.

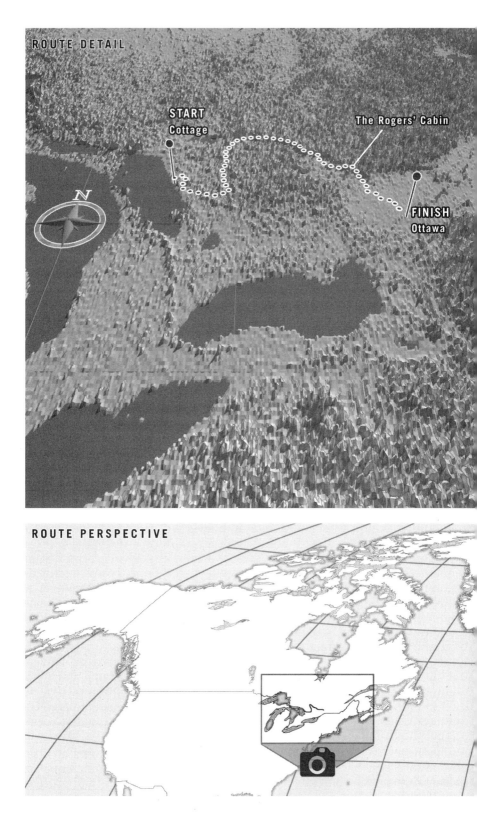

ROUTE DETAIL

START
Cottage

The Rogers' Cabin

FINISH
Ottawa

N

ROUTE PERSPECTIVE

Moving on Down the River

**A reflection on life and death during a
750-kilometre music tour by canoe.**

His bearded face is deeply coloured, its tan the combination of sun
and windburn typical of one who's lived outside for a while. His eyes
close and he stands, cocking his head and stamping his right foot to
the rhythm in his head as he sings his reworked uptempo version of
Leonard Cohen's "Suzanne." His fingers expertly pick at "Barry," his
baritone ukulele, making it sound like a virtuoso guitar. It's midnight,
and Peirson Ross is putting on an impromptu performance under the
cozy golden lights inside a log home along the Ottawa River to an
audience of two octogenarian music aficionados.

Jules and Dave Rogers had no idea we were coming tonight, or
even who Peirson Ross and I were — but now they are witness to the
"Wild Ones Tour." We are 18 days into a 24-day, 750-kilometre music
tour from Georgian Bay to Ottawa in support of Peirson's latest album
of the same name. No van, no support — just two dudes in a canoe,
paddling venue to venue through Ontario and Quebec.

Earlier this evening, at dusk, Peirson and I were at the top of a rapid
on the Ottawa River. We could hear the torrent but not see it, so we
looked to shore for a place to camp. A lone dwelling lay in the woods
with a beach off to its side that looked like a good spot. A man sat

in the balcony of the home, observing us as we pulled in. He walked around to meet us as we landed.

"Mind if we camp here?" I asked.

It was Dave Rogers, and he seemed suspicious at first. His big six-foot-four frame stood darkly before us, arms crossed as he eyed our outfit. He paused as his gaze fell on Peirson's guitar and uke cases.

"You play music?"

"I don't... he does." I jabbed my thumb in Peirson's direction. "We're actually on tour right now — Peirson's playing at Esprit Rafting in Quebec tomorrow."

"Oh, really?" Dave seemed suddenly quite jolly. His arms went to his side and he smiled broadly. "Well, you guys don't have to camp here on the beach — you can sleep in our bunkhouse. *And* you can play us some music tonight. My wife and I are both musicians."

After settling our stuff in the comfy bunkhouse (running water, bathroom, a full bed for each of us), we walked over to the main log home. The Rogers let us cook our dinner on their stove and fed us a couple of beers. Dave Rogers is a talker, regaling us with tales of his life as a geologist that took him to remote parts all over Canada. His passion now is wood carving, and he took us on a tour of the collection of carved figures that line the windows and shelves of their living room.

He stopped to show us a "natural" carving — one that hasn't been altered from its found state — for which he won a prize at a competition. Now that's the sort of art I can handle: carved by nature and claimed by you — simply sand and varnish, and you have yourself a winner. "I picked this one up off the beach and then stood back and looked at it and said, 'Gee, I don't need to do anything more to that.'" Dave pointed at the mounted sculpture. "That's an abstract — look at that. Isn't that perfect? See the head coming out, and the beak and the tail?"

It did look somewhat like an eagle, now that Dave had pointed it out. I guess natural carvings are similar to seeing figures in clouds — once someone describes to you what they see, it becomes apparent. Jules sat in the corner chair, mostly quiet except for the occasional sly rejoinder to things Dave said.

He paid her no mind and continued his soliloquy. He came to a shelf of small carved faces, any of which can be attached to the top of his prized musical instrument — a "tea chest bass," basically a two-foot-high box with a long wooden neck and single string. He popped a carved snowman head onto the bass and started to pluck away. Peirson gave it a go too, and mastered it quickly.

"He's got the hang of it already, Dave!" Jules remarked from her seat. Our talk turned to canoeing.

"That set of rapids you guys were looking at," said Dave, "I've seen every type of canoeist you can imagine try to run them. Once saw a group of eight canoes go down, and every one of them flipped. Most people who try to run them don't know a thing about canoeing — but you guys looked like you could handle a canoe, so I knew right away I'd like you." He showed us a picture of himself running the rapids at high water with his young grandson in the bow. Then he turned to Peirson. "You want to play a number with us?"

Ever gracious, Peirson agreed and soon found himself standing between Dave with his tea chest bass and Jules with her piano, following them along as they played an old ragtime tune. And now we end the night with Peirson's a cappella mini-concert.

We are in bed by one a.m., utterly tired out after a 14-hour paddling day and then partying with the 80-year-olds. It's a good tired, and we sleep well. Random occurrences on canoe trips are why you do them in the first place: you never know what's going to happen, so you just go with the flow — be it the river or circumstance.

The random experiences of a canoe trip or music tour are often the most memorable. Planned stops on the tour usually come with expectations — good sound, enthusiastic audience, free beer, etc. — and if any of those don't pan out, you end up somewhat disappointed. The lack of expectation with impromptu experiences is what makes them so unique, and somehow far more authentic than anything that's been set up in any way.

After a hearty breakfast of pancakes, eggs and bacon, Dave and Jules wave to us as we set off down the long set of Class 2 rapids, under a bridge and back into the wide, slow-moving expanse of the river. Peirson's concert that evening will be our first in Quebec. The manager of the operation there told me he'd have "a hundred people packed on the outdoor deck overlooking the river" where Peirson would be playing. We are excited at the prospect of a good turnout. So far the shows have been to intimate audiences in Nobel, Dwight, and Mattawa — about 20 to 50 people per show in small rooms that felt full with that many folks.

Ah, yes, I mentioned earlier that I don't play music — so what am doing here with this musician guy? Well, Peirson and I go way back to the early 1990s, when we worked at Onondaga, a summer camp where we guided kids on canoe trips. Peirson is a few years younger than me and was a "campfire god," one of those guys who would rip out the guitar and entertain the whole camp with ubiquitous campfire tunes by artists like Neil Young and Cat Stevens. Once I left that camp for good, I went deep into canoe tripping and adventure in general, while Peirson dove into his music, eventually making a career out of it.

I started making films about my adventures, and Peirson contacted me out of the blue one day and asked if I needed any music, and bingo — we reconnected. His tunes are perfect soundtrack music — melodic and organic, with plenty of instrumental stretches to set a nice tone for the thoughtful spots in my documentaries. His work appeared in my films On the Line and The Hand of Franklin, and we began to socialize regularly when I'd visit Toronto, where he's based.

His neighbourhood is in the Dundas and Ossington area of Toronto — a hub of music studios and venues for musicians to ply their trade. We met there one evening at a nice little dive/hipster bar called the Communist's Daughter, or ComDot if you're a regular. It was a conversation that began with Peirson saying, "Hey, imagine if we toured my album by canoe. We can ditch the touring van, the band, everything — just paddle to each show by canoe!" I think he expected me to laugh, but I was immediately intrigued. Inspiration doesn't just fall out of trees — you have to seize the moment when it arrives; it's how all great journeys start.

"Okay, I'm in — let's make this happen!"

"Really?!"

"Yeah, let's do it... this summer."

"Wow... we're going to do this."

"Yep."

It was pretty much that simple. I would plan the trip, navigate, be the roadie when it came to setup/breakdown, as well as act as road manager and documentary filmmaker. Peirson took care of the most important part — the music.

As the journey approached, my younger brother — who'd been diagnosed a year earlier with glioblastoma, an incurable form of brain cancer — took a turn for the worse. A few days before we were to depart from the cottage, I was visiting him in hospital, where he was waiting to be transferred to palliative care, as my mother and sister could no longer care for him at home.

It was a tough, tough time. My father had passed just over a year earlier, and now this. I felt bad having to leave on the trip, but the doctors thought my brother had a few months left, so I'd be back afterwards, most likely to say goodbye.

It's one of the inevitable things with going on long journeys, year after year, summer after summer. Bad things will happen to people you know while you're away, especially as you get older. I've missed most of my friends' and family's weddings and get-togethers — which in my opinion is fine, as they all end up being the same kind of thing after a while. But death is different. Death is serious. Death can derail anything — be it to someone on a trip or to someone you know while you're away on trip. You'll ultimately be left with a tough decision about whether or not to abort an adventure project you've worked so hard to achieve.

I try to control all aspects of expeditions as best as I can through good planning and decision-making — but extraneous circumstances are out of my control. This approach may sound a bit detached and heartless, but you have to understand where I'm coming from. These journeys are my life's passion, my life's work. I can't not do them. It was hard to leave for the music tour, but I had no other choice. I dealt with it by compartmentalizing the trip, separating it from what was happening outside of it.

Our paddle to Esprit was pleasant — a beautiful, sunny day, and easy paddling on a glassy river. It was June, and the maple, birch and willow along the banks were a bright green that contrasted with the dark and wispy pine and spruce trees intermingled with them.

Peirson sat in the front, singing songs and paddling along, his shirt off as he soaked up the sun. He'd began the trip quite plump, used to the "vampire hours" of a musician — late nights, drinking, toking and not much exercise. Now he was getting lean, shaping back into that kid I'd known to rock the campfire so many years ago. Peirson also knew my brother — better than he knew me, at one point. They also canoe tripped together at the camp a few years after I left — and tree planted together as well. He gets us confused sometimes, recollecting stories from times he had with my brother that he thinks were with me.

My brother and I look somewhat alike and speak similarly but are very different people. We both went to St. Michael's College School in downtown Toronto. You either come out of that place severely Catholic or an atheist. My brother is the former, I'm the latter and our paths diverged from there. It's typical of a Catholic upbringing, and of Catholic school.

The show that evening at Esprit is a disaster. The owner of the rafting company avoids us like the plague, refusing eye contact. We set up outside, and no one is there to see Peirson. It is indeed a beautiful deck, but the only people there are a family of five who randomly show up for dinner and talk throughout Peirson's first set. They leave, and a group of millennials come in — about ten of them — and chatter loudly behind him, paying him no mind at all as he finishes the set. What was it I said earlier about planned events never meeting expectations?

Peirson moves his second set indoors as the mosquitoes swarm the deck, driving the millennials inside. Soldiering on like a professional, he finishes his final song with the backs of the audience to him. The owner has long disappeared and never pays us the meagre amount of money he had agreed to beforehand. The shining light is Elizabelle St. Hilaire, a waitress there who feeds us free beer afterwards and is the sole person to compliment Peirson on a job well done.

We bounce back with a great show the next day at OWL Rafting, then shove off in the direction of Ottawa to play a Canada Day concert downtown.

The day before the Ottawa show, I wake up in the tent. It's June 30, and the rays of the sun at seven a.m. are already hot through the tent. Peirson still hasn't got the knack of this morning thing and will sleep soundly until I wake him. I get the stove going for our oatmeal and coffee. As Peirson emerges for breakfast, my phone rings. It's my mother. "Frank... Robin passed away this morning. His funeral is on Saturday."

"Okay, mom... I'm sorry. I'll be there."

It's all she can say, it's all I can say. His condition deteriorated suddenly in the past couple of days, and his life expectancy went from several months to a matter of a week or less.

The Ottawa show tomorrow will be our last one on the canoe tour. We'd originally planned on finishing in Montreal, but I no longer have a brother, and people need me. I have to compartmentalize the funeral and what just happened and keep moving this trip along. Being able to do something I love between now and then is the best I can do.

My brother's death is a random and wrenching experience for me — unplanned, but unlike the joyous experience with the Rogers, very hard to take. In both situations, I have something I'll hold with me forever.

In life and on trip, I have to keep moving on down the river.

Frank Wolf is an adventurer, filmmaker, writer and environmentalist. In addition to his film work, he is known for magazine feature articles and online columns that document wilderness expeditions around the world, with a focus on the Canadian North. His expeditions include being the first to canoe across Canada in one season and cycling 2000 km in winter on the Yukon River from Dawson to Nome. His films include *Wild Ones, The Hand of Franklin, Kitturiaq, On the Line, Mammalian and Borealis*, all of which are broadcast regularly on CBC's documentary channel in Canada. In 2012 he was named one of Canada's Top Ten Adventurers by Explore magazine, and in 2015 he was named one of Canada's Top 100 Explorers by Canadian Geographic. Frank Wolf lives in North Vancouver, BC. More of his adventures and work can be found online by visiting frank-wolf.net